The Handbook of Racial Equity in Early Childhood Education

by

Jen Neitzel, Ph.D.
Educational Equity Institute
Charlotte, North Carolina

and

Ebonyse Mead, Ed.D.
Educational Equity Institute
Savannah, Georgia

with invited contributors

·P A U L ·H·
BROOKES
PUBLISHING CO.®

Baltimore • London • Sydney

·PAUL·H·
BROOKES
PUBLISHING CO®

Paul H. Brookes Publishing Co.
Post Office Box 10624
Baltimore, Maryland 21285-0624
USA
www.brookespublishing.com

Copyright © 2023 by Paul H. Brookes Publishing Co., Inc.
All rights reserved.

"Paul H. Brookes Publishing Co." is a registered trademark of
Paul H. Brookes Publishing Co., Inc.

Typeset by Absolute Service Inc., Towson, Maryland.
Manufactured in the United States of America by
Integrated Books International, Inc., Dulles, Virginia.

All examples in this book are composites. Any similarity to actual individuals or circumstances is coincidental, and no implications should be inferred.

Purchasers of *The Handbook of Racial Equity in Early Childhood Education* are granted permission to download, print, and photocopy the Appendixes in the text for educational and professional purposes. This form may not be reproduced to generate revenue for any program or individual. Photocopies may only be made from an original book. *Unauthorized use beyond this privilege may be prosecutable under federal law.* You will see the copyright protection notice at the bottom of each photocopiable page.

Library of Congress Cataloging-in-Publication Data

Names: Neitzel, Jennifer C., author. | Mead, Ebonyse, author.
Title: The handbook of racial equity in early childhood education / by Jen Neitzel, Ph.D., Educational Equity Institute, Charlotte, North Carolina and Ebonyse Mead, Ed.D., Georgia Southern University, Statesboro, with invited contributors.
Other titles: Racial equity in early childhood education
Description: First edition. | Baltimore, Maryland : Paul H. Brookes Publishing Co., [2023] | Includes bibliographical references and index.
Identifiers: LCCN 2023000194 (print) | LCCN 2023000195 (ebook) | ISBN 9781681257204 (paperback) | ISBN 9781681257211 (epub) | ISBN 9781681257228 (pdf)
Subjects: LCSH: Early childhood education--United States. | Multicultural education—United States. | Toleration--Study and teaching (Early childhood)—United States. | Race discrimination—United States--Prevention. | BISAC: EDUCATION / Inclusive Education | EDUCATION / Schools / Levels / Early Childhood (incl. Preschool & Kindergarten)
Classification: LCC LB1139.25 .N45 2023 (print) | LCC LB1139.25 (ebook) | DDC 379.2/60973--dc23/eng/20230222
LC record available at https://lccn.loc.gov/2023000194
LC ebook record available at https://lccn.loc.gov/2023000195

British Library Cataloguing in Publication data are available from the British Library.

2027 2026 2025 2024 2023

10 9 8 7 6 5 4 3 2 1

Contents

About the Downloads

Purchasers of this book may download, print, and/or photocopy Appendixes for professional and educational use.

To access the materials that come with this book:

1. Go to the Brookes Publishing Download Hub:
    http://downloads.brookespublishing.com

2. Register to create an account (or log in with an existing account).

3. Filter or search for the book title *The Handbook of Racial Equity in Early Childhood Education.*

About the Authors

Jen Neitzel, Ph.D., Executive Director, Educational Equity Institute, Charlotte, North Carolina

Dr. Jen Neitzel is the Executive Director of the Educational Equity Institute. She received her B.S. degree in child development from the University of Pittsburgh and then began her career in the classroom in Pittsburgh as a teacher of young children with significant behavioral challenges. In 1998, she moved to Chapel Hill, North Carolina, where she worked in a group home for adults with autism. Following this, she began her studies at the University of North Carolina (UNC) at Chapel Hill, where she received a master's degree in early intervention. Dr. Neitzel then returned to the classroom where she was a teacher in a model demonstration classroom for toddlers with autism at the Frank Porter Graham (FPG) Child Development Institute. Her quest for knowledge was not finished, however. After 2 years in the classroom, Dr. Neitzel began her doctoral studies at UNC-Chapel Hill where she earned a Ph.D. in education in 2004, specializing in early childhood. Her oldest son, Josh, was 6 months old when she defended her dissertation. To maintain a healthy balance between work and being a mother, she worked on various projects at FPG focused on autism and response to intervention. Dr. Neitzel finally became a full-time researcher and technical assistance provider in 2012. During this time, she began work on a project focused on examining the disproportionality in suspensions and expulsions of young Black children, particularly boys. As a White person, she had two choices: she could act like she hadn't see the data because they did not affect her or her family in a meaningful way, or she could be a part of the solution. Dr. Neitzel chose the latter, and thus began her work in educational equity. As she delved deeper into this area, she started examining the role of implicit biases in early childhood, sources of trauma, culturally responsive practices, and systems change. In 2018, Dr. Neitzel started the Educational Equity Institute (www.educationalequityinstitute. com), a nonprofit based in Charlotte, North Carolina, that is focused on promoting equity and justice through racial healing and systems change. She is widely published in peer-reviewed journals and is the author of *Achieving Equity and Justice in Education Through the Work of Systems Change* (Lexington Books, 2020). Dr. Neitzel lives in Charlotte with her husband, Craig, and their three sons, Josh, Gabe, and Luke.

Ebonyse Mead, Ed.D., Clinical Instructor, Georgia Southern University, Statesboro

Dr. Ebonyse Mead is a clinical instructor in the birth-to-kindergarten teacher education program at Georgia Southern University and is president of the Educational Equity Institute. For 20 years, Dr. Mead has worked in communities to improve the health and educational outcomes for racially and ethnically diverse children and their families. She was born and raised in the North Lawndale community on the west side of Chicago. Seeing many inequities in her neighborhood, she felt a sense of social responsibility to be a voice for those children and families often marginalized and excluded based on their ZIP codes. Dr. Mead started her career as a parent educator working with teen parents in Chicago Public high schools. She has held numerous positions where she has advocated for the healthy development and well-being of families and children of color. Participating on a workgroup to help write North Carolina's preschool suspension and expulsion plan and raising a Black male child, Dr. Mead felt compelled to address the racial disparities in school disciplinary practices with Black children. Since 2016, Dr. Mead has provided training on racial equity with a particular focus on examining structural barriers to educational equity, implicit racial bias, positive racial identity development in young children, and culturally responsive instruction to the early childhood workforce.

Dr. Mead is a Certified Family Life Educator and holds a doctor of education degree in early childhood and a master's in human services from Concordia University Chicago. In 2015, Dr. Mead earned a master's degree in family studies from Texas Woman's University and completed a master's in inner city studies from Northeastern Illinois University in 2004. Recently, she completed a graduate certificate in Anti-racist Urban Education from the University of North Carolina at Charlotte. Dr. Mead has presented nationally and has published articles on racial equity in early childhood. She is deeply committed to creating brave spaces to talk about structural racism and promote equitable and just programs in early childhood.

About the Contributors

Rosemarie Allen, Ph.D., Associate Professor, Metropolitan State University, Denver, Colorado

Dr. Allen is currently an associate professor in the School of Education at Metropolitan State University of Denver. She has served in directorship roles with the Colorado Department of Human Services as the Director of the Division of Early Learning and in Youth Corrections. Dr. Allen also serves as the president and CEO for the Institute for Racial Equity & Excellence, which is the lead agency for ensuring equity in educational practices throughout the United States. She is a national expert on implicit bias and culturally responsive practices, speaking at conferences across the country. She also has the distinct honor of being appointed as a Global Leader, connecting with world leaders in early childhood across the globe.

Tameka Ardrey, Ph.D., Assistant Professor, Georgia Southern University, Statesboro

Dr. Ardrey is an assistant professor in the School of Human Ecology at Georgia Southern University. She studies the impact of educational inequities on the learning and development of low-income and minority students. Dr. Ardrey has authored several publications and has presented her work both nationally and internationally.

Walter Gilliam, Ph.D., Professor, Yale University, New Haven, Connecticut

Dr. Gilliam is the Elizabeth Mears and House Jameson Professor of Child Psychiatry and Psychology at the Yale Child Study Center, and he directs the Edward Zigler Center in Child Development and Social Policy. His research spans early childhood policy, preschool expulsion, bias and equity, and COVID-19 impacts on child care.

Iheoma U. Iruka, Ph.D., Research Professor, Department of Public Policy, Chapel Hill, North Carolina

Dr. Iruka is a research professor in the Department of Public Policy, a Fellow at the Frank Porter Graham Child Development Institute (FPG), and the Founding Director of the Equity Research Action Coalition at FPG at the University of North Carolina at Chapel Hill. Dr. Iruka is leading projects and initiatives focused on ensuring that minoritized children and children from low-income households, especially Black children, are thriving through the intersection of anti-bias, anti-racist, culturally grounded research, program, and policy. Dr. Iruka serves on numerous national and local boards and committees, including the National Advisory Committee for the U.S. Census Bureau; the National Academies of Sciences, Engineering, and Medicine; the American Psychological Association's Board of Educational Affairs; Brady Education Foundation; and Trust for Learning.

Doré R. LaForett, Ph.D., Senior Research Scientist, Child Trends, Bethesda, Maryland

Dr. LaForett is a senior research scientist at Child Trends and an advanced research scientist at the Frank Porter Graham Child Development Institute at University of North Carolina at Chapel Hill. She studies the contexts that shape the experiences of young children and families; educational, social-behavioral, and family-focused interventions; and early childhood programming.

Justin Perry, MSW, LCSW, LCAS, Founder, Perry Counseling Healing and Recovery, Charlotte, North Carolina

Perry is a racial equity facilitator, a sought-after speaker, and the founder of Perry Counseling Healing and Recovery, where he and his clinical team use talk, art, and movement modalities to treat mental health, substance use, and trauma, helping individuals and families struggling with shame, insecurity, and personal relationships.

Aisha White, Ph.D., Consultant, Fred Rogers Productions, Pittsburgh, Pennsylvania

Dr. White has held positions at many early childhood programs including Family Communications, Inc. (now Fred Rogers Productions), where she currently is a consultant to the *Daniel Tiger's Neighborhood* television show. She directs the Positive Racial Identity Development in Early Education (P.R.I.D.E.) Program at the University of Pittsburgh Office of Child Development.

Preface

In recent years, there has been an increased emphasis on racial inequities in early child-hood education, particularly related to the suspensions and expulsions of young Black boys. Throughout this book, we focus almost entirely on Black children and families for several reasons. First, the deepest disparities across every system in our country (e.g., criminal justice, housing, wealth, health care), including within early childhood, are with Black children and families. When we address the deepest disparities, we also will work to eliminate inequities with other racial and ethnic groups. The second reason that we are focusing primarily on Black children and families is that the discrimination and oppression that other groups of color experience is grounded in anti-Blackness—a construct born out of slavery to dehumanize Black children and families as a justifica-tion for their subjugation. As race was socially constructed, other individuals of color were absorbed into anti-Blackness and have been "othered." We have spent most of our history running away from anti-Blackness, which is a key reason that despite efforts following the Civil Rights Movement, the opportunity and achievement gaps persist.

In May 2020, there was an instantaneous shift within our society when George Floyd was murdered by a police officer in Minneapolis. Following his death, there were large-scale marches and protests meant to draw attention to the centuries-long oppression of Black children and families within our society. For many White people, this event forced an internal reckoning that we do not and never have lived in post-racial society. This is not to put blame on any one White person for not knowing. It is just a given within our society that our racial position greatly affects our ability to see racism. For example, White people do not need to be aware of oppression for it to exist. Since the social construction of race in 1705 with the Virginia Slave Codes (discussed in Chapter 4), our nation has put structures in place to advantage White individuals while oppressing Black children and families. We have been swimming in white supremacy culture (Chapter 4) for so long that is has become invisible to us—unless we choose to see it. After the murder of George Floyd, White people were forced to see the reality of racism within our society and the gross inequities within each system in our country, including within early childhood.

With this awakening, there has been a new-found emphasis on eradicating the disparities that exist between White preschoolers and young children of color, particu-larly Black children. Although this work is welcome and needed, we must be intentional and strategic about how we go about eradicating racism within early childhood. Cur-rently, too many educators, administrators, and policy makers are engaged in address-ing these inequities who do not fully understand that equity and justice work must be focused on transformation. Much of the equity activity going on within early child-hood is "check-the-box" work. For example, many organizations have begun providing diversity, equity, and inclusion (DEI) trainings to generate awareness about racism.

Although these trainings serve a purpose, they will not disrupt the root causes that have held racial inequities in place for centuries. The issues are too deep and complex to be solved in one training or a series of trainings. Instead, we need to be engaged in deep transformational change that requires commitment, determination, self-reflection, and internal work, not just at the individual level but also at the organizational level.

The first component of transformational work is to shift mind-sets and generate a shared language for early childhood professionals. We must push individuals from thinking that equity work is just learning more about diversity, inclusion, or how to be culturally competent. Again, these trainings do serve a purpose; however, they are not going to be sufficient in upending the centuries-long subjugation of Black children and families within our society.

In our work at the Educational Equity Institute, we provide two primary trainings: an introductory paradigm shift training and a historical and racial trauma training that are designed to alter the mind-sets of educators. The first training is focused on helping early childhood professionals develop a shared language, particularly because many terms are currently being used interchangeably when they are not interchangeable at all. Having a shared language allows us to be united in our quest to eradicate the inequities within early childhood. Another key aspect of this training is helping educators understand the root causes of the inequities within society, specifically focused on the structures (i.e., policies, practices) that have prevented equal access to resources and opportunities within our various systems. We must understand how we got here, so we know where to go moving forward.

With the historical and racial trauma training, we always ground the content within the history of the area or region where we are conducting the training. We recently began work in a county in North Carolina, where in 1860, 27% of the population were slaves. This is remarkable because at the height of slavery, only 25% of the South owned slaves. In this county, there were six known lynchings, two of them involving 11- and 13-year-old brothers. One of the other men was a family member of the murdered boys. The family still lives in that county of North Carolina today. This is only one community in the United States; however, each city and town has its own unique history of oppression and deep pain that is in the ground of that community. Racial equity cannot be achieved without racial healing.

We must heal from slavery, the American Genocide, and the legacies of Jim Crow. We all have been affected by those atrocities, whether or not we are willing to see that. Our nation has experienced a series of traumas, the original trauma being slavery, for which we have yet to acknowledge and atone. The second large-scale trauma is the American Genocide and displacement of Indigenous Peoples. The suffering of these two primary groups has been immense and deep. Yet, we continue to say that "it's all in the past."

Each community across the United States has its own unique history, which needs to be unearthed so that we can begin to identify how those histories are still influencing Black and Indigenous children and families' involvement with and access to various systems within the United States. Placing an emphasis on racial healing is the path toward equity and justice, which is why one DEI training will not solve the racial disparities that exist within our society.

For White people, racial healing means having a commitment to learning about race and racism within our society; reflecting on how they have been complicit in their personal and professional lives in upholding systems of oppression; and unlearning their whiteness in which all experiences, frames of references, and understandings of the world are seen through a "white is the norm" lens (i.e., the white experience is *the* experience within society). White people must become their own educators so that they can learn about the true history of our country and how racism is endemic within each of our nation's institutions. They can then reflect on the ways in which they can contribute to confronting racism within their spheres of influence.

For Black people, racial healing involves unlearning internalized racial oppression. Many Black Americans have internalized the negative messages, stories, and images about who they are as a people. Unlearning these false depictions and narratives includes acknowledging the ways in which they have been deeply impacted by white supremacy and racism. Black people must address the ways in which they unintentionally perpetuate racist ideas and beliefs, and ultimately passed them down from one generation to the next (i.e., colorism). Black people must redefine and reframe definitions of success, strengths, and accomplishments not rooted in whiteness and adopt frames of references that uplift their culture, protect their humanity, affirm their identity, and celebrate their resilience. Racial healing for Black people also means deconstructing anti-Blackness and embracing the diversity of their racial group as there is no monolithic way to be Black.

A second component of transformational work is an ongoing commitment at the organizational and individual levels. For organizations, this means reviewing current policies, handbooks, hiring practices, and so on. Early childhood systems also must be deeply committed to reviewing data disaggregated by race, class, gender, and ability to identify where disparities exist. After this, current policies and practices can be reviewed to identify specific structures that are contributing to the ongoing disparities between Black and White children and families. In their place, organizations can develop more equitable and just programs to ensure increased access to services, supports, and opportunities that have been routinely denied to Black children and families.

At the individual level, early childhood educators are committed to ongoing learning and developing a deeper understanding about how they can alter the ways they interact with families, provide services to children, and challenge the way things have always been done. Early childhood educators engage in this work to develop a keen awareness about how whiteness (Chapter 4) and anti-Blackness (Chapter 10) play key roles in perpetuating disparate outcomes for Black children and families.

Currently, we are being confronted with a unique opportunity to address racial inequities in early childhood head-on. This work will require a unique commitment and determination. Many existing obstacles will work against attaining equity and justice in early childhood. In our experience, there is a great desire among early childhood professionals to "fix" the problem immediately. This impatience is heartening; however, it can be counterproductive to the cause. In the work that we do, we always ask early childhood practitioners to commit to nonclosure. It took more than 400 years to get to this point; it is going to take time to undo what has been done.

We often say that achieving equity and justice in our society will probably take 11 generations, which is approximately how many generations of slavey there were. This paradigm shift work is the first, most essential step in all equity work. If we do not commit to this personal and professional growth, we are at risk of perpetuating the status quo and putting bandages on the wounds of racism and white supremacy rather than working toward deep, transformational change.

Our society is on the precipice of momentous change. We can choose to be a part of that effort, or we can continue to look away. The onus lies with each of us to make this critical decision. Equity and justice work is in deep need of individuals who are committed to upending the ongoing disparities while also honoring the unnamed souls who lost and continue to lose their lives to racism and white supremacy throughout our complicated and hypocritical history. We need more early childhood professionals who understand the moral obligation each of us has: we must create an early learning system that ensures equal access and opportunity.

Throughout this book, we will explore topics that we believe are the most pertinent and important in working toward transformational change. Our hope is that this book helps practitioners, administrators, and policy makers think deeply about the racial issues within our society and commit to personal and professional growth. Each chapter will conclude with strategies that educators can use to address the topic that was discussed. Our intention is that his book is truly a handbook—one that educators can come back to again and again to deepen their understanding of a specific topic and to use the specific strategies to work toward lasting change.

It is important to understand that a commitment to anti-racism is a journey, not a destination. Many of us want to check the box and move on; however, none of us will ever arrive at anti-racist. Anti-racism is a process of unlearning all that we have been taught about who we are as a country and who we are racially. Anti-racism also is a learning process, which is not a check-the-box activity. We must commit to continual learning through reading, podcasts, watching documentaries and movies, and so on. Anti-racism requires self-reflection, not only about who we are as social beings but also how we have been complicit in upholding and contributing to the status quo. Anti-racism is a letting go—of who we currently are and how we have existed in a racist society until this moment. Anti-racism requires shedding the skin of who we thought we were. As we do this, there will be great discomfort and unease. *Who am I? Where do I fit? How do I operate in this world?* However, this work will open new possibilities, new relationships, new understandings, and a new commitment to achieving equity and justice in early childhood. We welcome you to this journey and look forward to providing guidance and support as you commit to deep transformational change.

Jen Neitzel and Ebonyse Mead

Acknowledgments

This book came about through a chance meeting—Robert Clouse sat in on a virtual conference session and later contacted us about writing a book on equity. We gladly jumped at the opportunity because we always have a lot to say about equity and justice within our society. However, we envisioned something greater than just a book. We wanted to create a resource and guidebook for early childhood practitioners, administrators, policy makers, and all others who are focused on creating a more just and equitable early childhood system.

We are so grateful to have had this opportunity to expand our vision for young children and their families. First and foremost, we would like to thank Robert Clouse for attending that fated conference session. He has given us the freedom to pursue our vision for what this book should be. In today's world, too many people are afraid to "go there." Robert was never afraid to do that, and we appreciate his commitment.

We also would like to thank our contributors: Aisha, Doré, Iheoma, Justin, Rosemarie, Tameka, and Walter. You guys are the dream team, and we were honored that you said "yes" to being a part of this book. Your contributions are one of the main reasons we had so few edits. Thank you for being our brothers and sisters in this fight.

As we have moved through this work over the past few years, we have learned so much from our experiences with early childhood practitioners and others in education. We are grateful for the time we have spent learning and growing alongside each of you. With each training and experience, we have gained powerful insights into what is needed and how to approach this work. Without the work that each of you does on a daily basis, our work would not be possible.

Jen: I have always viewed my life as a series of steppingstones—with each new experience providing the basis for what comes next. I am eternally grateful for my early childhood professors at the University of Pittsburgh who always believed in me, supported me, and pushed me to do more. Without their guidance, I would not have gone on to pursue my advanced degrees in early childhood education.

My time at the University of North Carolina at Chapel Hill was foundational. My experiences were varied. I was a student, teacher, researcher, and technical assistance provider. I had several mentors during my time there who were my cheerleaders and pushed me to be bigger than I thought I could be. Mark Wolery, the late, great Deborah Hatton, and Dick Clifford were particularly important to me. They showed me what it means to be humble, kind, and a true leader. They were giants in the field, but they never saw themselves as bigger than anyone else. They believed in me in a way that I did not at the time. Their confidence in me still pushes me today.

I loved being a teacher. It was one of the greatest joys of my life. I loved being that guide and support to the children in my classroom so that they too could realize what they were capable of. I learned so much from my mentors during student teaching at Shady Lane School in Pittsburgh and Kate Sobocinski at PLEA Developmental Preschool (also in Pittsburgh). Their wisdom and expert teaching were foundational to how I viewed early childhood education and served as a model for how I wanted to raise my own children. I also am eternally grateful to the children and families who were a part of my life during my teaching years. I hold each and every one of those children in my heart and often wonder where they are now.

I also would like to thank my family. To my mom and dad, we have navigated many ups and downs over the years, and I treasure it all. Without all of it, I would not be who I am today. As a child, my mom was a teacher and showed me the power of education. She and my beloved Mammaw also instilled a sense of justice within me from a very early age that was foundational to who I am today.

To Craig, my biggest cheerleader, champion, and rock: You have supported me through it all and have not been afraid of any of it. You have grown along with me and provided space for me to be me. I could not ask for a better partner in this life. My boys, Josh, Gabe, and Luke—they are my heart. No matter where we were or what I was doing professionally, they have always been first. My hope is that they will be my greatest legacy.

I also want to thank the best team in the world, Justin, Leondra, Ebonyse, and now Sil. We are not just coworkers, we are family. I have learned so much from each of you, and I look forward to growing alongside you for years to come. Last, but not least, Ebonyse. The first time we met, it was like we had known each other our whole lives. I could not ask for a better partner in the work that we do. We support each other, learn from each other, and care for each other as friends and sisters. We have so much work left to do, and I look forward to doing it all with you side by side.

Ebonyse: Where do I begin? This journey we call life has allowed me to meet some incredible, amazing people, but I must first begin by acknowledging my ancestors. I wholeheartedly know I stand on the shoulders of a mighty people—my African ancestors who did not have a choice in coming to a "new world" and my ancestors who fought for equality and a better life for the generations to come, I sincerely thank you for your sacrifices, resilience, and tenacity.

To my grandmother, Vernal J. Henry, although you are no longer with us, I feel your spirit guiding me. I am forever grateful for your wisdom, love, and nurturance. To my parents, Laurena Henry and Edward Mead Jr., your love, nurturing, and support has made me the woman I am. My mama, Laurena Henry, is one of the strongest women I know. Your heart is pure, kind, and giving. You graciously instilled these traits in me, and they serve as the guiding principles of my life. I am truly blessed to have you as my mother and my best friend. My papa, Edward Mead Jr., your knowledge and love have been a tremendous motivating force in my life. You have always instilled racial pride within me. Even when the world dehumanizes Black folk, you always made it cool to be Black and Proud. For that, I am forever grateful. I wear my Blackness and my womanness as badges of honor because of my parents.

To my greatest gift, my NIA (purpose), Myles Fitzpatrick, you are an amazing son. You make parenting enjoyable and very rewarding. Your genuine nature and kind spirit give me hope for a better world. I am incredibly blessed that I have been able to share the past two decades with you. Our beginning as mother and son was humble, but through it all we loved each other, learned from one another, and worked together to build an awesome life for ourselves. I could not have completed any of my accomplishments without you being the amazing son you are. Thank you for always being loving and sincere. I am so very proud of the man you are becoming.

It is not by accident that I am deeply engaged in racial equity work, and in addition to my father, I must acknowledge my professors at Northeastern Illinois University and the Chicago Urban League. I would be remiss if I did not acknowledge the professors at Carruthers Center at Northeastern Illinois University. I send a special thank you to Drs. Conrad Worrill, Leon Harris, and Anderson Thompson for your guidance and leadership in cultivating my knowledge of the African Diaspora. May you rest well with the ancestors.

To my Chicago Urban League family, I love you all deeply. The work we did together supporting Black children and families in Englewood was life changing. Our purposes were divinely put together to do amazing work for the community.

To my Educational Equity Institute family, Jen, Justin, and Leondra, it has been a phenomenal experience working alongside each of you for the past few years. I am a better friend and trainer because of you. I have learned so much from each of you. I am excited about our continued work together.

To my friend, sister, and partner in crime, Jen, I could not think of anyone else I want to get into "good trouble" with. Our journey has been completely rewarding. We learn, support, care, and most important, love each other. And it is that love that makes our partnership and friendship dynamic. Writing this book with you has been one of the highlights of my 2021. Our brains are truly tied together. As we always say, we will not see the end of racism in our lifetime, but we will continue to plant the seeds of racial equity. We have a plethora of seeds to plant. I am truly excited about planting those seeds and getting into more good trouble.

1

Current Issues and Challenges

Jen Neitzel and Ebonyse Mead

W e (Jen and Ebonyse) entered equity work around the same time and for re- markably similar reasons. Our first entrée into equity in early childhood was the release of the Office of Civil Rights (OCR), U.S. Department of Education data regarding suspensions and expulsions for young Black children in public pre- school programs. The OCR has been collecting data regarding these types of exclusion- ary practices for decades; however, 2014 was the first time that they reported statistics for young children. According to the OCR report, young Black children are up to 4 times more likely to be suspended or expelled from early childhood settings than their White peers. Young Black boys, in particular, are disproportionately on the receiving end of these types of exclusionary practices (U.S. Department of Education, 2014b). The sta- tistics were so alarming, and they were hard to ignore.

For me (Jen, a White person), I knew that those data did not reflect my experience or the experiences of my three sons. However, as a non-Black person, I also recognized that I had a choice to make. I could (a) ignore the data and pretend that I had never seen them or (b) join the efforts to address the racial disparities in suspensions and expulsions and other inequities in early childhood. I chose the latter, which took me down a path that I never could have imagined. Through ongoing self-reflection, near-constant unlearning of my whiteness, and learning about racism and white supremacy in our society, I have grown, and continue to grow, personally and professionally. I have altered the ways in which I parent my children and how I operate in this world. For that, I am grateful.

For me (Ebonyse, a Black person), I was born and raised in the North Lawndale community on the west side of Chicago. Seeing many inequities in my neighborhood, I felt a deep sense of social responsibility to be a voice for those children and families who are often marginalized and excluded based on their ZIP codes. I started my career as a parent educator working with teen parents in Chicago public high schools. I have held numerous positions where I advocated for the healthy development and well-being of families and children of color. In 2016, I was asked to participate in a workgroup to help write North Carolina's preschool suspension and expulsion plan. After reviewing the data indicating that Black preschoolers are 3.6 times more likely to be suspended than their White peers, I felt compelled to address these inequities. Since that time, I have provided training on diversity, inclusion, and equity with a particular focus on exam- ining structural barriers to educational equity, implicit racial bias, and culturally re- sponsive instruction to the early childhood workforce. As president of the Educational Equity Institute, I am deeply committed to creating brave spaces to talk about struc- tural racism and promote equitable and just programs in early childhood.

CURRENT ISSUES RELATED TO EQUITY IN EARLY CHILDHOOD

Although we have been doing this work for more than 5 years now, both separately and together, we did not encounter a sense of urgency for addressing equity in early child- hood until May 2020. Following the murder of George Floyd, more organizations began to place an emphasis on finally facing the racism that has been present within our soci- ety since its inception. The current inequities within early childhood are framed within four fundamental issues: (1) suspensions and expulsions, (2) instructional practices, (3) teacher–child relationships, and (4) access to high-quality early learning programs. Each of these issues is interconnected, making it difficult for young Black children to succeed in a system that was not set up for them. We often get questions and comments about how other groups of color also face prejudice and discrimination within our various systems. Even though that is true, it is important to understand that the deepest

disparities, across every system in the United States (including early childhood), are with Black children and families. When we create and implement policies and practices that are designed to address the deepest inequities, we will also inherently help other children and families of color.

Preschool Suspensions and Expulsions

Chapter 6 provides an in-depth discussion about suspensions and expulsions, as well as the issues associated with disparities in early childhood. As such, we will not spend much time discussing the disproportionalities in the suspensions and expulsions of young Black children in early learning settings. As Allen and Gilliam discuss in Chapter 6, implicit bias, anti-Blackness, and adultification all play key roles in these ongoing statistics.

Instructional Practices

Existing research suggests that Black children may have different instructional experiences than White children, negatively affecting their academic achievement (Bodovski & Farkas, 2007; Early et al., 2010). Of additional concern is how much instruction teachers provide to students. For example, researchers have found that teachers spend less instructional time on math skills with young Black children, which is related to their later math achievement (Desimone & Long, 2010). Connor and colleagues (2005) found similar effects for children regarding literacy instruction and outcomes. Results from this study indicated that children who spent more time in academic activities with active teacher instruction demonstrated stronger vocabulary and decoding skills at the end of first grade. Because instructional practices are instrumental in promoting long-term academic achievement, the combined findings from these studies indicate a need for greater equity in providing high-quality instruction to Black children in early childhood classrooms and beyond.

There is a clear need within early childhood to focus on both the quantity and quality of instruction. Many of the current practices and ways for measuring quality are grounded in a White European ideology. When we think about the major theorists who have defined child development (e.g., Piaget, Erickson, Bandura, Vygotsky), we must also reflect on the ways in which those developmental theories laid the foundation for modern-day early childhood educational practices. Those theorists, or our current definitions of high quality, have been foundational in early childhood; however, additional viewpoints and understandings about child development within the context of diverse cultures must be considered. In recent years, culturally responsive anti-bias educational practices have gained increasing attention due to their emphasis on providing instruction and behavioral interventions that promote equal access to learning and success for all students. Chapter 7 focuses on culturally responsive anti-bias practices and how they can be implemented within early learning environments. With these practices, there is an emphasis on providing learning activities that build on and enhance the experiences of children's cultural experiences within their families. By viewing children and families within this strengths-based lens, early childhood programs can enhance learning and development for all children.

Teacher–Child Relationships

Research on teacher–student relationships shows a clear pattern around race, with Black children possessing weaker, less-positive relationships with their teachers (Hughes & Kwok, 2007). For example, several researchers have found that older Black children have more negative relationships with teachers than do White children (e.g., Hughes et al., 2005; Kesner, 2000; Murray & Murray, 2004). Study findings also indicate that early childhood teachers are more likely to rate relationships with Black children as higher in conflict and as more dependent than those with White children (Hamre & Pianta, 2001). Howes and Shivers (2006) also found that Black children formed less secure attachment relationships with their White and Latine caregivers. Additional studies have highlighted the importance of these relationships on child outcomes. Early teacher–student relationships are related to children's academic achievement, with more positive teacher–student relationships leading to better outcomes for children (Hughes & Kwok, 2007; Ladd et al., 1999).

As we move forward with equity work, we need to fully consider the role of implicit bias in the formation of these important relationships (i.e., unconscious and automatic attitudes or stereotypes that affect our understanding, actions, and decision making in daily life) (Carter et al., 2017; Gilliam et al., 2016a). Ongoing research demonstrates how implicit bias affects teachers' relationships with children (Cunningham et al., 2004; Staats et al., 2015; Sugai et al., 2012). Specifically, Kumar and colleagues (2015) found that teachers who held more implicitly favorable attitudes toward White students were more likely to endorse performance-focused instructional practices and less likely to engage in culturally responsive teaching practices. Furthermore, teachers tend to have an implicit preference for White or light-skinned individuals (Clark & Zygmunt, 2014; Kumar et al., 2015).

These research findings further illuminate the need for personal reflection and internal work that is grounded in unearthing our biases and challenging them—not only in our everyday lives but also how they play out within the work that we do with young children. Although addressing implicit bias is a key part of this work, we also need to learn about and gain a better understanding of the cultural norms and values of the children and families that we serve. For example, it is important to engage families in authentic ways so that educators can move beyond their own way of thinking about respect, appropriate/inappropriate behavior, what developmental skills are important at different ages, and how children form relationships with others, both adults and peers. This critical information will go a long way in supporting the development of positive relationships between young children and early childhood educators.

Access to High-Quality Early Learning Programs

Decades of research indicate that high-quality early childhood education is one of the biggest investments we can make as a society to level the playing field for all children. Findings suggest that children who attend a high-quality preschool program at age 4 are 9 percentage points more likely to be ready for school than are other children (Isaacs, 2012). However, recent statistics suggest that only 31% of Black children are enrolled in some type of full-time center-based program. Of these children, 43% are living in poverty. Studies also have shown that Black children are the least likely to have access to high-quality care and education. According to a recent report by the Education Trust, a considerable number of Black and Latino children lack access to state-funded preschool programs. In addition, rates of access to high-quality early care and education are lower for Black and Latino 3-year-old children than for Black and Latino 4-year-old children. Similarly, a 2005 report from the National Center for Education Statistics showed that almost half of center- and home-based child-care programs were rated as medium, and over 50% of center-based programs were attended by Black children. In addition, 53% of Black children and 63% of Latino children attended home-based programs with either a low or medium quality rating.

Research on accessibility to child care indicates that low-income neighborhoods often are "child-care deserts" where there is little to no access to high-quality programs.

In fact, the supply of affordable, high-quality child care often is influenced by neighborhood wealth, maternal employment, and education levels, as well as the presence of community-based organizations that advocate for state and federal funding (Fuller et al., 2002). As such, the supply of high-quality early childhood programs often is limited in high-poverty neighborhoods.

An additional factor that limits access for Black children and families living in poverty is that high-quality early care and education is expensive. The United States Department of Health and Human Services recommends that child-care costs should be no more than 7% of household income. According to a recent report, the average cost of center-based care is 11% for married parents and 36% for single-parent households, which exceeds monthly housing costs, tuition at a 4-year college, and monthly costs of food and transportation. Since 2018, child-care costs have risen nearly 4% nationally. In most regions of the country, child-care costs now exceed what families pay each month for housing (Child Care Aware of America, 2020). Low-income families, in particular, have difficulty finding and affording high-quality early care and education programs. People of color are more likely to be in low-wage jobs that have erratic and unpredictable hours, and they are unlikely to have employment benefits such as paid time off, which makes it even more difficult to access affordable child care that offers flexible, nontraditional hours (Johnson-Staub, 2017). Although child-care subsidies are available for low-income families, only 17% of eligible families access them due to a complex maze of program rules at the state level regarding waitlists, family co-pays, and provider reimbursement rates (Dobbins et al., 2016). Children of color and their families are particularly affected by these policies (Brooks-Gunn & Duncan, 1997).

Universal access to high-quality early childhood education is essential if we are to achieve educational equity. Providing young children with a firm foundation, which is geared toward meeting their unique needs (i.e., emphasis on social-emotional and mental health), before they enter kindergarten supports them as they move through elementary school and beyond. To achieve this goal, communities across the nation will need to make additional investments in high-quality early childhood education that maintains a keen focus on implementing culturally responsive anti-bias classroom practices.

BARRIERS TO EQUITY WORK

Working toward equity and justice in early childhood education is imperative. We all have a moral obligation to unearth the root causes so that we can create policies and practices that promote optimal outcomes for all children. This is the intellectual understanding about what needs to happen; however, the barriers to this work are numerous and growing more intense every day. Because of this, we cannot approach this work naively. If we do, our noble efforts will fail. Instead, we need to be realistic about the challenges we face when undertaking this work.

Siloed Efforts

One of the biggest challenges in ongoing equity work is the propensity to work in silos. That is, early childhood mental health does their own equity work, whereas prekindergarten programs go about addressing equity in a different way. These individual efforts, although essential, will not fully eradicate the ongoing disparities for young Black children and their families. The issues are too multilayered and complex for any one sector to address on their own. Often, siloed efforts are driven by a sense of urgency, which is a characteristic of white supremacy culture. According to Okun (1999), when individuals and organizations feel pressure to solve a problem, it is difficult for them to take time to be inclusive, to encourage democratic and/or thoughtful decision making, to think long-term, and to consider consequences. Having a sense of urgency regarding this work is important; however, if we are not strategic and do not have a firm understanding of the issues, we are going to be working against the very goals that we are trying to accomplish.

In our work with organizations, one of our main goals is to facilitate a shared language so that everyone can be on the same page regarding key terms (e.g., *racism, prejudice, diversity, equity, inclusion*). That lack of a shared language is a smaller, but still significant, barrier to this work. Too often, organizations and early childhood professionals do not have a firm understanding about what racism means, or even prejudice for that matter. For example, having a shared language allows us to identify prejudice when we see it and then address it.

Generating a shared language across organizations is also critically important so that there is no confusion regarding terms such as *equity* versus *equality*. Recently, we worked with an organization that partners with and shares staff with another early childhood organization—each is engaged in its own equity work. This is commendable; however, it is also counterproductive to what they are trying to achieve. These competing efforts can create confusion about specific terms and how to go about addressing equity in early childhood, which can lead to potential burnout for employees because they are being bombarded with too much information. All of this is driven by a sense of urgency.

The most important thing that early childhood organizations can do when starting to address equity is to commit to nonclosure. Yes, we want to eradicate racism and injustice within our society, including within early childhood; however, the issues are too deep and complex to be solved in a brief period of time. That is why it is critical that organizations let go of that sense of urgency, which is driven by the need to "fix" things. Instead, we can be impatient while also being strategic and thinking about the long-term consequences of the work that we are undertaking. Once individuals and organizations commit to nonclosure, then they can begin the work of equity and justice in early childhood.

Ending siloed work also requires that early childhood professionals communicate with other early learning organizations that are doing equity work in their communities. The issues are so vast, and the resistance to change is so virulent, that we need to combine our efforts toward a common cause. Working in silos allows us to be disjointed and disorganized, and it fosters an unhealthy competitiveness. Early childhood organizations should be working together to push back against the resisters who want to uphold the status quo. We live in a very individualistic society where each person, organization, and institution is working in isolation.

This individualism is also a characteristic of white supremacy culture. From very early in our lives, we are socialized to focus on individual achievement and advancement. As such, we have very little experience or comfort working as part of a team. In our work lives, this translates into believing that people and organizations are responsible for solving problems alone, which leads to isolation and competition (Okun, 1999). As a society, we need to move into collectivism where we are working together toward a common goal, which, in this case, is equity and justice in early childhood. When organizations combine efforts, they can think long term, combine resources, and generate more transformative change within communities. However, this requires setting aside individual egos, which is another barrier to change.

Egos

Because of the individualism within our society, we often are driven by our own need to advance, attain, or be recognized as the solver of problems. Being grounded in our egos gets in the way of transformative change. Ego-driven work is intertwined with siloed efforts in communities because individuals who are ego-based want recognition and power. This hoarding of power is another characteristic of white supremacy culture, which must be deconstructed if we are to achieve what we have set out to do. According to Okun (1999), those who are ego driven see little, if any, value around sharing power. Rather, power is seen as limited—there is only so much to go around. Individuals who are grounded in ego feel threatened when anyone suggests changes in how things should be done. This work will not be successful if egos and power struggles come into play.

That is why we must set aside our own personal agendas and our own needs for recognition and accomplishment. This work is about putting our own career advancement and our own egos aside to do what is right and necessary to disrupt the roots of inequity within the educational system. Again, this is why self-reflection and individual work is so important. Progress cannot coexist with ego. According to Deepak Chopra (1994),

> The Ego, however, is not who you really are. The ego is your self-image; it is your social mask; it is the role you are playing. Your social mask thrives on approval. It wants control, and it is sustained by power, because it lives in fear. (p. 11)

Reflecting on our need for approval and recognition pushes us to examine what we are afraid of. Are we afraid that we will not get the recognition we feel we deserve? Are we afraid that someone else will get that recognition? Are we driven by the need to be the "one" who fixes racism in early childhood? When we can identify what is driving our need for power, we then can begin to let go of the ego part of ourselves. There is so much work to do, and we need to be working together toward the common cause of equity and justice in early childhood. The challenge is to move beyond ourselves and realize that this cause is greater than any one person.

Failure to Explicitly Name Racism

Another significant barrier to equity in early childhood is our failure to explicitly name racism and the effects it has on children's learning and development. According to McCarthy (2020), racism can lead to continual stress for young children, which contributes to changes in hormones that cause inflammation in the body—a marker of chronic disease. A failure to explicitly name racism is often grounded in an unwillingness to engage in hard conversations and our own need to avoid any topic that causes discomfort. As such, many times, efforts to address the current inequities are focused on cultural competence or diversity and inclusion. These types of trainings and professional development activities do little to highlight the root causes of the ongoing disparities in early childhood education, which is critical if we are to achieve equity and justice. It is long past time to explicitly name racism and how it is a key contributing factor in upholding the status quo.

Bills and Laws

Currently, 26 states have anti-racism laws, bills, or other state-level actions that are designed to prevent transformational change. As of July 2021, the following states have signed laws that ban teaching students about racism and sexism: Arkansas, Arizona,

Florida, Idaho, New Hampshire, Oklahoma, South Carolina, Tennessee, and Texas. Seven other states have proposed this type of legislation: Alabama, Kentucky, Michigan, North Carolina, Pennsylvania, Ohio, and Wisconsin. In addition, three other states have other state-level action that is legally binding: Georgia, Montana, and Utah.

A common thread across all these states' actions is the focus on teaching critical race theory within schools. Kimberlé Crenshaw, among others, coined the term *critical race theory* (CRT) in the late 1970s and early 1980s. CRT is a framework that critiques how the social construction of race and institutionalized racism perpetuate racism and oppression within our society. CRT scholars assert that we must acknowledge the legacies of slavery, segregation, and Jim Crow (George, 2021).

Across all these states, there are commonalities regarding language and intent. In Arkansas, the law bars state agencies from teaching "divisive concepts" during racial and cultural sensitivity trainings, including teaching that America is an inherently racist nation (Bowden, 2021). Idaho has prohibited schools and universities from teaching that "any sex, race, ethnicity, religion, color, or national origin is inherently superior or inferior" (House Bill No. 377). Oklahoma's law (OK HB1775) prohibits teachers from instructing students that "an individual, by virtue of his or her race or sex, bears responsibility for actions committed in the past by other members of the same race or sex," and from making students feel "guilt" or "anguish" on "account of his or her race or sex." In general, these laws and bills are directly focused on K–12 education.

This leads to the question, "Why is it important for early childhood educators to understand what is happening in states regarding race and racism?" First, many offices of early education are housed within departments of public instruction, which means they are included in these bans. Second, we must understand that no school in this nation is teaching children in any setting about CRT, which is a graduate-level class. What is being proposed across the country is a revision of social studies standards to include a more accurate representation of our nation's history.

Although these social studies standards do not apply directly to early childhood, efforts are already underway to limit teaching young children about diversity in a developmentally appropriate way. For example, the Idaho Freedom Foundation suggests that CRT is "infiltrating" early childhood programs in the form of preventing the use of picture books that promote diversity and inclusion. In addition, they maintain that

> anti-bias education peddles the idea that America is systemically and irredeemably racist and sexist; that white children, especially boys, are complicit in that racism and sexism; and educators must discriminate in their treatment of white and Black, male and female students to erase perceived "biases." (Miller, 2021, p. 154).

Not only are these claims blatantly false in their description of anti-bias education, but these types of groups are also gaining steam and visibility in school district Board of Education meetings across the country.

These groups, in combination with state legislation efforts, present a considerable barrier in addressing equity and justice in education. This leads to the question, "What can we do to address these efforts head-on?" First, we must become knowledgeable about the legislation in our state to determine what is prohibited and for whom. Second, it is essential that early childhood educators push themselves more into advocacy. That is, organize efforts in your communities and show up at Board of Education meetings to counter the noise of groups, such as Moms for Liberty, who are actively working against diversity, equity, and inclusion. Become well-versed in what CRT is and is not. Knowledge is power, and we must control the narrative about equity and justice work rather than constantly being on the defensive.

We also need to know their talking points. For example, one of the main strategies that opponents to anti-bias education use is to take quotes by Martin Luther King, Jr. out of context. One common refrain is that Dr. King would be horrified by what is happening within education because anti-bias educational practices are divisive. The most frequent quote that is used is "I have a dream that my four little children will one day live in a nation where they will not be judged by the color of their skin but by the content of their character" (King, 1963). Contextually, Dr. King spoke these words in a time when overt racism was extremely commonplace. Today, many of us believe that we live within a color-blind society where we are hyperfocused on being loving and kind to all, regardless of their skin tone. The anti-bias opponents are weaponizing Dr. King's words for their cause, which would horrify him.

Another common strategy is to state that teaching history should be left to parents. This tactic is manipulative and designed to subvert the efforts to help our children develop a greater understanding about diversity, equity, and inclusion. The goal of these teaching efforts is not to make White children feel ashamed or bad about themselves, which is counterproductive to the cause. Our nation's youth are already learning about this history through social media (e.g., TikTok, YouTube, Instagram) and peers, even in the younger years. Our children need spaces where they can process what they are learning and gain a better understanding about what is and is not the truth.

This argument also is highly flawed because parents of public school students have not been protesting that they should oversee teaching their children how to read or do math. This tactic is grounded in white supremacy, racism, and white shame. Understanding the strategies that are being used to distract from the real work of equity allows champions for change to gain control of the false narratives that are being pushed. Again, it is imperative that early childhood educators, administrators, and policy makers understand the key components of culturally responsive anti-bias education

(Chapter 7) so that these falsehoods can be put to rest and we can get back to the work of addressing disparate outcomes within early learning programs.

Nice White People

In our trainings, we emphasize that kindness, compassion, and empathy are important traits; however, they will not advance the cause of equity and justice. As such, "nice White people" pose a significant barrier to our work. DiAngelo (2021) refers to nice White people as "white progressives," whereas Dr. King referenced "white moderates" in *Letter from Birmingham Jail* (1963). White progressives/moderates, or nice White people, "see themselves as racially progressive, well-meaning, nice" (DiAngelo, 2021, p. 2). There is a propensity within this group to say, "I treat everyone the same regardless of race" or "I'm not a racist," which can result in personal complacency or an unwillingness to do deep reflection about the ways in which they have been complicit in upholding systemic racism. According to DiAngelo (2021), "Niceness requires that racism only be acknowledged in acts that intentionally hurt or discriminate, which means that racism can rarely be acknowledged" (p. 49).

The issue with nice White people is that they are so focused on seeing racism as an individual act, or trying to prove that they are not racist, that they cannot, or refuse to, see all the racist policies and practices that are below the surface. Nice White people are so focused on maintaining their goodness and innocence in the form of kindness, compassion, and empathy, which halts any conversation around the topics of racism and white supremacy. More White people must start pushing through their own discomfort or fear of making a mistake so that they can start shouldering some of the equity and justice work that has been placed on the backs of Black people since the social construction of race. The beautiful thing about leaning into this discomfort is that White people can engage in deep personal growth that allows them to have a more positive racial identity in which they are not only able to engage in authentic cross-cultural relationships, but they are also able to join the growing number of people who are part of the movement to achieve equity and justice for Black children and families within our society.

MOVING FORWARD

We recognize that everyone is entering this work at different points. For some, you have just begun your anti-racism journey, whereas others are already committed to undoing the centuries-old systems. We also understand that we all enter this work with our own unique life stories—our upbringings, our families, our communities—that provide a lens from which we view the current issues. We honor and respect each of these experiences. Wherever you are on your journey, there are several key things that you can do to further commit to anti-racism.

1. *Educate yourself.* Read books/articles; listen to podcasts focused on race, racism, and racial healing; watch historical and current-day movies and documentaries. These activities are crucial because they facilitate the deep internal work that is needed to undo racism within ourselves and our society.

2. *Reflect.* Take time to reflect on what you are learning. You can journal or just take time to better understand our history and how you have been complicit in some way in upholding the status quo.

3. *Notice.* In your daily life, observe situations, news stories, and television shows and take note of discrimination and bias. Racism is insidious and shows up in many ways and takes many forms within our lives.

4. *Have grace.* As you embark on this journey, have grace for yourselves and others. We have all been socialized in a society where white is the norm. You may feel guilt or even shame. Whereas guilt is healthy because it allows us to atone, apologize, and do better, shame is stagnating. Guilt is *I did something bad.* Shame is *I am bad.* Healthy guilt is expected; however, you need to move through that guilt. Allow yourself to feel the pain, but do not let it define you.

Again, welcome to your anti-racism journey. This is not a sprint or a destination. Anti-racism work requires commitment and determination. With each commitment, we get closer to creating what Dr. King called the "beloved community" (King, 1957).

2

Racial Healing as a Pathway to Racial Equity

Ebonyse Mead and Jen Neitzel

P rior to the murder of George Floyd, the focus of our work at the Educational Equity Institute was on building cultural competence. We spent a lot of time in our trainings talking about implicit bias, cultural responsiveness, and culturally relevant teaching. Although this work was important at the time (because talking about race and racism in education was truly in its infancy), we were not engaged in the deep transformational work that is needed to advance the cause of equity and justice in our society. As we reflect on this time, we fully understand that we were complicit in many ways in upholding the power structures and inequitable systems.

George Floyd's murder was an awakening for many of us that racism does still, in fact, exist within our society. There was no way to ignore the role of racism and anti-Blackness in his death. Black individuals have been crying out about the atrocities of police brutality for most of our history, if we include slave patrols in this narrative. With the video, we could choose to pretend that it did not exist, or we could acknowledge the ever-present role racism, anti-Blackness, and white supremacy play within our society. Marches sprang up across the nation in support of Black Lives Matter. Streets and murals were painted, and many of us wanted to do something. This period brought about an urgent need to "fix" racism.

For us, we also engaged in some individual and collective self-reflection, which helped us realize that we needed to shift how we approach the work of equity and justice. First, we needed to revise our content to explicitly focus on racism, anti-Blackness, whiteness, and white supremacy. We also realized that our country was in pain. We began to realize that we all carry a deep shame that stems from our painful history. Slavery and the American Genocide were the original traumas that inflicted extreme pain and suffering on two groups of people within our nation. The ideology that was needed to conduct the atrocities of the American Genocide, slavery, and Jim Crow apartheid was the dehumanization of Black and Indigenous Peoples. With the passage of the Emancipation Proclamation, we freed millions of slaves; however, we never dealt with the trauma of slavery and how we nearly wiped out an entire race of people during the American Genocide. We moved on, pretending that it was something from the past. This defense mechanism continues to be a common refrain. "I didn't own slaves." "Why do we need to keep talking about slavery?" The avoidance in facing this trauma is deeply rooted in shame. Truth and reconciliation will require deep self-reflection and a reckoning that we have covered up the wounds of slavery and the American Genocide through a false narrative that the ideals of our country have been achieved.

Throughout our history, we have continued to place bandages on the wounds created by slavery and Jim Crow. *Brown v. Board of Education*, the Civil Rights Act, and the first Black president created an atmosphere of avoidance where we convinced ourselves that we live in a post-racial society. We point to these accomplishments because they allow us to avoid our past and how our own actions prevent us from evolving and moving forward as a nation. However, our society is far from post-racial. If we look deeply at the true history of our country, we begin to understand that our government (federal, state, and local) has systematically put a variety of structures in place within each of our institutions to create a racial caste system in which a select number of White Americans with wealth (mostly men) maintain power and privilege.

When we begin to face the shame of our past, we start to see how the underlying ideology that White people are superior to Black people and other people of color has permeated every aspect of our society, including our subconsciouses. The social construction of race and the dehumanization of people of color has morphed over time—to the point that many of us just accept our society as is. This "White is the norm" mentality ensures that we remain complacent and complicit in upholding the status quo.

Just like with individual trauma where we try to the fill the holes to avoid facing the pain, our country has used up all its coping mechanisms. There are no more. Avoidance is no longer working. The bandage approach to equity is not working (and has never worked). Blame and deflection are no longer working. Our past has finally caught up with us. We have entered a state of urgency in which we have two choices. We can continue trying to fill the holes of shame, or we can open ourselves up to a healing that needs to take place within our society if we are to work toward freedom and justice for all. The latter choice is by far the harder one because it requires educating ourselves, deep self-reflection, personal responsibility, and commitment. However, it is the only choice currently. If we choose denial and willful ignorance, our country will continue down the path of self-destruction. That is the consequence of unhealed trauma.

RACISM AS TRAUMA

One of the key takeaways as the world watched in horror the murder of George Floyd and the protests that ensued is the need for racial healing in our society. Discussions of racial healing are often lacking in racial equity and justice work. Since the inception of the United States, structural racism and white supremacy have been deeply entrenched in American society and continue to be a pervasive problem in the United States.

Racism plays a significant role in the everyday lived experiences of Black people and other people of color, which deeply affects their physical and mental well-being. Given the insidious nature of racism, we all have been victimized by and internalized racist ideologies and messages. Engaging in racial equity and justice work goes beyond educating White people about white privilege and reflecting on implicit racial biases. Although those efforts are a great starting place, racial equity and justice work requires an atonement of past harms and an intentional need to center racial healing. Even though Black people and other people of color are continuously traumatized and hurting from the legacies of slavery, Jim Crow, and present-day racial injustices, White people too are harmed by racism and white supremacy because it robs them of their humanity. Racial equity and justice are not possible without racial healing. The time for all of us to heal is now.

BLACK PEOPLE AND RACIAL HEALING

Racial healing creates the path toward racial equity and justice because it provides the opportunity to process the wounds of historical, intergenerational, and current racial trauma. A key first step in the healing process is to have common definitions and understandings of some key terms. Historical and intergenerational trauma refers to the collective emotional and physical harm caused by momentous events that affect entire communities and is transmitted across generations (Statman-Weil, 2020). The African American community's survival of slavery and Jim Crow and Indigenous people's survival of genocide and forced displacement are examples of historical trauma in the United States. The pain of the unhealed traumas, Jim Crow apartheid, American Genocide, and mass displacement then gets passed on from one generation to the next in the form of intergenerational trauma (Chapter 6 provides a more in-depth discussion of historical trauma).

Racial trauma, on the other hand, refers to the "emotional and/or physical pain or threat of physical and emotional pain that results from racism" (Carter, 2007, p. 88). Racial trauma is often associated with intergenerational trauma because remembering the vestiges of slavery, Jim Crow, genocide, forced displacement, and other crimes against humanity, as well as the ongoing stress related to current racial issues, are very triggering for Black people and other people of color. As programs, schools, and classrooms seek to create equitable learning environments, it is imperative that White school administrators, teachers, and other school personnel understand the effect that historical and racial trauma have on children and families of color.

Because racism and White supremacy permeate our society, it is critical that we unpack the ways in which Black people have internalized racism and White supremacy. For example, Black people can experience internalized racial oppression, which refers to the internalizing and acting out (sometimes unintentionally) of the constant messages that you and your group are inferior to the dominant group (Sensoy & DiAngelo, 2017). Examples of internalized racial oppression can include a sense of inherent inferiority, low self-esteem, or feelings of shame and rage. For Black people, internalized racial oppression can manifest itself in colorism, anti-Blackness, and stereotype threat. These concepts also play a role in the outcomes for Black children. Having a deeper understanding of these issues is a key component of racial healing.

Colorism

Colorism is the process of discrimination that privileges light-skinned Black people (and other people of color) over their darker-skinned counterparts (Hunter, 2005). Whereas racism is tied to race and ethnicity, colorism is uniquely associated with skin tone. Like racism, colorism has its roots in Eurocentrism, slavery, and colonialism. One of the ways in which slavery was able to thrive in America was through a divide-and-conquer strategy. Slave owners divided enslaved Africans by their skin tone, giving lighter-skinned slaves more privileges than darker-skinned slaves. For example, lighter-skinned slaves typically worked inside the slave master's house, whereas darker-skinned slaves worked in the fields. Additionally, light-skinned slaves were occasionally provided the opportunity to gain experience to read and write (Davis, 1991). These privileges were given based on the idea that if your skin tone was akin to white skin, you were somehow better, smarter, more worthy, or more beautiful than dark-skinned individuals. This divide created deep-seated intragroup conflict between dark-skinned and light-skinned slaves that transferred through generations and is present in the Black community today. These intragroup conflicts also can be found within the Latine[1] community. In a recent study, 41% of Hispanic individuals with darker skin say that they have personally experienced discrimination, have been treated unfairly, or have heard racially insensitive comments from someone who is Hispanic (Pew Research Center, 2021). One reason for this is because lighter-skinned Latine individuals often are able to "pass" as White, which gives them more privileges within society (Quiros & Dawson, 2013).

The complexities of racial and ethnic identity development within the Latine community are a direct by-product of white supremacy and have their roots in colonialism. For example, "In Mexico, light-skinned Spaniards had access to more resources and power, whereas darker-skinned Indians were routinely oppressed, rendered powerless, and dispossessed of their land" (Hunter, 2007, p. 239). In Asian countries that have histories of colonialism, lighter skin tones are valued because of the European values that have been imposed (Hunter, 2007).

Colorism has been perpetuated in families, communities, and the media. In our work, we have heard countless stories from people of color about their experiences with colorism and the trauma it has had on their lives, from stories of mistreatment by family members to microaggressions such as "You are pretty for a dark-skinned girl." Colorism must be a part of racial healing conversations.

Colorism is also sustained through the media. For example, the popular television show *Martin* depicted Gina, whose character is very light skinned, as smart, educated, pretty, funny, and well mannered. Whereas Pam, her best friend who is dark skinned, was portrayed as loud, obnoxious, unable to find a man, sassy, and perceived as unworthy. Like racism, colorism has real and perceived consequences and implications on people's lives.

Colorism and anti-Blackness are uniquely tied together because of their origins in slavery and colonization, which were based on racist ideologies that White people are inherently superior to all other groups of people. To maintain this idea, science, religion, and laws were used to uphold and maintain the idea of white superiority. The maintenance of white superiority is evident in the racial caste system in America where White people, primarily White men, are on the top followed by lower-class White people, people of color, and then Black and Indigenous Peoples at the bottom.

European intellectuals and world travelers wrote extensively about Africans as being subhuman (Kendi, 2016). The need to dehumanize Africans was necessary to justify their enslavement. Theories such as climate and curse theories emerged and circulated throughout Europe. They perpetuated false narratives that Africans were naturally "slave material" and lacked civilization. Not only were these theories circulating through Europe, but they made their way to America. Several European books

---

[1]In U.S. academic circles, *Latinx* is being used as a gender-inclusive term to refer to people from Latin American backgrounds, but Spanish speakers find that Latinx is unpronounceable in Spanish. Therefore, we have opted to use the gender-inclusive term *Latine,* commonly used throughout Spanish-speaking Latin America (Melzi et al., 2020).

about "beastly Africans" were translated into English, and Americans interested in slave trading took hold of these racist ideologies and false narratives. These racist ideas fueled slavery in America and served as the beginnings of the social construction of race and anti-Blackness.

Anti-Blackness

Anti-Blackness is a form of racism that dehumanizes and devalues Black people across the globe. It has its roots in the social construction of the White identity. As Whiteness was being socially constructed, so was anti-Blackness as it became the justification for the enslavement of Africans. Anti-Blackness dictates the social position of Black people in America. Although non-Black groups of color also experience racism, Black people are disproportionately affected by every social aspect within our institutions (e.g., health care, education, wealth, housing, criminal justice, the food system). For this reason, the investigation of anti-Blackness is not only central to conversations about race and racism, but it is critical to racial healing.

It is imperative to understand that anti-Blackness occurs in all races and ethnicities. Black people both experience anti-Blackness and perpetuate it. For example, some family members told me (Ebonyse) not to choose a historically Black college or university for college because I would receive a better quality of education and have greater job opportunities if I attended a predominantly White university.

Anti-Blackness and colorism are forms of racial trauma that are not only passed down across generations, but they are normalized within our families and communities. It is imperative to Black liberation that we begin to deconstruct anti-Blackness and colorism in our families and communities. We must discuss the ways that anti-Blackness and colorism show up in our families and in our communities. We must explore strategies to combat and heal from anti-Blackness and colorism. We must adopt new attitudes, beliefs, and practices that celebrate Blackness in all its shades regardless of race and ethnicity.

Anti-Blackness, colorism, and stereotype threat are all interconnected because they influence the social identity of people of color, especially young Black children. According to Sensoy and DiAngelo (2017), stereotype threat is the fear one has that they will be evaluated negatively due to the stereotype of the identity they possess or the group to which they belong. This fear can cause an individual or group of people to perform poorly because they have internalized the stereotype. Stereotype threat may influence the way an individual, especially individuals from minoritized groups, see themselves. Internalizing the negative stereotype(s) that are associated with their group could negatively affect their sense of self, including their self-efficacy and self-concept. For example, too often Black children are bombarded with daily messages from individuals and institutions that they are not good enough, as smart, valued, or as beautiful as White children (White & Wanless, 2019).

In school, too many Black children have experiences that devalue their Blackness, thus impacting their sense of self and self-esteem. Barbarin and Crawford (2006) concluded that the stigmatization of preschool Black boys as "bad" or "troublemakers" negatively affects their self-worth. Teachers who mispronounce or shorten the names of students of color send the message that the students are not important enough to learn the correct pronunciation of their name. Other microaggressions such as "You are pretty for a Black girl" or "You speak so well" are the consistent reminders telling Black children and other children of color that they do not belong and are different from the dominant group. When children of color internalize these negative messages and/or stereotypes about their group, they are also experiencing internalized racial oppression. As educators responsible for the well-being of the whole child, we must create safe spaces where children's multiple identities are respected, valued, and celebrated. Altering our definition of "safe spaces" and creating them must be an integral part of racial healing in educational settings.

LATINE PEOPLE AND RACIAL HEALING

Non-Black groups of color also experience anti-Blackness and are absorbed into it through the idea of "othering" (meaning other than White). Research suggests that colorism, in-group prejudice and discrimination, and color blindness are widespread. According to Chavez-Duenas and colleagues (2014), the roots of these issues began during the conquest of Latin America in the 1500s, which resulted in massacre, domination, and oppression of Indigenous Peoples in the Caribbean as well as Central and South America. During the postcolonial period, a foundation of white supremacy, including the denial of inequality, was laid down.

The concept of *mestizaje* was initiated during this time and was a strategy that socialized all Latine people, including formerly enslaved Africans, that they were all mixed Indigenous, African, and European heritage (Soler Castillo & Pardo Abril, 2009). During this time, "whitening policies" also were instituted in Latin America. For example, European immigrants were encouraged, particularly in areas with high concentrations of Indigenous and African Peoples, and White prostitutes were sent to areas with high concentrations of Afro-descendants (e.g., Colombia) (Castellanos Guerrero et al., 2009). The elites believed that these practices would whiten and improve the race.

Whiteness plays a significant role in Latine identities, with about 10% of the U.S. population identifying as both White and Latine. According to Casey (2021), those who are able "to pass as white are more often able to live more financially secure lives than those who are not," highlighting some of the complexities within the Latine community between lighter- and darker-skinned individuals (p. 361). Because of this, people within the Latine community must navigate "a host of intraracial and intraethnic tensions" based on their identities. For example, individuals who identify as both White and Latine are more likely "to experience identity-based oppressions regardless of their racial affiliation as white" (Casey, 2021, p. 362). Non-Black groups of color with more European physical features and skin tone can assimilate more easily into American culture. Therefore, they are more likely to benefit from anti-Blackness because they can gain access to power within American institutions.

More than half of the Hispanics in the Pew Research Center survey (2021) identified their race as White (58%), whereas 27% selected "some other race" category. Only 2% selected Black or African American. Bonilla-Silva (2018) found that White-identified Latine individuals were less likely to view Black people positively because of anti-Black messages received that include criticisms of darker skin, African features, and elevation of whiteness (Araujo-Dawson & Quiros, 2014). However, in a recent study Latine individuals who identified as White were more likely to skip questions on a questionnaire that related to their white privilege (Fernandes, 2017).

This inclination to identify as White, but with an unwillingness to acknowledge white privilege based on lighter skin, may be related to the color-blind ideology that is promoted within the Latine community that has its roots in mestizaje. Chavez-Duenas and colleagues (2014) noted that many revealing statements exist within Latine discourse: 1) We are all mestizos (racially mixed); 2) in Latin America, social class "matters more" than skin color; and 3) there is no racism in Latin America. However, there tends to be an emphasis on white as superior through comments such as "We need to better the race by marrying a White individual" and "Oh! How pretty your daughter is—she's so beautifully white!" (Chavez-Duenas et al., 2014). Adding to this narrative is that Latine individuals with medium dark to very dark skin are more likely to identify as White, although socially they would be considered non-White (Darity et al., 2008). Diving into the contradictions and internalized oppression, as well as internalized superiority, are key issues that need to be addressed as part of the healing process within the Latine community.

The complexities of the history within the Latine community regarding skin color and color blindness are reflected in their attitudes about racial justice in the United States. In the Pew Research Center survey (2021), they found that a little over one third of Latine adults, regardless of skin tone, said that there is not enough attention paid to race and racial issues in the United States, whereas the same said that there is too much attention given. Of the respondents, younger Latine people were most likely to say that race gets too little attention. However, 55% of Latine adults say that too little attention is given to race issues concerning the Asian community, whereas 51% said that too little attention is given to issues experienced by Latine children and families.

The reckoning that must occur is that prejudice, discrimination, and oppression of other groups of color within the United States are grounded in anti-Black racism. White supremacy and the othering that was needed to justify slavery also othered immigrants of color as they entered our nation. We must move beyond comparing oppression within our society to deem who has it worse. That is exactly what white supremacy wants us to do—pit ourselves against each other so that we do not face the real enemy. For the Latine community, healing will require reconciling the complicated past of Latin America as well as that of the United States. There will need to be an acknowledgment of similar but competing ideologies that are harming their positive racial identity development. As with other racial and ethnic groups, this will require learning, unlearning, and deep self-examination and self-reflection. This is the foundation of healing.

INDIGENOUS PEOPLES AND RACIAL HEALING

Indigenous Peoples in the United States have been referred to by many different names throughout our nation's history: Indians, Native Americans, First Nations Peoples, and American Indians. These terms can be problematic, however, because they assume that there is a shared culture and practices. For specific tribes, identification means a people, a language, and a physical place that they are native to (Casey, 2021). As such, European notions of land, property, and language are "fundamentally at odds with many Indigenous Peoples' ways of knowing and living" (Casey, 2021, p. 33).

As Europeans landed on their shores, so did whiteness. The American Genocide "left devastation on a scale never before recorded in human history" (Casey, 2021, p. 33). Tens of millions of people lost their lives in the name of individualism, capitalism, and westward expansion. The Catholic Church played a significant role in the fate of Native Peoples. For example, in 1493, a papal bull declared that all lands in the Western Hemisphere were open to European plunder and conquest. It is important to note that the Native tribes were not consulted or considered as Europeans forced Peoples off their lands. Starting in 1537, the Catholic Church ruled that Indigenous Peoples were, in fact, human and should be converted to the Catholic faith, which was seen as a blessing for them by the Church.

The colonization of Native tribes did not end there. In 1851, the U.S. Congress passed legislation that created the Indian Reservation System, which often forced them off their lands to places that were not part of their ancestral homes. In addition, Indigenous Peoples received fewer resources and were not allowed to leave the reservations. By the end of the 19th century, American Indian Boarding Schools were created, starting with the Carlisle School in Pennsylvania. Indigenous children were taken from their families; forced to cut their hair, take new Christian names, and adopt Western-style dress and behaviors; and give up their languages and customs (Casey, 2021). As a result of this mass trauma and loss, Indigenous Peoples today face the highest rates of diabetes, suicide, and death by injury in the United States. Rates of addiction and alcoholism also are higher within these communities. A significant healing must occur that requires reclaiming their native languages, dress, and histories. However, we, as a nation, also play a key role in their healing process. Honoring native lands and engaging in atonement for past harms will be critical.

WHITE PEOPLE AND RACIAL HEALING

According to Resmaa Menakem (2017), white supremacy is "in the air we breathe, the water we drink, and the culture we share" (p. xix). Many White people often get triggered by the phrase *white supremacy*. The reason for this is because the phrase has become synonymous with the Ku Klux Klan, white nationalists, and so on. However, we must understand that white supremacy is a cultural way of being within society, which is based on the notion that White people are inherently superior to people of color.

White supremacy as a construct has its roots deep within the history of our country. For example, the early Europeans who came to the newly discovered continent were ruled by White, Christian men with wealth. Although the elite were White, they did not identify as such. Rather, they identified with their ethnic, national, and/or religious roots (e.g., English, French, Dutch Protestant, Catholic, Puritan). When they came to the new world, they were intent on profiting and prospering at the expense of Native Peoples. Over time, the ruling class elite and their families were outnumbered by the Indigenous Peoples whose lives and land they were stealing and Africans whom they forcibly kidnapped for enslavement and forced labor.

Because the ruling class elite were outnumbered, they had to persuade newly arriving immigrants from Europe, who were mostly White indentured servants, to cast aside their ethnic, national, and/or religious differences and associate themselves with the ruling class. This category of "white" and whiteness (i.e., straight, White, elite male) consolidated the idea of white supremacy to organize these immigrants into a singular and unifying racial category.

Throughout our history, the ruling elite, or the power elite, who traditionally have been wealthy White men, have knowingly or unknowingly upheld whiteness and a hierarchy of racialized value to disconnect and divide: (1) White people from Black, Indigenous, and People of Color; (2) Black, Indigenous, and People of Color from each other; (3) White people from other White people (i.e., classism); and (4) each of us from ourselves (Okun, 2021).

For us to move forward collectively, we must heal from the wounds of our past. We must begin to acknowledge our brokenness. South African scholar Jonathan Jansen (2009) refers to brokenness as "the idea that in our human state we are prone to failure and incompletion, and that as imperfect humans we constantly seek a higher order of living. Brokenness is the realization of imperfection" (p. 269). In her book, *The Gifts of Imperfection* (2010), Brené Brown said:

> Owning our story can be hard but not nearly as difficult as it is spending our lives running from it. Embracing our vulnerabilities is risky but not nearly as dangerous as giving up on love and belonging and joy—the experiences that make us the most vulnerable. Only when we are brave enough to explore the darkness will we discover the infinite power of our light. (p. 6)

Confronting our nation's darkness may invariably bring about feelings of guilt or shame, which is why we work so hard to keep the true history hidden. According to Thandeka (2006), brokenness is connected to white shame, which is this "feeling of inner turmoil over recognition of the ways one has rejected aspects of their full humanity in order to become white" (Casey, 2021, p. 78). White people work so hard to prove they are not racist while continuing to benefit from racist policies and practices within society. Wildman and Davis (2016) contend that too many White people conflate racist actions within a racist system with personal "badness." White people become consumed with how to avoid the label "racist" instead of working to dismantle systemic inequities within our society. This laser focus on proving their goodness allows them to avoid self-reflection about how they have benefited from a system of white supremacy.

Currently, we are seeing the manifestations of this white shame across our country, but particularly within the field of education where there has been a battle against teaching critical race theory (CRT) within schools. Attacks on the fictional CRT bogeyman are a direct manifestation of white shame. The battle against CRT is code for "Do not teach the real history of our country because I do not want to acknowledge the falsehoods of our nation and how I and my children directly benefit from the narrative that *all men are created equal.*"

According to Brown (2010), "Shame hates it when we reach out and tell our story. It hates having words wrapped around it—it can't survive being shared. Shame loves secrecy" (p. 9). The power of shame overshadows and prevents progress within our country. It "corrodes the very part of us that believes we can change and do better" (Brown, 2018, p. 129). This is a primary reason White people must heal from racism and white supremacy. In her book, *all about love,* bell hooks (2001) talked about the notion that a key part of healing is "not about forgetting about the past but seeing it in a new way. We go forward with the fresh insight that the past can no longer hurt us" (p. 209).

For White people, they must move from individualism (i.e., focus on self, including needs and interests) into collectivism. This will require that they lean into the discomfort of how whiteness and white supremacy show up within themselves. When they commit to critical self-reflection and self-examination, they will move into collectivism. Brown (2010) refers to this as true belonging, which she describes as "the innate human desire to be part of something larger than us." She goes on to say that "true belonging only occurs when we present our authentic, imperfect selves to the world, our sense of belonging can never be greater than our level of self-acceptance" (p. 126). That self-acceptance is cultivated through sitting with ourselves, our emotions, and our discomfort in a space where we can move through the negative feelings into a place where we feel intertwined because of our shared humanity. When we can do this, we have started on our quest for racial healing.

White Supremacy and White People

When we think of racial trauma, most of us will not intuitively think of White people. However, we must move into the conscious understanding that we all have been affected by racism and white supremacy in diverse ways. White supremacy is uniquely tied to the experience of a straight White male with money (i.e., the patriarchy). The focus on power and success has allowed White people to buy into it from our nation's inception at the expense of their full humanity. To achieve this false notion of success, White people must knowingly or unknowingly categorize and label individuals of different races, ethnicities, abilities, gender identities, and sexuality as "other" because they do not adhere to the definition of whiteness. This has provided White people with a very narrow understanding of what it means to be human within our society. Consequently, many who do not fit into this notion of whiteness have sacrificed who they are at their core so that other White people will accept them.

So, White people adhere to and uphold characteristics of white supremacy culture, such as individualism and perfectionism, that force them to fit into specific ways of being that sacrifice the very authentic experience of what it means to be human—vulnerability and a feeling of truly belonging, to ourselves and others. Brené Brown (2017) ponders: "What will it take to get to the place in our life where we belong nowhere and everywhere—where belonging is in our heart and not the reward for 'perfecting,' 'pleasing,' 'proving,' and 'pretending'" (p. 35). White supremacy has fed White people false narratives about who they are supposed to be (e.g., success, woman, man) and hindered their positive identity development.

That elite notion of success also was fed to lower-class White people in a very intentional way. The elite needed them to buy into whiteness so that they could maintain their power and control in our nation's institutions. As waves of immigrants from Europe came to the United States, they faced discrimination; however, they quickly realized that they were not on the bottom rung of the ladder. It was particularly easy for European immigrants to morph into whiteness by shedding their names, customs, and languages. By doing so, they could benefit from the societal rights and privileges afforded to White people that were denied to Black children and families. For example, White working-class people were paid a "psychological wage" that allowed them to

"freely go throughout town, attend public parks, be seen at public functions without fear of retribution, ostracism, or refusal" (Bierdz, 2021, p. 711). As such, White people have been stripped of key pieces of their humanity so that White elites could maintain their privilege and power. It has always been about that, which is hard for a lot of people to accept because of our views on patriotism in our country. However, there is nothing more patriotic than recognizing our nation's hypocrisies and working to overcome them. Racial healing is a key part of that journey.

COLLECTIVE HEALING

To heal ourselves and our nation we must understand that racial equity work goes beyond educating White people about white privilege and reflecting on implicit racial biases. Currently, we are surrounded by individuals and organizations that are engaging in so-called equity work. However, they are just putting a bandage on the problem by focusing on empathy, kindness, and compassion. Others continue to implement diversity, equity, and inclusion trainings, or emphasizing the need for cultural sensitivity. These efforts, although important, are not enough to achieve racial justice.

Because many people think that examining implicit biases or becoming culturally competent is all that is required, they ignore the need to address anti-Blackness, institutional and structural racism in our society, and work toward creating equitable and just systems for all. True racial equity work requires an atonement of past harms, reconciling present injustices, and building a socially just future. This work is not easy. It is draining and discouraging at times; however, it is necessary if we are to continue to work toward the "beloved community" that Dr. King talked about.

Acknowledgment

The first stage of racial healing is acknowledgment. To heal from White supremacy and racism, there must be an acknowledgment of the atrocities of slavery and the legacies of Jim Crow and other crimes against humanity, including forced displacement and the genocide of Indigenous Peoples. The truth must be told about the construction of race, racism, White supremacy, slavery, and colonization. We must tell the truth in our families, communities, and local, state, and national governments.

Engagement

Engagement is the second stage, which must take place on personal, interpersonal, and organizational levels. Racial equity and healing take an incredible amount of work. Individuals must be completely engaged in *listening, learning,* and *acting.* It is imperative that people participate in racial equity and racial healing in their spheres of influence (work, home, community), but also cross-culturally. These efforts can be small or large (e.g., reading *How to Be an Anti-Racist* [Kendi, 2019], attending racial equity training).

Reconciliation and Atonement

The third stage involves reconciliation and atonement, which requires changes in society's identity. During this stage, we change society's narrative and require a moral obligation to do so. Given America's narrative of freedom, self-determination, and opportunity for all who work hard, America must first apologize for the intentional subjugation, discrimination, and oppression of liberty and freedom. America must confront its hypocrisy. The goal of this stage is to initiate a shift in power dynamics.

Restoration and Transitional Justice

Finally, we promote restoration and transitional justice, which refers to the ways in which countries emerge from periods of conflict and repression by addressing large-scale or systematic human rights violations so numerous and egregious that the normal justice system will not provide an adequate response (see the International Center for Transitional Justice; www.ictj.org). Examples of transitional justice include establishing accountable institutions and restoring confidence in them; advancing the cause of reconciliation; making access to justice a reality for those harmed and violated; and ensuring that those who have been most affected play a primary role in the pursuit of a just society.

    The four phases of racial healing are not linear. People will move back and forth through each phase as they continue to learn and engage more deeply with authentic racial equity work that focuses on deconstructing anti-Blackness and whiteness. Racial healing within our society is imperative and imminent. Black people and other people of color are simply exhausted, need reprieve from consistent racial trauma, and are tired of fighting for humanity and dignity in a country our ancestors helped build. As a society, many of us are overwhelmed and discouraged by the blatant racial injustices and the lack of accountability. We want things to go back to the way they were before 2016. The fact of the matter is that we cannot go back to a society that was benefiting one group but oppressing another. We must dig in—to our own discomfort, to discuss hard topics of race and racism and heal from racial trauma. That is the only path forward, and it is going to take time. Only when we commit to healing will we be able to achieve the ideals of "liberty and justice for all."

3

Creating a Shared Language

Jen Neitzel and Ebonyse Mead

Racial equity work is fluid and ever changing, mostly because our rapidly changing world demands it. When we commit to advancing equity and justice for young Black children and their families, we must fully recognize that these efforts cannot serve to just check a box. Racial equity and justice work requires that we pledge to deep personal learning and unlearning of what we have been taught about who we are as individuals and a nation. Engaging in racial equity efforts also means that we must understand key terms that define the current situation regarding race and equity within our society.

Many have become fearful about talking about race and racism because of the ever-increasing number of states that are working to outlaw the teaching of critical race theory. The term *critical race theory* (CRT) has been harnessed by a subset of individuals within our society to generate fear so they can maintain and expand their political power. Those within this small group have pushed a false narrative that CRT is being taught in our nation's K–12 system, and even in early childhood education. This false narrative is intended to play on the fears of affluent White families that talking about race and racism will make their children feel bad about themselves and ashamed for being born white. This could not be further from the truth.

First, CRT is a theoretical framework typically taught in graduate school. CRT has its origins in legal studies and has been used to understand the complexities of institutional racism. Second, our children are being exposed to and are already learning about race and racism; there is nothing that anyone can do to prevent that from happening. What CRT does is provide us with a lens for having a broader understanding about race and racism within our current society. CRT theorists posit that racism is deeply enmeshed within our society and has become so commonplace that many of us unknowingly fail to acknowledge the deep effects that it has on the lives of young Black children and their families (Hunter, 2016). This normalization of racism is evident within both historical and current events that have shown how pervasive racism is within our nation's institutions, including education, government, criminal justice, the food system, and health care.

Having a common language allows us to address structural racism and deconstruct whiteness and anti-Blackness in educational settings. Having courageous conversations about race and racism, as well as developing a shared language, is important because it gives us the terminology to name racism when we see it, challenge false narratives, and have tools to fight against it. The purpose of this chapter is to provide definitions for common terms that can be used in racial equity dialogues that will serve as the foundation for addressing inequities within the early childhood system.

RACE

According to York (2016), race is a contrived sociopolitical way to categorize people based on physical differences, such as skin color. Chaddock (2021) notes that the term *Caucasian* was first used to describe White individuals during the 18th century colonization of what is now the United States. During this time, Europeans created a system for placing individuals within specific racial types for the purpose of "annihilation, domination, enslavement, and the production of free labor" (p. 15). The social construction of race allowed White landowning men to create structures that subjugated groups of people based solely on the color of their skin, hair texture, and physique, which still permeates society today.

RACISM

When many of us think of racism, our minds often wander to the Ku Klux Klan or someone who uses racial slurs. We all know what an individual racist looks like; however, we must move beyond this definition to one that grounds itself in systems thinking. According to the University of California, San Francisco Multicultural Resource Center (2022), racism is

> a system (consisting of structures, policies, practices, and norms) that structures opportunity and assigns value based on the way people look. It also unfairly disadvantages some individuals and communities. Yet even more profoundly, the system of racism undermines the realization of the full potential of our whole society. (para. 4)

Racism is built into the United States systems and institutions, and it is deeply woven into the economic, political, and social structures of America (York, 2016).

In early childhood, we often think we are beyond the clutches of racism, but when we look at the disproportionalities in suspensions and expulsions for young Black children as well as the inequities in access to high-quality early childhood programs, we begin to understand that no system within American society is immune. A key part of racial equity work is fully understanding racism and how it shows up within early childhood education.

Structural Racism

There are four levels of racism that we need to unpack so that we can begin to disrupt the inequities that exist in early childhood. According to Lawrence and Keleher (2004), structural racism is a system of hierarchy and inequity, characterized by white supremacy that provides the normalization and legitimization of racial group inequity that routinely advantage White people while producing cumulative and chronic adverse outcomes for people of color. Although there is no "official" definition of structural racism, a collective understanding is that it is "produced and reproduced by laws, rules, and practices, sanctioned and even implemented by various levels of government, and embedded in the economic system as well as in cultural and societal norms" (Bailey et al., 2021, p. 768). In other words, there is a cumulative and compounding effect of various governmental policies that produce inequitable outcomes for Black children and their families. For example, redlining and racialized residential segregation made mortgages less accessible to Black families, which made access to home ownership nearly impossible, and deprived these communities of "an asset that is central to intergenerational wealth transfer" (Bailey et al., 2021, p. 768).

In early childhood, similar structures have been put in place over time, which limits positive outcomes for young Black children. Current policies regarding access to high-quality early childhood education limit families' abilities to acquire key services for their children that are critical for later life and academic success. Studies also have shown that Black children are the least likely to have access to high-quality care and education. For example, 36% of White children who are enrolled in childcare attend high-quality programs, whereas only 25% of Black children attend such programs (Barnett & Nores, 2013). Head Start, which is meant to serve children from extremely poor families, is focused on implementing high-quality early childhood services; however, only 26% of programs that serve Black children are considered to be high quality, whereas 48% of programs where White children receive services are high quality. This is particularly alarming considering that Black children make up 54% of all children served in Head Start programs across the country (Schmit & Walker, 2016). Improving quality and access for Black children is imperative to disrupt the structural racism within early childhood education.

Institutional Racism

Sometimes, the different definitions of racism can get confusing, particularly when talking about structural and institutional racism; however, they are uniquely different. In general, institutional racism can be defined as the dominant group's (i.e., White people) traditions, beliefs, opinions, and myths that are firmly ingrained in every aspect of society—so much so that they are accepted as common facts and understood to be normal. These attitudes and beliefs, which have been absorbed into White people's subconsciouses, serve as the basis for formulating policies and practices that marginalize and oppress people of color (primarily Black children and families). Institutional racism has been practiced in American culture for so long that racism is continually perpetuated (knowingly and unknowingly) and is practiced as normal social behavior in the educational, governmental, political, and even religious arenas (Boutte et al., 2011). The compounding effects of these racist policies and practices in our nation's institutions is structural racism.

Individual and Interpersonal Racism, Implicit Bias, and Microaggressions

When most of us think of racism, we often think of individual and interpersonal racism. With individual racism, these are the internal beliefs that lie within individuals that are not necessarily knowingly acted upon. Interpersonal racism, on the other hand, occurs between individuals. This is when our private beliefs play out in our interactions with others (Lawrence & Keleher, 2004).

A more subtle form of interpersonal racism is implicit bias. According to the Kirwan Institute for the Study of Race and Ethnicity (n.d.), implicit bias refers to the attitudes or stereotypes that affect our understanding, actions, and decisions in an unconscious manner. Everyone is susceptible to these biases, or associations, which include both positive and negative assessments about people and are

activated involuntarily without an individual's awareness or intentional control (Rudman et al., 2004). The unconscious feelings and attitudes we harbor toward people based on race, ethnicity, age, gender, and appearance develop at a very early age through direct and indirect messaging; however, they are malleable and can be unlearned through conscious effort (Blair et al., 2001; Dasgupta & Greenwald, 2001; Rudman et al., 2004). Implicit biases influence individual behaviors and decision making, which can result in inequitable outcomes for different groups. Recent research on implicit bias suggests that stereotypes about Black students are still prevalent and influence the way schools administer disciplinary actions on a daily basis (Cunningham et al., 2004).

Microaggressions are another, more subtle form of interpersonal racism, which include "the everyday slights and insults that minoritized people endure and that most people of the dominant group don't notice or take seriously" (Sensoy & DiAngelo, 2017, p. 226). In general, researchers have identified eleven thematic categories of microaggressions, such as intelligence (e.g., "a credit to your race," "You speak so well"), assumption of criminality or deviance, color blindness, denial of individual racism, objectification, environmental invalidation, and the meritocracy myth. Although microaggressions occur daily, their effects on an individuals' well-being have been minimized because they have become such a normal part of cross-racial interactions. However, microaggressions have been found to contribute to anxiety, depression, substance abuse, and educational performance (Keels et al., 2017).

The use of these microaggressive code words may not seem to be overtly racist to those who use them; however, they do imply that White is superior and Black is inferior. Neighborhood schools are good. Urban or diverse schools are bad. It is important to understand that this coded language did not simply appear out of thin air. It is part of a long history of denigrating Black children and families that has morphed over time and seeped into our collective memory (Neitzel, 2020).

ETHNICITY

Many times, we confuse the terms *race* and *ethnicity*. Even though they share many common characteristics, they are uniquely different. Race is externally imposed and is based on external characteristics such as skin color and hair texture. Racial identities often include a cultural heritage; however, these cultural attributes often are based on stereotypes held by the dominant cultural group (i.e., White people). According to Hinton (2000), a stereotype has been defined as overgeneralized attributes associated with the members of a social group (e.g., Black children and families) with the implication that it applies to all group members. Again, these cultural attributes are externally imposed on a group of people.

Ethnicity also includes a person's cultural heritage, including language, religion, values, food, music, traditions, and holidays that bind people together; however, people of different ethnic groups have power over where they see themselves belonging (Coles, 2006). According to Burton and colleagues (2005), human groups are constantly moving and mixing, which provides individuals with a great deal of freedom to choose their cultural and ethnic identities. Because of this, ethnic identity is becoming increasingly dynamic and based on the differing interests, ideas, and choices of individuals.

COLOR BLINDNESS AND COLOR-BLIND RACISM

Color blindness is the racial ideology that posits that the best way to end racial discrimination is by treating individuals as equally as possible, without regard to race, culture, or ethnicity (e.g., "I love all my children the same," "I don't see color. I just see my kids") (Schofield, 2007). The era of color blindness emerged during the Civil Rights era and promoted the belief that there is no racial hierarchy, which is sustained by a failure to consider the permanence of race's role within our nation's institutions. According to Fergus (2016), a color-blind mind-set sustains White as the norm and ensures this cultural frame of reference for all behaviors, interactions, and experiences. However, color blindness is problematic because it imposes whiteness on everyone and fails to acknowledge the unique, rich, and lived experiences of various racial and ethnic groups.

Color-blind racism is a direct offshoot of color blindness that rationalizes racial inequality using nonracial language. With this type of racism, specific policies and practices that maintain racial inequalities and white supremacy are legitimized because we have been operating under the assumption that racism no longer exists. Examples of color-blind racism include notions of meritocracy, opportunity gaps in education, housing discrimination, and voter disenfranchisement (Bonilla-Silva, 2018).

COLOR BRAVE

In response to color blindness, American businesswoman Mellody Hobson coined the term *color brave* in her TED Talk "Color Blind or Color Brave?" that has been viewed more than 4.5 million times. Hobson contends that we all must lean into being color brave. This means that instead of ignoring racism, we need to be proactive by having honest and courageous conversations about race with others. Becoming color brave means that white people continue to learn about racism, white supremacy, and white privilege while also challenging the ways in which these characteristics show up within themselves. As white individuals commit to being color brave, they also begin to identify how they can influence change and challenge racism in their spheres of influence (e.g., early childhood programs, state policy, early intervention services). (Retrieved from https://www.pwc.com/us/en/about-us/colorbrave.html).

MERITOCRACY

Meritocracy is a strong belief within American society, particularly within White communities, which suggests that individuals can achieve whatever they want if they work hard enough and are talented enough (e.g., pulling yourself up by your bootstraps) (McNamee & Miller, 2014). Inherent in this ideology also is the notion that the system is fair and provides enough opportunity for anyone to get ahead if they put their minds to it. However, this myth of meritocracy is in complete contradiction to the realities of systems where specific structures have been put in place over time that prevent Black people from achieving the same outcomes as their White counterparts (Sensoy & DiAngelo, 2017). The problem with the notion of meritocracy is that it ignores systems and structures put in place to safeguard the privilege of one group over another.

PREJUDICE

Social psychologists contend that since the earliest expressions of racial prejudice, there has been a pattern of derogation, attempting to negatively differentiate Black people, in an explicit manner, as a "race" that is lazy and not intelligent (McDonald & Crandall, 2015). Due to a shift to more implicit forms of racial behaviors during our post–Civil Rights era of color blindness, overtly explicit racism has declined and given space for the development of prejudgments about "a person, a group, an event, an idea, or a thing" (Lawrence & Keleher, 2004, p. 5). While overt forms of racism are not as prevalent as they were during slavery and Jim Crow, we all have absorbed thoughts and feelings regarding race, gender, age, and ability into our subconsciouses that can unknowingly affect our behaviors and decisions on a daily basis. When we act on our prejudices, we engage in discrimination.

DISCRIMINATION

According to DeGruy (2009), discrimination is "the unfair or prejudicial treatment of different categories of people or things especially on the grounds of race, ethnicity, age, or sex" (p. 60). Racial discrimination can be both overt and more subtle. Examples of overt discrimination include (a) a Black person receiving a longer prison sentence than a White person who committed a similar crime or (b) Black people getting pulled over by police at a higher rate than White people (Li, 2019; Pierson et al., 2020). There are many examples of subtle forms of racial discrimination as well. In employment, it can take the form of failing to hire, train, mentor, or promote a person of color, or they may find themselves subjected to excessive performance monitoring or may be more seriously blamed for a common mistake.

POWER

Power is a relational term between human beings that is best understood within the context of specific historical, economic, political, and social settings. In other words, to understand power in today's society, we must look back at our history and the transmission of power across generations (Lawrence & Keleher, 2004). At the formation of the United States, power was held by White, straight, landowning men. Through their monetary, societal, and political power, they were able to (1) have control of and prevent access to institutions sanctioned by the state, (2) own and control the major resources of a state while also having the capacity to make and enforce decisions based on this

ownership and control, (3) decide what they want and to act in an organized way to get it, and (4) define reality and to convince other people that it is their definition.

To maintain this power, White men with wealth knowingly limited the rights and privileges of anyone who did not fit into the combined categories of (a) White, (b) straight, (c) landowning, and (d) male. Over time, our nation has expanded who can be included in those categories of power; however, White men with monetary wealth have had a collective power that is just now beginning to be challenged. It is important to understand that when we are talking about power, we are talking about a collective power that can alter policies and practices in a way that advances the rights and privileges of those people who have been traditionally excluded from the power categories. Within society, we are looking for a shared power where a diverse group of individuals collectively work toward advancing equity and justice.

OPPRESSION

Racial oppression occurs when those individuals with collective institutional power (e.g., political, economic, social) act on their prejudices and actively discriminate against those who do not have that type of power. According to Sensoy and DiAngelo (2017), "oppression occurs when one group is able to enforce its prejudice throughout society because it controls the institutions" (p. 226). An uncomplicated way to understand oppression is this equation: prejudice + institutional power = oppression (e.g., racism, sexism, ableism, classism).

EQUALITY, EQUITY, AND JUSTICE

Equality, equity, and *justice* are the most misunderstood of all the racial equity terms. For example, they often are used interchangeably when they are not at all interchangeable. According to the Annie E. Casey Foundation (2021), equity involves digging

deeper into the issues. With equity, we give people what they need to thrive. Equality, in contrast, works to give *everyone* the *same* things to enjoy full, healthy lives. Like equity, equality aims to promote fairness and justice; however, it is built on notions of meritocracy that posit that we are all starting off at the same place.

Many of us who are currently working to promote better outcomes for Black children and families are stuck within an equity lens; however, we want to move into a racial justice framework where we are engaged in the "proactive reinforcement of policies, practices, attitudes and actions that produce equitable power, access, opportunities, treatment, impacts and outcomes for all" regardless of race, ethnicity, or the community in which they live (Lawrence & Keleher, 2004, p. 2). Implementing a racial justice framework allows us to be more proactive and preventive, rather than reactive to the ongoing inequities. This means we are working to understand the root causes of the inequities while also listening to people with lived experience to understand the context for the ongoing inequities in society, including within early childhood education.

INTERNALIZED RACIAL OPPRESSION

Internalized racial oppression is experienced by Black individuals and other people of color when they take on and act out (sometimes unintentionally) the constant messages that they and their group are inferior to the dominant group (i.e., dominant white culture) (Sensoy & DiAngelo, 2017). Examples of internalized racial oppression include a sense of inherent inferiority, low self-esteem, or feelings of shame and rage. Children's racial and ethnic culture shape how they see themselves in the world and greatly influences their sense of self, identity, and self-efficacy.

When young children experience internalized racial oppression, their positive racial and ethnic identity is threatened. Developing a positive sense of self and identity is a journey for Black, Indigenous, and People of Color (BIPOC) that starts in early childhood. Strategies such as racial socialization are often used by Black families and other families of color to promote positive racial and ethnic identity. Racial socialization has been referred to as the developmental process by which children acquire specific verbal and nonverbal messages about values, attitudes, behaviors, and beliefs of their racial group (Lesane-Brown et al., 2006). Racial socialization often includes messages that (a) counteract the negative connotations associated with being Black in America, (b) teach Black children how to navigate a racist society, (c) demonstrate the racial inequalities in society, and (d) emphasize racial pride. Teachers play a pivotal role in developing the social and emotional well-being of young children. Using racial socialization to promote positive racial and ethnic identity in young children is a promising strategy that helps children deal with internalized racial oppression.

INTERNALIZED RACIAL SUPERIORITY

Internalized racial superiority, on the other hand, is experienced by individuals within the dominant White culture when they take on and act out (sometimes unintentionally) the constant messages that they and their group are superior to a minoritized group (Sensoy & DiAngelo, 2017). Examples of internalized racial superiority include normalizing whiteness, defensiveness, a sense of entitlement, or white fragility. York (2016) argues that racism harms White children's development just as it does children of color. Denial of reality, rationalization, rigid thinking, superiority, fear and hatred, and fragility are ways in which racism harms White children. When White children experience internalized racial superiority, it creates a falsehood that normalizes whiteness. It sends a message of a shared experience of whiteness that prevents White children from taking the perspective and understanding the experiences of Black children and other children of color. When White children lack exposure to Black people and other people of color, they are unable to empathize with the stress of racism (York, 2016). Thus, White children grow up unable to understand the complexities and nuances of racism and the implications it has on the lives of Black people and other people of color. It is imperative that educators talk about race and racism with young children to avoid both internalized racial oppression and internalized racial superiority.

ANTI-RACISM

With equity and justice work, each of us must commit to anti-racism. This ideology includes ideas and actions that are meant to challenge and confront racial prejudice, systemic racism, and the oppression of people of color, particularly Black children and families. Anti-racism is grounded in conscious efforts and deliberate actions that are intended to create equal opportunities for all people (Derman-Sparks & Phillips, 1997). For White people, committing to anti-racism can be particularly challenging because when they do so, they must engage in deep, personal work in which they acknowledge personal privileges, confront how they have been complicit in racism, and work to change their personal racial biases.

The tricky part for White people is that they cannot simply declare themselves "non-racist." According to Derman-Sparks and Philips (1997), "People cannot choose to remove themselves from the racist system and become 'non-racist,' because it is impossible not to participate in an institutionally racist system." They go on to say that individuals can, however, "choose to change it—to consciously seek to reduce and eventually eliminate racism, and in its place to create new institutional relationships not dependent on domination and subordination of any racial group" (p. 23). For White people, this involves moving beyond "nice racism," which prevents White people from acknowledging their role in upholding racism within our society and systems because they are so intent on proving that they are "one of the good ones," "not racist," "nice," and "kind." Derman-Sparks and Philips (1997) say that there is a great need for White people to put this exhausting effort aside because (1) it prevents their own healing and personal growth and (2) it allows them to ignore the fact that White people are "the problem with race, that racism is carried by White power, closed structures, and ethnocentric culture" (p. 25). What we need right now is more White people who are committed to redistributing power and creating more equitable resources and institutions. This will require that White people sit in the ambiguity of "White privilege while fighting White privilege" and understand that White people do not need to feel ashamed of something that they did not create (Derman-Sparks & Philips, 1997, p. 25).

Being anti-racist is different for White people than it is for people of color. For White people, being anti-racist evolves with their racial identity development. They must acknowledge and understand their privilege, work to change their internalized racism, and interrupt racism when they see it. For people of color, it means recognizing how race and racism have been internalized and whether it has been applied to other people of color (Derman-Sparks & Philips, 1997). Committing to anti-racism is ongoing. We all will continue to learn and unlearn throughout our lives. There is no destination for anti-racism. It is all about the journey.

INTERSECTIONALITY

Intersectionality is a term coined by legal scholar and sociologist Kimberlé Crenshaw in 1989. The concept of intersectionality describes the ways in which multiple identities interact and shape the experiences of individuals from oppressed and marginalized groups. Intersectionality is a useful framework to address inequities within education because it allows us to see the many ways children may experience discrimination based on their multiple identities. For example, the disproportionate rate at which Black girls are suspended compared with other girls can be understood through the lens of intersectionality. Intersectionality is also useful in understanding the trauma experienced by traditionally marginalized and oppressed groups. Understanding the layers and the intersections of multiple identities provides a holistic picture to enact policies that address discriminatory practices based on multiple identities.

BIPOC AND PEOPLE OF COLOR

BIPOC is a term that is used to highlight the unique relationship Indigenous and Black (African American) people have to whiteness and how it shapes their experiences of and relationship to white supremacy (www.thebipocproject.org). The term *BIPOC* is typically used among activist groups and other organizations leading racial justice efforts that are mindful of and want to explicitly highlight the unique experiences of racism among Black and Indigenous Peoples in the United States. Using *BIPOC* illustrates the awareness that not all people of color have a shared experience of racism in America. However, it should be noted that when promoting diversity, equity, and inclusion efforts using the term *BIPOC* may be useful. For example, when creating a diverse parenting advisory board, it may be useful to encourage all BIPOC families to attend. On the other hand, using *BIPOC* may not be ideal when addressing issues that disproportionately impact one group of people (i.e., police brutality among Black males).

The terms *people of color* and *BIPOC* can be useful when describing similar experiences of racial discrimination and suffering experienced by racialized people. However, the terms are also problematic because they do not give space to the unique experiences of racial discrimination, injustices, and biases experienced by different racial and ethnic groups. The term *people of color* often lumps all racialized people's experiences together and does not give way to the necessary investigation and injury experienced by each group.

WHAT TO DO NEXT

Having a shared language and understanding of key terms is a critical component of racial equity work because it allows groups of individuals to begin addressing inequities without having ongoing discussions about what each term means. This chapter provided a broad overview of the most important terms that are used within racial equity dialogue at this time. For all of us, we must continue our learning because anti-racism is never ending (see the resource guide in Appendix A for continued learning opportunities). There is too much to unpack and understand as we engage in disrupting centuries-old issues. Begin or continue to have conversations with those in your sphere of influence. Organize monthly coffee talks to discuss issues around microaggressions, implicit bias, or colorism. Racial equity work must be intentional, or we will just continue to uphold the status quo and "how things have always been done." Be impatient but intentional with the process. Having a deep understanding of these terms and how they show up in early childhood education is critical to the success of racial equity work.

4

Whiteness in Early Childhood Education

Jen Neitzel

In December 2018, I lost my job as a researcher and technical assistance provider because of a lack of funding. This was an incredibly difficult and painful experience because I had been with this organization for more than 18 years—not only as a researcher and technical assistance provider, but also as a student and teacher. My time there had been foundational to who I was. I learned a great deal from mentors who had become pseudo-parents to me. Being told that there was no more funding for me was not how I anticipated leaving this place that had become home. Looking back now, I realize that this experience was necessary for me to truly engage in transformational equity work. I had to transform individually before I could help facilitate that same transformation in others. During that time, and even now, I reflect on this quote by the Franciscan friar Richard Rohr (2018):

> Looking back, I see how the job I lost pushed me to find work that was mine to do, how the "Road Closed" sign turned me toward terrain that I'm glad I traveled, how losses that felt irredeemable forced me to find new sources of meaning. In each of these experiences, it felt as though something was dying, and so it was. Yet deep down, amid all the falling, the seeds of new life were always being silently and lavishly sown.

For those 18 years, I had been in the white towers of academia, removed from the real-life experiences of the children and families whom I was dedicated to serving. I was not proximate to their lived experiences. I was swimming in whiteness and white supremacy culture. Losing my job stripped me of everything that I knew that I was and my identity at that time: research scientist and technical assistance provider at a prominent Research I university. I had been lured into this false identity because of whiteness—the identity that promotes individual achievement and success. Now I was just Jen. I went through a period of depression and intense anxiety. I took time to grieve and began to unlearn everything that society told me I needed to be.

So much of my professional life had been caught up in status and titles, mostly driven by the antiquated and archaic standards for promotion in academia but also by my own need to finally be recognized for making something of my life. Professional success is defined by how many publications you have, how much grant money has been brought into the university, or how many principal investigator positions you have. I was part of the system that was tied to an affluent White notion of success. I was caught up in my own whiteness (i.e., accepting that the White experience is the norm) and the whiteness of the entire system—even though I was working toward achieving equity in education. Or so I thought. I now realize that I had to be stripped of my worldview regarding success and achievement to truly do the work of equity.

Currently, within our society, we have a skewed idea of what success means, which is primarily driven by what White people (predominately White men) have defined it to be. On top of the false notions of success, many affluent White people place value on where their children attend school, whether their children are on the top sports team, the neighborhoods where they live, and which country club they belong to. These affluent White measures of success are really driven by our need to achieve, to place ourselves in positions higher than others, and to create separation between "us" and "them." What I have found in the months after I lost my job was that these false notions of success (e.g., publications, principal investigator positions) and the desire to attain them do not matter. When those of us who are working toward equity get proximate, as Bryan Stevenson, founder and Executive Director of the Equal Justice Initiative, says, we begin to see that our current definition of success does little more than to maintain the status quo.

Those of us who are working toward equity must get out of our offices, our institutions, and our systems so that we can truly understand the issues that we are working so tirelessly to overcome. To do this, however, requires a significant amount of humility. We must be willing to accept that we, with our PhDs and fancy titles, do not have all the answers. In fact, the very answers that we seek are waiting to be heard. We just need to be willing to step aside and provide seats at the table for those who are most affected by the structural barriers and inequitable systems.

These principles do not apply just to those who are doing equity work. When we allow ourselves to buy into a narrow definition of what it means to be successful, we perpetuate the ongoing divides and notions of otherness within our society. We sustain the ideal that only those who are "successful" should have access to privilege and power. Relinquishing this longstanding worldview requires a willingness to look deeply and conclude that, although important for survival, many of the materialistic possessions that we hold dear are not the ultimate markers of success. What is needed now within our society, more than ever, is a leveling of the playing field—that underneath all the bravado and show—we are all humans worthy of dignity, respect, and the right to have our voices heard and be a part of the solutions to our very pressing problems.

I now realize that I needed to be humbled. I needed to lose my job. I needed to be stripped of my titles. I had to become "nobody" to understand that our current definition of success and achievement allows our egos to lead the development of policy and the implementation of practices within our systems, most notably education. If we were just willing to accept that we are not better than those we seek to serve, we would find that the path to equity becomes much clearer. It is not just about understanding the issues and having knowledge about the research. When we ignore the voices of those who are most affected, we create a power dynamic—one that is very paternalistic at its core. It is one that says, "I know what is best for you." Doing true equity work requires a willingness to strip ourselves of our titles so that we can begin to engage in relationships that are more authentic, genuine, caring, and more human—relationships where we listen, learn, and allow others to lead the way.

I realize now that I was so ego driven. Even though it is difficult to admit, those titles and credentials were incredibly important to me and defined how I operated in this world. I needed to be stripped of all of that so that I could move through this work with humility and an understanding that none of these external achievements matter and that they are counterproductive to the cause. My title, where I worked—none of it matters. My preoccupation with ego-driven accolades prevented me from doing true equity work. Those things are not the point of all of this, and focusing on those outcomes prevented me from achieving "real success," which is actually the work itself.

WHAT IS WHITENESS?

In our work at the Educational Equity Institute, we have found that understanding and deconstructing whiteness can often be difficult for White people. A major reason for this is because White people have been socialized within a society that values their "perceptions, feelings, and emotions" (Bonilla-Silva, 2018, p. 104). In other words, the experiences of White people are seen as the norm, which limits their ability to comprehend the experiences of people of color, particularly of Black people within our society. Whiteness is an incredibly complex construct that requires an unpeeling of many layers to fully understand its hold on our society. Gaining a better understanding about the social construction of race is essential before we can unpack how whiteness shows up within the early childhood system.

The Social Construction of Race

In the past few years, there has been a growing awareness by many White people that race and racism are interwoven into the fabric of our nation's DNA. In 1619, twenty African souls arrived on the shores of the Virginia colony of Jamestown after being captured in Luanda. They were herded onto the privateer *White Lion* and forced to make the long journey through the Middle Passage to the colonies. Ibram X. Kendi (2021) refers to August 20, 1619, as the birth of "African America"; however, "Life was not promised for this newborn in 1619. Joy was not promised. Peace was not promised. Freedom was not promised. Only slavery, only racism, only the mighty Atlantic blocking the way back home seemed to be promised" (p. xvi).

During this time, many White indentured servants also were arriving from Ireland and Scotland to escape war, famine, poverty, and torture as sport. They were coming to the North American continent in search of a better life. After 7 years of domestic servitude, they would be free to build lives, wealth, and privilege. This experience was quite different from the African indentured servants in 1619 (chattel slavey did not yet exist) who were torn from their villages, their lives, and their families so that they could be transported to the colonies to provide free labor on newly formed plantations. Already wealthy White landowning men could use their bondage to amass even more wealth and power.

In the late 1600s, nearly 40% of the indentured servant population lived in the Virginia colony. The Africans, in combination with the White indentured servants, built houses and buildings, planted and harvested crops, and worked in houses as servants for the wealthy elite. These White and Black indentured servants lived together, worked together, and eventually rebelled together against the horrible living conditions and treatment they experienced. This uprising became known as Bacon's Rebellion (1676) because of landowner Nathaniel Bacon's support of White and Black indentured servants rebelling against other plantation owners (McGhee, 2021).

Following this rebellion, landowning men in the Virginia colony realized that the only way to maintain their power and wealth from further uprisings was to divide and conquer. Thus, the social construction of race began. As such, they instituted the Virginia Black Codes in 1705, which coincided with ongoing talk about whether Africans were fully human and entitled to the protection of God's love (Wright, 2021). In "An act concerning Servants and Slaves" (known more informally as the Black Codes), passed in October 1705, the Virginia General Assembly stated the following:

> All servants imported and brought into the Country . . . who were not Christians in their native Country . . . shall be accounted and be slaves. All Negro, mulatto and Indian slaves within this dominion . . . shall be held to be real estate. If any slave resists his master . . . correcting such slave and shall happen to be killed in such correction . . . the master shall be free of all punishment . . . as if such accident never happened.

These harsh codes reinforced the nonhumanity of enslaved Africans.

It is important to understand that before Bacon's Rebellion, race (i.e., Black, White) did not exist. People in the colonies referenced and categorized each other according to where they came from (e.g., Ireland, England, Scotland, African tribe). The Assembly decided that, whereas White servants could own property, all property owned by African servants was to be seized and sold, with profits "applied to the use of the [white] poor."

Thus, the White poor materially benefited from additional oppressions put upon enslaved Africans. The Black Codes further provided White landowners with the "legal order to control the unruly and growing Black workforce upon which the colonies' wealth extraction depended" (Wright, 2021, p. 80). In this way, the legal construction of race helped diffuse the threat of insurrection. Poor White people would now see themselves as allied with those far wealthier than themselves and would define themselves by race rather than by class. This social construction of whiteness was intended to hinder class solidarity; however, it also ushered in anti-Blackness—the notion that Black people are subhuman, undeserving, unworthy, and in need of control (Boehm-Turner & Toedt, 2021).

POST-RACIAL SOCIETY?

Before the murder of George Floyd in May 2020, many White people were operating as if we were living in a post-racial society. Many events over the past several decades have perpetuated this color-blind reality that racism no longer exists in the United States.

In 1954, the U.S. Supreme Court had ruled in *Brown v. Board of Education* that segregation within our nation's public schools was unconstitutional. Even though many of us associate that landmark case as groundbreaking (which it was), "many communities failed to fully implement the court-ordered plans or deliberately subverted the plans due to fear of social disruption or deeply rooted racist beliefs" (Mattheis, 2021, p. 86). To this day, the ideals of *Brown* have not been fully realized in our nation's public schools. Predominantly Black schools remain woefully underfunded, whereas White schools become overfunded, primarily because of "capital campaigns" initiated within wealthier suburbs to provide additional resources and equipment (e.g., playground equipment, computers). According to Mattheis (2021), "The impact of the case on public opinion and as legal precedent has perhaps been much stronger than in effecting true and lasting change in education" (p. 81). The myth of *Brown*'s success remains an ever-present reality within our nation's psyche.

The beginning of the Civil Rights movement directly coincided with the *Brown* ruling. The Montgomery Bus Boycott, the Selma March, the Freedom Riders, and the March on Washington were the impetus behind monumental legislation that provided equal protection under the law and were designed to protect the voting rights of Black Americans. The murder of George Floyd was a wake-up call for many White Americans that, although these pieces of legislation were progress and were cause for celebration, Black Americans are still fighting for their lives to simply matter in this country. Police brutality, voting restrictions, and other repressive policies, particularly from 2016 to 2020, persist despite the efforts of Marcus Garvey, Dr. King, Malcom X, Angela Davis, and others. The power of whiteness continues to inhibit the work of equity and justice within our society.

WHITENESS IN SOCIETY

We live in a very individualistic society. Americans tend to view every person as a self-sufficient individual, and this idea is important to understanding the American value system. Individualism implies that everyone is their own person, not a representative of a family, community, or any other group. Americans are more likely to prioritize themselves over a group, and they value independence and autonomy (Rosenbaum, 2018). Some scholars suggest that the roots of this individualism are within the American Revolution, particularly within the elite ruling class. However, the masses were much more focused on the success of the group as a whole (Grabb et al., 1999; Lipset, 1996).

Understanding our history and the origin of thought and narratives within our country provides us with such a unique perspective about the issues and problems we are facing today. According to these scholars, the "rugged individualism" that has become synonymous with our cultural values was only present within the elite ruling class in the colonies. Going back to the social construction of race allows us to gain a bird's eye view as to when this ideology became mainstream. As the elites used race to divide and conquer the lower-class White indentured servants from the Black slaves and indentured servants, this individualistic narrative seeped into the psyches of newly freed White indentured servants as they morphed into whiteness.

That affluent White whiteness ensured that "white cultural and behavioral norms" were "taken for granted as the neutral standard for society." From the inception of whiteness, it was equated with "rationality, orderliness, self-control, and empirical thinking." In contrast, anything non-White was seen as "violent, chaotic, and irrational" (Baker, 2021, p. 251). As such, whiteness, that affluent White whiteness, became an aspirational goal in the United States. According to Baker, "What ensued was a nationwide game of cultural assimilation for those with white skin. Physical appearances, methods of education, work ethic, religious values, and standards of behavior took on a homogenized hue while racial segregation intensified." He goes on to say, "By the 1950s, a new message emerged for all to witness first-hand: whiteness was attainable for those with white skin, but never for those without it" (p. 252). So, what began as the historical and legal construction of whiteness turned into the invisible system of white privilege. Harkening back to the roots of whiteness, "the largest contemporary factor determining who gets access to the privilege of whiteness is largely decided by social and economic capital" (p. 253). Because of the strength of anti-Blackness within society, there is a constant pull for White people of all socioeconomic classes to be encompassed within that affluent White whiteness.

Since the election of 2016, we have seen the historical roots of whiteness and anti-Blackness rise to the surface after decades of willful ignorance and color blindness to avoid acknowledging our complicated history and to maintain the status quo. What we are seeing right now is a desperate attempt to uphold whiteness within our society. This "invisible system of white privilege" has fed us false narratives about who we are as individuals and as a country.

Whiteness places value on certain experiences within society, including social, educational, and financial. Whiteness tells us that superior education, wealth, and materialism are the gold standards of success in our society. Whiteness dictates dress, hairstyles, attractiveness, tone of voice, behavior, and how to show respect. Whiteness tells individuals what it means to be a boy/man or girl/woman within society. Many people do not understand that gender is also a social construct. For generations, boys and girls have come into the world with predetermined standards about who they are supposed to be. We hold gender reveal parties with pink and blue decorations. We give dolls to girls and trucks to boys, not understanding that we must allow our children to determine their own course and interests. We need to honor our little girls who do not want to wear dresses or bows in their hair, which are the unspoken standards of femininity within our society. We must honor our sensitive boys who love baby animals and pink. Too often, we expect our boys to be emotionless alphas who can only show anger, not sadness or other "weak" emotions. Moving out of whiteness means deconstructing all these characteristics, including how they show up in our own lives.

Whiteness has also created the false narrative that we should not make things political. However, everything within our country has always been political. Education, including early care and learning, is intertwined with whiteness politics. Early childhood education and public education have never been valued within our country. White people, particularly affluent White parents, often view public education as a service that they are entitled to and should serve their aspirations for their children to apply to and attend elite universities, thus completing the circle of white achievement and advancement at the expense of others. According to educational historians, compulsory education has always been how "the ruling class sought to invest the working class with bourgeois attitudes, values, and habits. . . . while teaching its children to identify with and aspire toward the bourgeoisie" (Falk, 2021, p. 689). Public education has never been about teaching critical thinking and problem solving; it has always been a way for elite White people in power to uphold the status quo. That is one of the main reasons we are seeing such a backlash against teaching children about racism and the true history of our country. Educating our children about our nation's past is seen as a direct threat to the status quo.

During the pandemic, we also watched as waves of White parents pulled their children from public schools and enrolled them in private schools, which had the financial resources to acquire safety materials and technology to stay open in a way that minimized the spread of COVID-19. Many White families, particularly affluent White families, criticized public school systems across the United States for not keeping schools in session, not recognizing that public education has been woefully underfunded by state legislatures for decades. Currently, in North Carolina where I live, we have a $6.5 billion budget surplus; however, the majority Republican state legislature is withholding the state budget because they have been court-ordered to fully fund public schools. Public school teachers, who are already underpaid, have not received a raise in 3 years, whereas those in positions of leadership in the Department of Public Instruction were recently given hefty raises. As such, the public education system is crumbling under the weight of decades of devaluement, underfunding, and the ongoing pandemic.

Whiteness also tells us that early care and learning is nothing more than glorified babysitting. Currently in North Carolina, the governor has recognized that the child-care system is crumbling, just like it is across the country. He is offering grants to child-care programs to help keep them open so that families can go to work. Like public education, child care has been devalued and underfunded for decades. Those of us working in the field of early childhood have advocated for increased funding for child care because (1) it has become increasingly expensive and (2) access to quality programs continues to be an issue for families living in low-income households.

We can see the devaluing and underfunding of child care playing out before our eyes in the ongoing discussions about President Joseph R. Biden's Build Back Better Plan. We have seen paid family leave eliminated, which is particularly detrimental for parents who are working hourly jobs that do not provide these types of benefits. Originally, the compromise in the plan was that paid family leave would be provided for 4 weeks; however, that has been eliminated. This is harmful for low-income families because (a) it limits their ability to form positive attachments with their newborns because they must return to work immediately so they will not lose their jobs and (b) child-care centers do not admit babies until they are 6 weeks of age, leaving families with few options. Child care and early education have always been political.

This leads us back to the notion of whiteness and individualism. Because everything is and always has been political in our country, we must look at how we vote. Typically, White Americans vote for themselves—what benefits them and what benefits their family. However, we must move into a collectivism where we are motivated by group goals and long-term relationships. With collectivism, people easily sacrifice individual benefit for the benefit of others. This is what theologian Kate Bowler refers to as the "wild project. . . .about love." I listened to a 2021 *On Being* podcast episode featuring her that was focused on hope and optimism. As she was talking about this wild project of human existence, she said, "It was always about all of us. We belong to each other" (Bowler & Ali, 2021).

It is long past time for us to move into that mentality within our country; however, that will require that we relinquish whiteness—that we sacrifice our own self-interests for the common good. It will require that we move into the collective where we are all working toward the common goal of our shared humanity. It will require that we are building a movement that is designed to disrupt the status quo of whiteness so that others may have access to the same opportunities and resources that have been denied to them since the inception of our country. This will require "a true revolution of values" as Dr. King called it. In his 1967 speech, *Where Do We Go From Here,* he said,

> America, the richest and most powerful nation in the world, can well lead the way in this revolution of values. There is nothing to prevent us from paying adequate wages to school teachers, social workers and other servants of the public to ensure that we have the best available personnel in these positions which are charged with the responsibility of guiding our future generations. There is nothing but a lack of social vision to prevent us from paying an adequate wage to every American citizen whether he be a hospital worker, laundry worker, maid or day laborer. There is nothing except shortsightedness to prevent us from guaranteeing an annual minimum—and livable—income for every American family. There is nothing to keep us from remolding a recalcitrant status quo with bruised hands until we have fashioned it into a brotherhood.

I recently had a discussion with my 18-year-old about the importance of voting. He is quite cynical about politics and rightfully so. However, I told him that voting is not only about him. He must vote for the bus driver and for the person who works at McDonald's, for affordable child care, and for full funding of our public schools. We must move into that brotherhood that Dr. King talked about. That is when we will begin to transform our systems, including early childhood.

WHITENESS IN EARLY CHILDHOOD

I think that we, as early educators, often have a challenging time admitting that we are not immune from the reach of whiteness. Just like every institution within our society, we have been touched by its cultural norms and values. According to E. Miller (2021), Euro-American research over the past 300 years has compartmentalized, generalized, and labeled "'appropriate' behaviors for various maturational phases of childhood as if they were universal, objective, and neutrally experienced by various groups of racialized people" (p. 152). Just like other institutions within the United States, the White worldview has provided the foundation for how we determine what high-quality early childhood education looks like. I know this can be a hard concept for us as early childhood educators to grasp; however, we need to do some critical analysis of our current practices.

For decades, we have relied on developmentally appropriate practices (DAP) by the National Association for the Education of Young Children (NAEYC) to guide us in how we educate our youngest children. According to NAEYC (2020), DAP "constitutes an approach to teaching grounded in what is known about effective early education" (p. 4). Engaging in equity work requires that we do a lot of holding two things in our hands at the same time. For example, I remember doing a White processing session, and one of the women said that she was having a tough time loving her country while also understanding the true history of it. For her, and many of us, it is possible to hold love of country in one hand and its hypocrisy in the other. Within early childhood, we can acknowledge the goodness of DAP while also understanding that we need to include additional voices in the conversation about what high-quality early childhood education looks like and how it can be more inclusive of racially and ethnically diverse children and families.

Whiteness shows up in many ways within early childhood. According to E. Miller (2021),

> Racialized bias seeps through early childhood curricula and assessments oft-used in the education of young children, the effects of which can be devastating on children's academic trajectories if they do not measure up to the idealized white norms for child development. (p. 155)

In their work, Feinberg and colleagues (2011) found that Black children who qualified for services at 24 months based on developmental delay alone were less likely to receive services. However, no differences by race were found among children who qualified based on established medical conditions.

These findings are particularly important because they reveal the objectivity often associated with some diagnoses within early childhood education. For example, established medical conditions are highly objective. It is easy to diagnose hearing or visual impairments in children regardless of race or ethnicity. However, subjectivity and bias come into play with other diagnoses, such as developmental or language delay. E. Miller (2021) noted that we often view Black children from a deficit lens in which they experience less rich language in their homes, indicating they need to catch up to White middle-class norms. This deficit lens and assessment practices serve as a gateway into special education as children enter public school. For instance, as Black children move into the K–12 system, they are twice as likely to be identified as having emotional disturbance and intellectual disability as their peers (Feinberg et al., 2011).

In our approach at the Educational Equity Institute, we always emphasize that when we address the deepest disparities, we will address the inequities for other children and families of color. Even though the deepest disparities tend to be with Black children, we often overlook Indigenous children and the inequities with that population. Feinberg and colleagues' findings (2021) indicate that American Indian students are twice as likely to be identified as having specific learning disabilities and are 4 times as likely to be identified as having developmental delays. Understanding and addressing the disparities within the Native American population is another critical need within our society. A part of the reckoning is to acknowledge that the introduction of disease, particularly smallpox, wiped out nearly 90% of the population of Native Peoples (Patterson & Runge, 2002). Today, most Indigenous children and families live in 10 states where little has been done to atone for past and current harms, including within the educational system.

Within early childhood, whiteness also shows up in the behavioral expectations we have for children, what social skills are important, how we expect children to interact with teachers, and what we mean when we say "school readiness." Because our current system of early care and learning was set up within this frame of whiteness, we must acknowledge that we have forced, and continue to force, young Black children to learn in an educational system that was not set up for them. Our current early education system does not allow Black children and other children of color to be free in who they are.

For early childhood educators, it is essential that we begin asking ourselves and others some key questions:

- What curricula do we use? Who designed them? Do they represent a strengths-based approach or a deficit model?

- How do we determine academic achievement? What assessments do we use? What worldview do they represent?

- How do we determine high-quality education? What worldview does the instruction represent?

- What ideal of achievement are we promoting? The right college? The right job?

- What school readiness skills are important?

- In our social-emotional curricula, how do we define safety and trust? What does it mean for young Black children and their families to feel safe and develop trust?

- Are we knowingly, or unknowingly, generating practices that require Black children to alter who they are so that they "fit" into our current system?

- How do we educate future teachers?

- Is academic achievement the primary goal of education?

- Does our educational system promote conformity to whiteness?

- Does our educational system, knowingly or unknowingly, perpetuate hierarchies within our society (e.g., patriarchy, class, race)?

WHAT YOU CAN DO

Challenging whiteness, not only in ourselves but within the early childhood system, is a critical component of anti-racism and equity work. Many times, White people do not know where to begin in their efforts to dismantle inequitable systems. Following are some things that you can do right now to begin challenging whiteness.

1.   *Move beyond allyship. Commit to being a co-conspirator.*

I am going to challenge White people a bit now. Often, we (meaning White people) say that we are allies in this work; however, this can be a performative gesture that makes us feel like a "good White person" because we are essentially saying, "I am not a racist," which is not enough. Self-proclaimed allyship allows us to check a box without committing to the deep, internal work of anti-racism. A first step is to acknowledge that Black people cannot avoid racism. White people have numerous escape hatches that allow them a way out of situations and conversations that might make them uncomfortable. Instead, White people must commit to being co-conspirators. This means that we do our own anti-racism work. We create spaces where White people can do the work together that moves beyond White book clubs reading about racism and then moving on with their daily lives. This means that we must read, listen, examine, and reflect on the ways that whiteness shows up within us, within our daily lives, and within the early childhood system. Becoming a co-conspirator means committing to deep, transformational change.

One escape route for White people is to avoid talking about racism because we fear that we will be attacked for speaking out. We must understand that none of this work is about us. The issues that we are trying to address are bigger than any one of us and our fragile egos. Those who oppose anti-racism by challenging or attacking us are not targeting us—they are targeting the message. I challenge White people to commit to deep growth so that we can strengthen our vocal cords and armor up to do this work. Black people have been shouldering the work of equity and justice since the beginning of our country. It is long past time for White people to carry some of that burden.

2.   *Deconstruct whiteness in ourselves, in our daily lives, and in the work that we do.*

Self-examination and self-reflection are challenging but necessary tasks in the work of equity and justice. White people, particularly affluent White people, must confront the ways in which whiteness shows up for us on a personal level but also within our daily lives. For example, what language do we use to talk about people from different racial and ethnic backgrounds? Where do our belief systems come from? Examining our families and how our upbringing has influenced how we view the world is critical. Are we knowingly, or unknowingly, trying to live up to a false notion of success within our society? Are we promoting that notion of success in our children? Where and how do we spend our time? Who do we surround ourselves with? What are our values regarding public education, teachers, and child-care providers? Are we willing to identify whiteness within early childhood values, practices, assessments, and curricula? These are all important questions that we must begin to ask ourselves as we move through this work. Committing to our own personal growth allows us to show up in a way that does not continue to harm Black children and families, and other children and families of color.

3.   *Be humble.*

The definition of humility is "a modest or low view of one's own importance; humble-ness." For White people, we must commit to humility. That is, we must acknowledge that we are not the experts on race and racism. For many of us, we have lived our entire lives not fully understanding racism and how it permeates every aspect of our society because we have not had to. White people can choose to not see racism. As we commit to anti-racist work, it is essential that we remain humble. That is, we listen, we learn, and we grow. There is a fear within our society surrounding racism. Much of this fear comes from a fear of ourselves. We are afraid that we might come across as racist. We are afraid to admit that we have been complacent and complicit in upholding racism. That fear, however, holds us back from significant personal growth. We have an opportunity to learn and unlearn ways of being that prevent us from being our authentic selves. White people often do not understand that they have been harmed by racism as well. We have a unique opportunity here to free ourselves from that fear and to grow in ways we never thought imaginable. The journey of anti-racism is long and winding, but it is a neces-sary one. C. P. Cavafy (1974) writes in his poem *Ithaka,*

> Keep Ithaka always in your mind.
> Arriving there is what you're destined for.
> But don't hurry the journey at all.
> Better if it lasts for years,
> so you're old by the time you reach the island,
> wealthy with all you've gained on the way,
> not expecting Ithaka to make you rich.

The challenge for all of us is understanding that anti-racism is not a destination, it is a journey. It is not easy work, but it is necessary work. The undoing of everything we have been taught about ourselves and society is the first step in the work of equity and justice.

5

Historical Trauma

Jen Neitzel and Justin Perry

Our historical trauma training is by far the most challenging training that we offer because we push participants beyond their idealized conception of the United States to one that recognizes and acknowledges our complicated past. With this training comes a heaviness that is grounded in an understanding of the atrocities committed on our soil for which we have yet to atone. Participants begin to comprehend that for all our nation's strengths, we are deeply flawed. In this training, our goal is to help individuals move beyond the "blame the victim," paternalistic mentality where we place the responsibility on the individuals who are experiencing trauma rather than shifting the responsibility back to the communities and systems that originated and sustain the structural barriers that created the initial trauma. In this country, there is a propensity to treat individual family problems, affect disorders, or substance abuse issues rather than working to heal the hidden wounds of racial oppression (Hardy, 2013).

With each training, we work to understand the larger picture of slavery, Jim Crow apartheid, and the American Genocide while also individualizing the content for the specific area where we are conducting the training. This individualization is important because we must help community members understand that historical trauma is not an abstract "that was them" issue. This is particularly relevant in the North where many see themselves as the "good guys" because they were not actively engaged in widespread slavery. We all need to recognize that none of our communities are immune from the atrocities that took place across every inch of our nation. We want our participants to understand that they did not create slavery, Jim Crow apartheid, and so forth, but we have all inherited the legacies from them. That is why it is critical to individualize the history for each community. It is incumbent on each of us to acknowledge, atone, and reconcile our nation's collective trauma.

Individual communities must understand that historical trauma and the ongoing pain are in the ground. For each individual community, we always research the history of slavery, Jim Crow, and Indigenous Peoples. For slavery, the 1860 Census is particularly important because (a) this was the height of the transatlantic slave trade (plantation owners needed more and more slaves to keep up with cotton production) and (b) this was the last census before the South seceded from the Union in 1861. For a rural community in North Carolina, we found out that 26% of the population were enslaved Africans in 1860. We continued our research and found six "known" lynchings, two of whom were young boys, brothers, ages 11 and 13. When conducting the training, one of the participants noted that another man who was lynched in this county had the same last name as the boys. Another participant said, "He was their uncle. Their family still lives here." Their family still lives here. The pain and the trauma are in the ground in that community, just like they are in every community across this nation. Each community has a racial history buried below the surface, often deeply so that we can mask the shame that many of us feel for what our ancestors did in the name of capitalism and white supremacy.

Throughout this chapter, we will provide a greater understanding about historical trauma, including the roots of that trauma in our nation's past. We, as early childhood educators, must understand the ramifications of slavery, Jim Crow apartheid, Indian boarding schools, and the American Genocide on the families and communities that we serve. As we move through the nation's history, we also will provide a greater context for improving how we address trauma, as well as how the early childhood system can be expanded to promote more positive attachments with children and families.

RETHINKING THE CURRENT TRAUMA-INFORMED MOVEMENT

In the current trauma-informed movement, much attention has been given to helping children develop resilience—to "bounce back" from the adversities they have faced. A key flaw of this approach is that it is grounded in deficit thinking—that children and families who have experienced trauma need fixing. According to the *Oxford Dictionary* (2021), *resilience* is defined as "the capacity to recover quickly from difficulties; tough." When we use a strengths-based approach, we acknowledge that children and families who are experiencing trauma are highly resilient already.

Data collected by the National Survey of Children's Health (NSCH; 2016) indicate that Black children were found to experience more adverse childhood experiences (ACEs) than any other racial/ethnic group—with poverty being the most prevalent ACE for this group of children and their families. Hispanic children also disproportionately experience more ACEs than White children nationwide (NSCH, 2016). In their report, Sacks and Murphey (2018) stated that "Discriminatory housing and employment policies, bias in law enforcement and sentencing decisions, and immigration policies have concentrated disadvantage among Black and Hispanic children, in particular, and leave them disproportionately vulnerable to traumatic experiences like ACEs." These discriminatory and oppressive practices have their roots deep within our nation's history. Because of these factors, the current trauma-informed movement must move beyond focusing solely on individual trauma into a more nuanced understanding of historical trauma and the complex nature of multigenerational trauma, including the ways in which our systems perpetuate harm to traditionally marginalized groups of children and families.

HISTORICAL TRAUMA

The term *historical trauma* first emerged in the 1990s through the work of Debruyn and Brave Heart. According to Brave Heart and colleagues (2011), historical trauma is the cumulative emotional and psychological wounding across generations, including the life span, which is the result of massive group trauma. Historical trauma responses associated with this collective group trauma are often characterized as historical unresolved grief or a soul wound that is experienced as a "wounding down to the level of being" (Avalos, 2021).

In our historical trauma training, we ask participants to name some of the traumas that our country has experienced. Most often, the first response is 9/11, followed by COVID-19. Other responses include gun violence, slavery, lynchings, and the Trail of Tears. Throughout our history, the United States has produced a wide variety of historical traumas that are the direct result of white supremacy and colonization. Specific populations of people within our nation have been psychologically affected by the legacies of colonialism and their structural violence over time by limiting their access to resources (Avalos, 2021). The policies and practices within our systems were set up to cause trauma to Indigenous Peoples and Black Americans in particular. Over time, the systems have evolved; however, they continue to cause harm and regulate access to services and resources within society, such as high-quality early childhood education.

HISTORICAL TRAUMA AND INDIGENOUS PEOPLES

From its inception, the Europeans who came to what is now the United States were intent on settling this new land. According to Dunbar-Ortiz (2014), "Settler colonialism, as an institution or system, requires violence or the threat of violence to attain its goals." She continues, "People do not just give over their land, resources, children,

and futures without a fight, and that fight is met with violence" (p. 8). The land that the colonialists were trying to acquire belonged to Indigenous Peoples that today include more than 500 federally recognized tribes with their own distinct languages, shared beliefs, cultures, and governing structures that were based on collectivism and consensus building. Indigenous tribes had also created towns, farms, monumental earthworks, and networks of roads that served as trading routes throughout the United States (Dunbar-Ortiz, 2014). According to recent estimates, the overall population of Indigenous Peoples in the United States was around 10 million in 1492. Today, that population is 6 million (Koch et al., 2019).

American Genocide

Scholars now refer to this drastic decrease of Indigenous Peoples as the American Genocide, which included torture, terror, sexual abuse, massacres, systematic military occupations, removal of Indigenous Peoples from their native lands, and removal of Indigenous children to military-like boarding schools (Dunbar-Ortiz, 2014). A well-known example of this is the Trail of Tears, in which all Native tribes east of the Mississippi were relocated to "Indian Territory," specifically Oklahoma, which has the second largest population of Indigenous Peoples in the United States today. This forced removal was also met with violence by U.S. troops who fired on the surrendering Black Hawk. The Wounded Knee Massacre in 1890 also resulted in the deaths of 250–300 Lakota men, women, and children. Although these events are the most well-known within our history, documented genocidal policies can be found in at least four distinct periods: the Jacksonian era of forced removal, the California gold rush in Northern California, the post–Civil War era of the "Indian wars" of the Great Plains, and the 1950s termination period.

What is so devastating about the genocide is that Indigenous Peoples were not given space and time to properly grieve their friends, leaders, and family members. According to Brave Heart and colleagues (2011), traditional Native American mourning practices and cultural protective factors were prohibited around 1883 until the 1978 American Indian Religious Freedom Act. Indigenous Peoples have their own burial practices and ceremonies they use to honor their dead. For example, the Lakota have an extended sense of "family" so that mourning and grief are expanded to include larger numbers of the deceased. Manifestations of grief might include cutting one's hair, or even one's body, to symbolize the loss of part of oneself. Following the mourning period (typically 1 year), called "spirit keeping," the Lakota would then "release the spirit" and "wipe the tears" to resolve their grief (Fast & Collin-Vezina, 2010). At the Wounded Knee Massacre, bodies of men, women, and children were thrown into a mass grave, and survivors were not allowed to engage in their traditional grieving rituals, which compounded the effects of the trauma on their emotional well-being.

Indian Boarding Schools

In the early 19th century, the United States instituted policies designed to "educate" Indigenous children and prepare them for mainstream society. The first federally funded boarding school was the Carlisle Indian Industrial School in Pennsylvania, which served as the model for subsequent institutions. Young children were separated from their tribes and forced to assimilate into whiteness. Their hair was cut. Their names were changed. They were forbidden from engaging in traditional practices and using their native languages. Between 1860 and 1971, the Bureau of Indian Affairs established nearly 100 boarding schools in 18 states (Ryan, 2021). The Indian Boarding schools were devastating to Indigenous Peoples. Children lost their sense of identities and self. Families lost their sense of power and extended family. Tribes lost their sense of community, language, and traditions.

Today, approximately 1 in 3 American Indian and Alaska Native children live in poverty. Their high school graduation rate is 67%, the lowest of any racial or ethnic group in the United States. Suicide is the leading cause of death—2.5% higher than the national average—for Native youth ages 15–24 years (White House, 2014). American Indians and Alaska Natives born today have a life expectancy that is 5.5 years less than all races and ethnicities in the United States (73.0 years and 78.5 years, respectively), and they continue to die at higher rates than other Americans in many categories, including chronic liver disease and cirrhosis, diabetes, unintentional injuries, assault/homicide, intentional self-harm/suicide, and chronic lower respiratory diseases (Indian Health Services Fact Sheet, 2019).

Healing for Indigenous Peoples

Ongoing racism, both interpersonal and structural, continues to affect the self-image and self-worth of Native Peoples while also causing anxiety and depression (Avalos, 2021). Recently, Native American researchers have developed new ways of helping children and families heal from historical trauma by engaging them in traditional grief ceremonies and reestablishing their connection to the natural world, including plants, animals, and their ancestors. Another part of the process is to name and validate the emotional suffering of Indigenous Peoples throughout our long and complicated history as well as the continued oppression that occurs at the societal level. For truth and reconciliation to occur, we as a society must address the structural factors that disrupt traditional patterns of subsistence, undermine community autonomy, and continued occupation of native lands and resources (Kirmayer et al., 2014). Helping children and families heal is a multi-pronged approach: (1) focus on individual and familial healing using culturally relevant practices that honor the belief systems of Indigenous children and families; (2) facilitate collective healing by engaging in traditional grief practices, reclaiming cultural traditions and language, and reconnecting with nature; and (3) disrupt structures within society that continue to harm Indigenous families, including within early childhood education (Fast & Collin-Vezina, 2010).

HISTORICAL TRAUMA AND BLACK AMERICANS

Having worked in the mental health field treating trauma since 2004, becoming a licensed clinical social worker in 2009, I (Justin) have had extensive experience working with children, adults, and families of various backgrounds with significant trauma histories and attachment challenges. In recent years, our society has made a commitment to having a deeper general understanding of trauma and posttraumatic stress disorder that goes beyond the experience of combat veterans. Despite these efforts, little widespread attention has been paid to understanding historical and racial trauma, especially that of Black Americans. However, Black social workers, historians, and researchers have taken steps to create a paradigm shift in this space.

Dr. Joy DeGruy (2005) wrote the book *Post Traumatic Slave Syndrome: America's Legacy of Enduring Injury and Healing* to discuss the impact of slavery, Jim Crow, and subsequent discrimination on multiple generations of Black Americans. DeGruy's (2005) thesis is that the historic trauma of slavery, Jim Crow, systemic discrimination in our nation's institutions, and even microaggressions of today have led African Americans to experience intergenerational psychological trauma that has produced traumatic retentions culminating in reduced self-esteem and persistent anger, as well as beliefs tied to internalized racism.

Many conceptualizations of slavery in the United States have essentially minimized it to an arrangement of people farming while not being paid. Commonly, comparisons are made to experiences of indentured servitude of Irish and other Europeans who may have faced various levels of exploitation and violence but were always counted as human. At the end of their contract, they typically had the opportunity to build a life and wealth. In one of the most egregious cases of slavery mischaracterization (following complaints from a Black parent), McGraw-Hill was pushed to issue an apology due to labeling enslaved Africans as "workers" in Texas textbooks (Weber, 2015).

To truly appreciate the traumatic impact of historical and racial trauma on the core beliefs and coping strategies of African Americans, it is important to have a fuller conceptualization of chattel slavery and the Black experience in the United States. Beyond unpaid labor, chattel slavery and the transatlantic slave trade involved kidnapping, torturing, and raping of Africans and systematic separation of families and individuals who shared language, culture, and connection—all while preemptively labeling them and their descendants as permanent property. Unlike Europeans, Africans' names and languages were stripped from them and there was no opportunity to eventually become free. The dehumanization of Africans involved propagating racist myths, such as the idea that Africans and those with Black skin do not feel pain as those with fair skin do (Kendi, 2016).

Similarly, the idea that Africans did not experience emotional pain like Europeans served as justification for slaveowners not honoring their marriages and families. This culminated in the separation and selling of family members, as well as slaveowners raping wives and mothers on the same plantations where their husbands lived, which was done with the full intent to produce biracial children who were also enslaved but given

more favorable placement in the house due to complexion differences and biological ties
to the slaveowner. This created tension, emasculating the man who was unable to protect his wife without fear of losing his life. It also promoted distrust and resentment between enslaved husbands and wives. Separately, selling of children led to the traumatic
retention of mothers and parents downplaying the strengths of their children as they
sought to protect them by making them less appealing and marketable (DeGruy, 2005).

Kendi (2016) highlights the ways in which Black people were promoted as physically superior specimens to carry out labor, while also using the notion that they did
not physically experience pain to justify having them work as much as 18 hours per day
on plantations and then brutalizing them for "falling short" of extreme labor expectations. This brutalization occurred at the hands of White people of lower economic class
who served as overseers (read more about the social construction of race in Chapter 4
on whiteness). If the enslaved sought to escape for freedom, they were tracked down
by the original police force, runaway slave patrols. As egregious as the above is, little
personified the disregard for Black humanity as clearly as the experiments of the 1840s
by J. Marion Sims, the father of gynecology, where he performed invasive procedures on
enslaved African women without anesthesia before later using anesthesia to perfect his
practices when operating on European women (Kendi, 2016).

Unfortunately, the conclusion of chattel slavery following the Civil War in 1865 did
not mean an ending of racial trauma. The promises of Reconstruction offered hope of
opportunity for economic and political participation for newly freed Black southerners.
However, these promises also were accompanied by Black massacres to dissuade Black
political and economic progress. Starting in 1866, many massacres were initiated to
prevent Black citizens from participating in the United States political process. For
example, in Wilmington, North Carolina, in 1898, White and newly freed Black men
elected politicians advancing their shared economic interest. In response, the elite

massacred Black citizens and destroyed their businesses and staged the only successful coup d'état in United States history. This was immediately followed by restrictive voting rights during the Jim Crow era that used a multitude of practices to suppress Black voting. Reconstruction had glimmers of hope; however, this hope ended as quickly as it began following the withdrawal of Federal troops in the South following the election of 1877 (Kendi, 2016).

In the Jim Crow era, actions such as looking a White person in the eye, not stepping aside if a White person was walking in your direction, and not displaying significant deference could lead to repackaged slavery in the form of convict leasing or even murder in the form of lynching (DeGruy, 2005). This distinction is significant; often, the way the story of slavery in the United States is told is that the end of chattel slavery meant a soft transition into segregation. To many, segregation simply meant inconveniences like separate water fountains and some modest limitations in opportunity that were overcome by the efforts of Martin Luther King, Jr. before we peaked with our first Black president, Barack Obama, proving finally that everyone can do whatever they put their minds to.

Unfortunately, the execution of segregation and the Jim Crow era was one of subjugation accompanied by violence to ensure buy-in. As such, the descendants of the enslaved faced their own waves of trauma, leading to internalized messages about themselves, while often using harsh forms of discipline to get their children to fall in line (DeGruy, 2005). DeGruy also discussed symptoms consistent with posttraumatic stress disorder, including discomfort around White people, poor health outcomes, and distrust of systems. What DeGruy makes clear, however, is that these symptoms, as well as behaviors including parental practices and coping strategies, often were a combination of internalized trauma and adaptive responses to prepare Black children for a world that quickly "adultified" them and was unforgiving and harsh.

During our historical and racial trauma training, one of the things we do is intentionally lay out the difference between resilience and healing. Although resilience is a valuable concept, when discussing the experience of enslaved Africans and their descendants it is important to recognize that we are talking about the strongest personification of resilience, much like Black families navigating poverty today. The timeline of white supremacy we use illustrates the long road from slavery that became convict leasing and felony disenfranchisement, culminating with mass incarceration. All the while, we systematically excluded, and continue to exclude, Black people from most legislation designed to support the White middle class, such as the Homestead Act, the GI Bill, and the New Deal, with restrictions in the spaces of other safety nets such as food stamps and health care. In recent years, we have added in displacement via urban renewal and gentrification of underinvested areas that Black people have inhabited, while continuing a war on drugs that fueled mass incarceration from the 1970s into the 2000s (Alexander, 2010). The mental health of Black children and families is further minimized because of the near-daily experience of microaggressions that continue to "put them in their place." All these factors together have placed Black people under a constant state of disconnection and/or trauma on American soil. Adding to this trauma, many Black Americans have experienced these events with a pressure to not appear angry, hostile, or aggressive due to fear of feeding stereotypes of Black people as dangerous threats that were created during chattel slavery while they were on the receiving end of violence (DeGruy, 2005).

Many of the previous acts, especially during Jim Crow, in their purest form represent terrorism. And yet, if you asked the average American what they think of when they think of terrorism, without hesitation they would likely say, "9/11." The question I always ask is this: "Why is it that we will forever use the phrase 'Never forget' for 9/11, but when it comes to slavery, Jim Crow, and other terrorism against Black people, we say, 'Get over it'?" Why is it that we fly the flags of the confederacy and name things after Robert E. Lee and others associated with the confederacy to remember that history, but we do not feel the need to fly ISIS flags and name schools and roads after Osama Bin Ladin to remember 9/11? Why is it that our monuments for the end of slavery center those who fought to preserve it instead of operating like the 9/11 memorial, which honors the actual victims? Is it the fact that 80% of the victims of 9/11 were White, whereas those who carried it out were brown-skinned foreign Muslims? These factors make it easy to mobilize strong feelings against this type of terrorism, in comparison to the faces of domestic terrorism and slavery preservation, which were "regular Americans."

Perhaps it is like the way the nation has committed to a holistic "We can't arrest our way out of it" public health response to the opioid crisis where 80% of the overdose victims are White, whereas the response to Black Americans with crack cocaine was aggressive mandatory minimum sentences, felony charges, and mass incarceration. When I look at the responses to 9/11 and to the opioid epidemic, it tells me this country knows what to do in the face of trauma if it sees the victims as worthy. As someone who has long treated mental health, trauma, and addiction in various communities, what I have learned is that although everyone bleeds, not all blood is honored the same way. And when it comes to Black pain and blood, it has been ignored at best and criminalized at worst.

DeGruy (2005) aptly points out that the cycles of trauma for Black Americans have not been accompanied by acknowledgment and the support to heal, but often by minimization and misdirection. She uses her book *Post Traumatic Slave Syndrome* to help Black Americans understand the roots of certain challenges and practices and to eliminate the idea that we are "crazy." Instead, she illuminates traumatic retentions as something that once served a valuable purpose in survival but now at times can be less useful and even maladaptive. She notes, however, that knowledge such as this can be the starting place of healing for the descendants of the enslaved.

Resmaa Menakem (2017) builds on this foundation, laying out pathways of healing for Black bodies whom he describes as having been victimized by what he calls "white body supremacy." First, Menakem acknowledges the internalized oppression that Black people experience as a form of what he calls "dirty pain." Examples of Black dirty pain include (a) self-hate, (b) internalized oppression, (c) favoring light skin over dark, (d) teaching our kids by "whupping" them, and (e) reflective denigration of those who have achieved success.

Menakem (2017) incorporates body-centering exercises while also laying out pathways to what he describes as "clean pain," moving through the trauma into acts of healing. Four critical stages include (1) confronting historical trauma and embracing our history, (2) understanding trauma, (3) releasing our pain, and (4) transcending the pain. Critical elements of the healing process for Black people include:

- Raising up leaders, artists, writers, and elders who have addressed some of their own racialized trauma.

- Learning and teaching about traumatic retentions—and grow out of them.

- Learning and teaching about historical and intergenerational trauma.

- Learning and teaching about African history and cultures.

- Invoking the power of names ("Where did my name come from?").

- Teaching children the basics of body awareness and anchoring practices (Menakem, 2017, p. 197).

As a practitioner, part of what resonates about Menakem's healing practices is that not only does it tap into psychological and emotional components, but it also acknowledges the psychosomatic aspect of the healing process. From the time many people inhabiting Black bodies set foot on this soil, their bodies have not belonged to them. Controlling of the Black body that began with the transatlantic slave trade exists today in child-care classrooms and subsequent schools, stores with security guards, nonprofits and corporations, and lastly jails and prisons, the modern-day plantations.

Even as a 41-year-old Black man with no legal history beyond speeding tickets, I was taught from the age of 5 that outside of protecting myself from abuse, my body did not *really* belong to me. At times, I had to make it smaller to be less threatening to White people. I had to reduce the bass in my voice and smile to be less intimidating. And I certainly had to "watch my temper" because I would be judged more harshly with more severe consequences. As I raise my own children, I seek to balance the implementation of traumatic retentions that were passed down through generations of my family to me with offering my children a still prepared but more autonomous knowledge and ownership of their beautiful, curious, innocent, and joyful Black bodies. One generation at a time, I remain committed to the healing of the Black mind, body, and soul. Regardless of how others see us, it is critical now more than ever that we see our multiple dimensions and open ourselves up to the healing that our strong and resilient ancestors deserved but did not always fully pursue.

ADDRESSING HISTORICAL
TRAUMA IN EARLY CHILDHOOD EDUCATION

Historical and racial trauma are distinct but also intertwined with the individual trauma that is often found within predominantly high-poverty Black and Indigenous communities. Any discussion about trauma within the current resilience-based trauma-informed movement must also include a large focus on historical trauma, including how it plays out within the early childhood system. This will require a significant paradigm shift about the goals and purpose of early childhood programs, the role of educators in maintaining the status quo, and how we can provide spaces for healing for children and families (Neitzel, 2020).

Within early childhood, there must be a commitment on the part of policy makers, administrators, and practitioners to help children and families heal from racial oppression within our society. For policy makers, this means advocating for (1) increased access to affordable, high-quality early childhood education; (2) expanded hours for families who work nontraditional hours; (3) increased pay for child-care providers (who often have their own unhealed trauma); (4) increased funding for ongoing professional development regarding race, racism, and equity; and (5) working with other systems to address oppressive practices that perpetuate intergenerational poverty and trauma.

For administrative staff, this means providing comprehensive professional development activities focused on historical trauma, race and racism, and culturally responsive anti-bias practices. Every early childhood program must be a place for healing for all who enter, including staff. Programs should provide opportunities for staff to engage in self-care and mindfulness to prevent burnout and a reliance on inappropriate teaching practices (Bartlett et al., 2017). Administrators also can help facilitate the development of positive relationships and connections among staff members. Building a staff community is critical because relationships with others provide a context for acquiring the support needed to work in environments that serve young, trauma-exposed children.

Finally, early childhood providers must focus on working to heal from their own trauma so that they can move to helping children and families heal. Self-awareness and understanding about the ways in which historical oppression has affected their own emotional well-being are critical so that they can focus on (1) helping young children of color develop positive identities; (2) facilitating family and community pride about languages and cultures; (3) building community within classrooms and programs that include caring authentic relationships among children, staff, children and staff, and staff and families; and (4) helping young children develop connections with nature and the natural world. Through these efforts, we can all begin to heal from our past into a new way of being where we are no longer ashamed of who we are.

6

Suspensions and Expulsions in Early Childhood Education

Rosemarie Allen and Walter Gilliam

E very year, young children enter preschool excited, enthusiastic, and full of joy. For many, it is their first day of school. Some come donning new clothes or a new backpack, and many carry a lunch box with their name on it. By the end of each school day, 250 of these children will be suspended or expelled from their early childhood programs (Malik, 2017). Some will be suspended for a day or more, whereas others will be expelled or asked to leave, never to return. Overall, preschool children are suspended 3 times more often than those in kindergarten through 12th grade. For those enrolled in child-care programs, the numbers are much higher (Gilliam, 2005a, 2005b). The 2016 National Survey of Children's Health revealed that suspensions may occur more frequently than previously reported. It showed approximately 174,300 suspensions and over 17,000 expulsions of children from early childhood programs during a single year (Zeng et al., 2019).

It is unfathomable that young children, from infancy through 5 years of age, are expelled from programs that are proven to enhance their lives and improve long-term outcomes. How is it that we have made young children dispensable at a time when we can have the greatest positive impacts on their development? How is it that we have allowed what should be an incredibly positive experience for young children and families to become an extremely damaging one for so many of them? This is the broken promise of the benefits of a quality early childhood program. Studies show that children, specifically African American children living in poverty, benefit from participating in high-quality early childhood programs (Barnett, 1998; Magnuson & Waldfogel, 2005). Long-term benefits include increased income as adults, decreased involvement with law enforcement, higher educational attainment, and better health outcomes (Belfield et al., 2006). It is important to note the history of these programs, the racial backdrop during the 1960s, and the prevailing belief that Black children and their families were profoundly deficient (Allen et al., 2021). Despite the racial underpinnings of the research, gains were made and lives were improved, especially when deficit-oriented frames of "fixing" young Black children and remediating "cultural deprivation" were replaced with strengths-oriented efforts to partner with Black families and communities (Derman-Sparks, 2016). Although African American children made the greatest gains, it has been proven that all children can benefit from high-quality early childhood programs. The participants that provided the data in the three studies most cited to build the case for the effectiveness of early education, (a) the Perry Preschool Project, (b) the Abecedarian Study and, (c) the Chicago Child–Parent Centers Study, were nearly all African American children (100%, 98%, and 93%, respectively; Gilliam, 2016). Unfortunately, African American children have little access to the same high-quality early childhood programs that were proven beneficial to their development and overall outcomes (U.S. Department of Education, 2016a, 2016b). When Black children can gain access to high-quality early childhood programs, many are pushed out through suspensions and expulsions, denied the opportunity to benefit from the very programs their data were used to create (Gilliam, 2015, 2016; Meek & Gilliam, 2016).

DISPARITIES IN SUSPENSIONS AND EXPULSIONS

Research on racial disparities after the *Brown v. Board of Education* (1954) decision, forcing the integration of America's schools, showed that Black children were twice as likely to be suspended from school than their White counterparts (Children's Defense Fund, 1975). Suspension rates for all students have doubled since the 1970s. In 1973, the national suspension rate was 3.7% compared to 7.4% in 2010 (Losen & Gillespie, 2012).

During the 2017–2018 school year, 4 million K–12 children received at least one school suspension (U.S. Department of Education, 2021). Forty years of research has consistently shown that Black children, specifically Black boys, are more likely than any group to be suspended from school. Black boys are the most suspended group of children in America (Office for Civil Rights, 2021), and relative to their White elementary school peers, Black boys are more than twice as likely to be referred to a principal's office because of their behaviors, even when the behavioral concerns are similar in severity to those of White children (Skiba et al., 2011). Moreover, the racial disparity in behavioral response is independent of socioeconomic status (Skiba et al., 2002). In other words, these disparities faced by our Black boys are driven primarily by biases regarding their race, not their families' resources (Allen, 2022a, 2022b).

The first suspension report regarding the expulsion of young children revealed the prevalence of expulsions of young children in public prekindergarten settings as reported by early educators in 2002–2004 (Gilliam, 2005a, 2005b). It was found that these children were expelled at 3 times the rate of children in K–12 settings. Boys were expelled at more than 4 times the rate of girls, Black preschoolers were expelled at nearly twice the rate of White preschoolers, and therefore Black boys were expelled at the very highest rates (Gilliam, 2005a, 2005b). The degree of gender and race disparity in expulsion from U.S. preschools in 2002–2004 mirrored that of U.S. adult incarceration in 2019, roughly 16 years later (Zeng & Minton, 2021).

When the U.S. Department of Education released the results of its 2011–2012 Office for Civil Rights Data Collection, surveying school superintendents, it contained preschool data for the first time (U.S. Department of Education, 2014a, 2014b). The data included the number of preschool children who had one or more suspensions, those who had at least one expulsion, and those who received corporal punishment. The results of the report were consistent with the overall findings from Gilliam (2005a, 2005b), conducted nearly a decade earlier. The 2013–2014 data collection 2 years later provided further confirmation of stark gender and race disparities (U.S. Department of Education, 2016a, 2016b). Boys, who were only 54% of the preschool population, comprised 78% of those suspended. Black boys were 45% of males suspended despite being only 19% of the male preschool population, whereas Black girls were 54% of females suspended from preschool but comprised only 20% of the female preschool population (U.S. Department of Education, 2016).

The most recently released Civil Rights Data Collection report in July 2021 showed children with disabilities are disproportionately expelled from preschool programs (U.S. Department of Education, 2021). Children served under Part B of the Individuals with Disabilities Education Act (IDEA) comprised 22.7% of total enrollment and nearly 60% of preschool students expelled. This report also shows the same patterns of gender and racial disparities as previous reports. Black preschoolers are 2.5 times more likely to be suspended than White children. American Indian/Alaskan Native and multiracial children are 1.5 times more likely to be suspended. Black girls continue to be disproportionately suspended relative to other girls, and Black boys are more than 3 times more likely to be suspended than their White peers.

Early childhood programs are often the referring agencies to early intervention programs, early childhood mental health, and other necessary services and supports. When children are excluded from early childhood programs through suspensions and expulsions, they may lose access to these services (Meek & Gilliam, 2016). It is the failure of adults to take advantage of this time in a young child's life when the brain is evolving rapidly and competencies are being developed at astronomical rates (Gilliam, 2009).

Imagine the lost opportunities to enhance the lives of these children and the benefits that could be realized if the promises of high-quality early childhood programs were preserved.

THE ROLE OF IMPLICIT BIAS AND ANTI-BLACK RACISM IN SUSPENSIONS AND EXPULSIONS

To understand racial inequities in suspensions and expulsions, it is important to examine the history of the exclusion of the Black population from the American educational system. From the 1600s through 1954 there were laws, practices, and policies designed to ensure Black people were not allowed access to education. From the time they were enslaved through 1865 when slavery was banned, laws prohibited enslaved and free Black individuals from engaging in any educational activities, including reading, writing, and other forms of schooling (Erickson, 1997). Following emancipation, as Black citizens began to build schools to educate their newly freed population, laws were enacted to prevent equitable education. Funding was intentionally withheld or critically restricted for Black schools, and so-called "separate but equal" laws during the Jim Crow era denied Black children access to well-resourced schools within their neighborhoods (Butchart, 2010).

In sum, the Black experience in America has been one of roughly 250 years where literacy and education were illegal during their enslavement, followed by another roughly 100 years of Jim Crow and segregation-by-design educational experiences—altogether about three and a half centuries of systemic educational exclusion and oppression. Currently, just about 70 years following the *Brown v. Board of Education* (1954) decision, schools are still highly segregated, and academic and discipline gaps persist (Reardon et al., 2012). Black children have little access to high-quality educational programs. African American students continue to be victimized by racist

policies and practices embedded in an educational system that was not designed for their participation or their success (Pine & Hilliard, 1990). Individual, institutional, and structural racism must be recognized as a contributing factor in the disproportionate suspensions of children of color, specifically Black children. In addition, implicit bias is a critical factor in the perception of children's behaviors that often lead to exclusionary discipline.

Implicit Bias in Early Childhood Programs

Implicit biases are unconscious beliefs, judgments, and associations that influence perceptions and behaviors toward others (Banaji & Greenwald, 2013; Eberhardt, 2019). They are based on unconscious messages received over one's lifetime and are supported by stereotypes and overgeneralizations about groups of people. They are exacerbated by limited exposure to contact with and knowledge of those who are perceived as different or other (Smolkowski et al., 2016). Most teachers believe they see and treat children equally; however, it has been shown that implicit bias influences how early childhood educators perceive children and their behavior.

A 2016 study examined the role of implicit bias in how children's behaviors are perceived by early educators (Gilliam et al., 2016a). The study was conducted at a national early childhood conference where teachers were asked to watch a video to anticipate challenging behaviors. The video included a Black boy, White boy, Black girl, and White girl. Participants did not know the children were child actors, and there were no challenging behaviors in the video. Eye-tracking devices were used to determine which children were being watched, although participants were not aware of this aspect of the research. Once it was revealed that eye-tracking devices were used, participants were given the opportunity to withdraw from the study. One participant withdrew their data. The results of this study showed that Black children were watched more than White children, especially the Black boy. Also, 42% of the teachers reported that the Black boy required more of their attention. This expectation of challenging behavior from Black boys provides great insight on racial and gender disparities in exclusionary discipline. This study showed that teachers anticipate more challenging behaviors from Black boys and actively look for those behaviors. This may contribute to the disproportionate numbers of Black boys that are removed from early childhood programs.

Anti-Black Racism

Childhood is a time in life where one is supposed to be afforded the protections of being a child. During this period, most children are viewed as innocent and in need of guidance, compassion, and support. Childhood is where undesired behaviors are forgiven and guidance is provided to replace behavior deemed inappropriate. It is a season of second chances, an opportunity to learn from mistakes, while being supported by adults. When children are stripped of the innocence of childhood, they are subjected to adult consequences and deemed culpable for their actions as if they were adults, while engaged in childlike behaviors (Goff et al., 2014).

Unfortunately, Black children are often denied this experience of childhood. Young Black children indeed are afforded fewer second chances for misbehavior, with a much quicker escalation of discipline compared with other children exhibiting the exact same behavior (Okonofua & Eberhardt, 2015). Other studies show harmful, dehumanizing perceptions of Black boys that result in the loss of the innocence widely afforded children of other races. Black boys are viewed as less innocent than their White peers and are thought to be 4.5 years older than they are. They are also viewed as more culpable for their behaviors and receive more severe consequences for their actions (Goff et al., 2014). Simply put, Black children are not allowed to be children. When Black boys are viewed as older, less innocent, and more culpable, they are robbed of the benefits and innocence of simply being children.

Black girls are also dehumanized and criminalized, not only in K–12 settings but also in early childhood. They are suspended from preschool at disproportionate rates, and by the time they enter K–12 programs, they are nearly 6 times more likely to be suspended than White girls. Black girls are 3 times more likely to receive corporal punishment and are often suspended for subjective reasons such as defiance, noncompliance, and failure to adhere to dress codes. Black girls are often viewed by others in hypersexualized ways, perceived as aggressive, and believed to need less nurturing than same-age White girls (Morris, 2016; Onyeka-Crawford et al., 2017). These perceptions of Black children contribute to the high rate of exclusionary discipline beginning in preschool and continuing throughout their K–12 experience (Allen, 2022a).

Myths and Attitudes Toward Children with Disabilities

Teacher biases toward children with disabilities may be grounded in the fear that they are not equipped to teach such children. Many believe children with disabilities require more attention, have more behavioral problems, and should be in self-contained classrooms (Saloviita, 2020). Many teachers are not confident in their ability to effectively meet the needs of children with disabilities and have preconceived notions about how they will fare in an inclusive environment (Barton & Smith, 2015). Research supports the benefits of children with special needs in inclusive, high-quality early childhood settings. Studies show that when children with disabilities are engaged in interactions and relationships with typically developing peers, the advantages are far greater and the developmental gains exceed those of children who are placed in ability segregated classrooms.

A crucial factor in promoting full inclusion and decreasing suspensions of children with disabilities in early childhood settings is dispelling the myth that they fare better in segregated settings. Other prevailing myths related to segregating children, especially those with autism, include the belief that children with disabilities (a) need one-to-one instruction, (b) become overstimulated in typical settings, and (c) have needs that exceed those in typical classrooms and teachers cannot provide the interventions necessary to address their challenging behaviors (Strain et al., 2001). The success in meeting the needs of children with disabilities in inclusive environments lies in ensuring staff members are well trained, parents are informed, and administrators and other leaders provide adequate support (Strain et al., 2001).

OTHER FACTORS THAT CONTRIBUTE TO SUSPENSIONS AND EXPULSIONS

Professional development activities focused on addressing challenging behaviors is the number one request of preschool teachers (Fox & Hemmeter, 2009). Teachers consistently request assistance and tools to respond to undesired and difficult behaviors in their classrooms (Children's Equity Project, 2020). Unfortunately, only 20% of the early childhood workforce has received training on social-emotional learning. When teachers lack the skills to address these behaviors, exclusionary discipline is more likely to be used. One of the most common reasons for removing a child from the classroom is noncompliance. Persistent problematic behavior that preschool teachers find difficult to manage often results in suspensions and expulsions (Quesenberry et al., 2014). Teachers report feelings of powerlessness working with children they experience as consistently defiant or oppositional. This may result in frustration and resentment toward the child, making evidence-based interventions less effective (Keat, 2008).

Teacher stress is elevated in early childhood classrooms where challenging behaviors are perceived to be out of control. Higher rates of expulsion were associated with reports of teachers' stress, depression, and feelings of hopelessness (Gilliam, 2005a, 2005b). Teachers who exhibit depressive symptoms have unfavorable classroom climates and more children engaging in challenging behaviors. These teachers were significantly more likely to suspend or expel a child (Callie Silver & Zinsser, 2020). Classrooms with high numbers of 3-year-olds and those with larger group sizes have higher incidents of suspensions and expulsions. Teachers are 4 times more likely to expel a child if they have many children in the classroom and are experiencing elevated levels of job stress and depression (Gilliam & Shahar, 2006).

The decision to suspend or expel a child is often initiated at the classroom level by the child's teacher. A 2018 study examined circumstances that influence a teacher's decision to expel a child from its program. It examined the factors that predicted the likelihood of removing a child from the classroom and the thinking process teachers engage in that leads to early childhood expulsions. Three factors were identified: "(a) a teacher's perception that the child's behaviors are disruptive to the learning environment; (b) a teacher's fear of being accountable for the child's behaviors that may cause harm to self or others; and (c) a teacher's perceived level of stress caused by the child's behavior" (Gilliam & Reyes, 2018, p. 104). Another study examined predictive factors for a teacher's use of exclusionary discipline and found the most prevalent reason was related to concerns about safety. Teachers who feared for the child's safety and the safety of other children were much more likely to engage in exclusionary discipline. The study also found that experienced teachers were less likely to suspend or expel a child compared with those who were newer to the field (Chow et al., 2021).

PREVENTING EARLY CHILDHOOD SUSPENSIONS AND EXPULSIONS

As discussed previously, children are being suspended from early childhood programs at astronomical rates. Children who are expelled or suspended experience negative outcomes such as negative school attitudes, lower achievement, academic failure and grade retention, and as much as a tenfold increase in high school dropout rates and an eightfold increase in incarceration or other involvement with the juvenile and adult justice systems (American Psychological Association, 2008; Council on School Health, 2013; Fabelo et al., 2011; Petras et al., 2011). When children are removed from the classroom, the child–teacher relationship may be fractured. It can negatively affect the child's perception of school, resulting in the child feeling estranged, rejected, and unwelcomed in the classroom (Children's Equity Project, 2020). Moreover, young children of incarcerated parents are at a threefold increased risk of being expelled from preschool (Zeng et al., 2019). Therefore, preschool expulsion, disproportionately applied to young Black boys, increases their risk of later school failure, dropout, and incarceration, and the incarceration itself increases the risk that their own children will be expelled from preschool, continuing this vicious cycle intergenerationally.

Racial disproportionality in early childhood disciplinary practices has reached a critical mass. Immediate action must be taken to decrease the number of children of color and those with disabilities from being excluded from participating in the education process. The solutions must include training on racism and implicit bias, access to early childhood mental health consultation, and training on behavioral management programs such as The Pyramid Model for Supporting Social Emotional Competence in Infants and Young Children. Policy recommendations to reduce class size, child-to-teacher ratios, and length of time children attend the center should also be considered.

Addressing Implicit Bias

To prevent early childhood suspensions and to create an equitable classroom require discussions about race, power, and privilege. It is important that teachers are aware of the role of implicit bias in their perception of children's behavior and how it shapes decision-making processes. Many of today's teachers and students in teacher preparation programs live in racial isolation with very little interaction with those who do not share their cultural and ethnic background (Delpit, 2012). This isolation, coupled with unquestioned racial and cultural beliefs, may result in a myopic worldview and even denial that injustices and inequities exist in early childhood classrooms (Cannella, 1997). It has been shown that teachers possess a higher degree of bias than those who are not teachers (Hinojosa & Moras, 2009). Acknowledgment of personal bias and intentionally engaging in de-biasing activities reduces implicit bias. Activities that are proven to reduce bias include (a) stereotype replacement: using an alternative nonstereotypical response to replace a stereotypical response; (b) counterstereotypical imaging: imagining a realistic, detailed counterstereotype to dispute an existing stereotype; (c) individuation: acknowledging individuals as separate beings rather than as part of a stereotyped group; and (d) increasing opportunities to engage with others who are different culturally, socially, or in any category of diversity (Devine et al., 2012).

Awareness of implicit bias and anti-Black racism is a critical first step in reducing disproportional practices but may not be sufficient to ensure long-term, substantive changes.

Complete transformation of racial attitudes and perceptions develops over extended periods of time. A 2011 study showed participants experienced transformation in racial bias after completing a 2-year course of study. The curriculum included activities related to linguistic diversity, culture, challenging assumptions, critical reflection, and moral competence. Substantive change in attitudes did not occur until the beginning of the third year (Shockley & Banks, 2011). Professional development activities related to race, racism, and implicit bias must take place over time, allowing participants the opportunity to reflect and process the content and challenge their beliefs. They must learn about individual, historical, institutional, and systemic racism and develop skills to challenge racism on all levels. This may lead to in-depth changes in practice that can be sustained throughout their teaching career.

Early Childhood Mental Health Consultation

When teachers have access to early childhood mental health consultations (ECMHC), suspensions and expulsions are greatly reduced (Gilliam, 2005a, 2005b). Early childhood mental health consultants work with children, teachers, and administrators at the child, classroom, and program levels. They partner with teachers to identify underlying causes of the child's behavior and reflect on teachers' responses to the behavior. The goal of ECMHC is to increase the efficacy of teachers, programs, and families to promote sound practices, prevent challenging behaviors, and provide intervention strategies to promote positive social-emotional outcomes (Zero to Three, 2017).

Programs participating in ECMHC not only experience a decline in behavioral incidents and expulsions, but they also see an increase in children's prosocial behaviors and improved peer-to-peer relationships. The confidence of teachers to prevent and address challenging behaviors increases and their overall stress levels reduce (Zero to Three, 2017). Indeed, ECMHC has now been shown in two separate rigorous statewide randomized controlled evaluations in Connecticut and Ohio to be effective at decreasing the child behaviors that most often lead to expulsions and suspensions (Gilliam et al., 2016b; Reyes & Gilliam, 2021).

The Pyramid Model for Supporting Social Emotional Competence in Infants and Young Children

The Pyramid Model for Supporting Social Emotional Competence in Infants and Young Children is an adaptation of the Positive Behavioral Interventions and Supports framework (McIntosh et al., 2021) that is specifically designed to meet the needs of very young children (Fox et al., 2003). The multi-tiered system of support provides strategies and techniques at the universal level to promote social-emotional competence in all children. The secondary level provides additional targeted teaching practices that promote social skills, and the tertiary level provides individualized supports to the few children who continue to display severe and persistent behaviors that are inconsistent with expectations.

The Pyramid Model is proven effective in promoting social-emotional competence, as well as preventing, decreasing, and addressing challenging behaviors. A 2021 study showed that directors of community child-care centers using the Pyramid Model were less likely to suspend and expel children (Clayback & Hemmeter, 2021). The Pyramid Equity Project, implemented over a 2-year period at two demonstration sites, used the Pyramid Model with an enhanced focus on implicit bias, cultural alignment between program and family expectations, and inequities in disciplinary practices. Over the 2 years, no exclusionary discipline methods were used and tools were developed to address issues of bias and enhancing culturally responsive practices. This project shows promise in reducing racial disparities in exclusionary discipline and decreasing early childhood suspensions and expulsions overall (Allen, 2022a, 2022b; Fox et al., 2021).

CONCLUSIONS

Throughout the nation, our youngest children are pushed out of their early childhood programs through suspensions, expulsions, and other exclusionary disciplinary practices. Those who historically have been most denied an inclusive educational experience—our Black, Indigenous, and other children of color, as well as those with disabilities—are disproportionately excluded (Office for Civil Rights, 2021). Research shows that these children are not engaging in more egregious behaviors but are subjected to more severe consequences for the same behaviors of their White and typically developing peers.

Implicit bias is a huge factor. We know that preschool teachers, like all people, have biases and perceive children's behavior based on race (Gilliam et al., 2016a, 2016b). It is critical that teachers are aware of the role of implicit bias in shaping their perceptions, expectations, and actions (Allen, 2022a, 2022b). Implicit bias can be understood, addressed, controlled, diminished, and interrupted. Taking implicit bias tests and engaging in critical reflection may heighten the awareness of implicit bias (Boscardin, 2015). Teachers must also engage in de-biasing activities that retrain the brain (Devine et al., 2012), and they should intentionally work to reduce bias and its impact on decision making (van Ryn et al., 2015).

When teachers are secure in their ability to address the behaviors they find challenging in the classroom, their capacity to use evidence-based models, strategies, and techniques is amplified (Allen, 2016). Models such as early childhood mental health consultation and the Pyramid Model focus on partnering with families to place the child and their needs at the center of all interactions, teaching, and learning. Together, families and teachers ensure cultural congruence to maximize the child's cultural agency to authentically engage in building strong, positive relationships with others. When children are known, understood, and valued, they become more engaged and challenging behaviors decrease, leading to fewer suspensions and expulsions of young children from their early childhood programs (Allen, 2022a, 2022b; Brown-Jeffy & Cooper, 2011).

7

The Role of Culturally Responsive Anti-Bias Education

Tameka Ardrey

I f you have attended an early childhood conference over the past few years, it is highly likely that you have heard a keynote speaker pose the question, "And how are the children?" This is a simple but powerful phrase that derives from the traditional greeting, "Casserian Engeri" (Hunt Institute, 2016) of the Masai people in Africa. Although it is often used as an attention grabber by many keynote speakers, this phrase is so much more than that for the Masai people. It is a declaration, a way of life, an acknowledgment that the future prosperity and health of the nation is directly connected to the condition of the children in the present. It signifies a commitment to ensure that children are nurtured, protected, and positioned for future success. I have heard this question posed many times and found myself looking around the room wondering how various individuals would respond to the question.

Although it is a direct and simple question for the Masai, it is loaded and complex for us here in the United States. The answer depends on whom you are asking and the children to whom you are referring. It is contextually located in the intersectionality of race, class, and gender. It is associated within the contexts of power and privilege. It is subjective and embedded in the positionality and the awareness of the responder. As an African American woman who fully embraces the intense conviction to be a voice and advocate for my people, my response to that question would be a resounding, "NO!" They are not well. In fact, they are disregarded, devalued, mistreated, and misunderstood in our schools. They are being held to unfair and often unreasonable standards that were designed to marginalize them and not to uplift them. So, until we are committed and intentional about transforming what we teach and how we teach it, our children, Black children, will continue to be in a state of emergency. Now, I know to some this may sound harsh. It may even sound biased, but the facts speak for themselves:

- More than 1 out of 4 Black children are living in poverty and are twice as likely to live in food-insecure households than their White peers (Children's Defense Fund, 2021).

- Black children are more likely to attend preschool but experience lower-quality care than any other group, regardless of the type of program (Barnett et al., 2013; Magnuson & Waldfogel, 2005).

- Black children are more likely to attend a high-poverty school (Children's Defense Fund, 2021).

- Black kindergarteners were ranked by teachers as having the least amount of school readiness skills and behaviors positively linked to higher academic achievement (Kena et al., 2015).

- Black children are twice as likely to be expelled from preschool than their Latine or White peers and 5 times more likely than their Asian peers (Gilliam, 2005a, 2005b).

- Nearly 80% of Black fourth- and eighth-grade public school attendees were rated incompetent in reading and math in 2019 (Children's Defense Fund, 2021).

Now, does that sound like children who are well to you? Each of these statistics serves as a glaring reminder of the inequitable treatment of children of color and the dire need of education reform as traditional educational approaches are inadequate in addressing the needs of culturally diverse learners.

Although these statistics are disheartening, they are not insurmountable. The good news is that many of them can be easily addressed from directly inside the classroom, which means that change can happen relatively quickly. Early educators can be powerful change agents for our field as they are on the front lines of creating equitable early learning opportunities for young children and their families. However, to effectively navigate this role, there must first be (1) an acknowledgment that these statistics are not mere coincidences but the lasting ramifications of a long history of structural and institutional racism and systemic inequalities and (2) a commitment to transform traditional, yet ineffective, early education practices.

However, it is impossible to adequately do so without addressing race. In fact, Michie (2012) declared that race must be positioned as a central theme in the process of education reform rather than perpetuating a color-blind approach in which we ignore the existence of racism and inequities while also upholding White middle-class culture as the status quo within education. As advocates for equity, early educators must be willing to accept the fact that schools were never designed with Black children in mind and thus are not structured for them to thrive and develop with ease. Furthermore, we must realize the notion that teaching models are neutral is a false narrative, problematically reflecting a single perspective focused on members of the most privileged group, thus marginalizing everyone else. Traditional teaching models use whiteness as the analytical lens through which all learning and development are assessed. Accordingly, Darling-Hammond (2005) emphasized that before education policies can be effective for all children, these critical issues must be addressed. Otherwise, they will continue to harm children of color by identifying them as the cause of their own failure.

Since 1986, the National Association for the Education of Young Children's (NAEYC) framework of developmentally appropriate practices (DAP) has been the metric for evaluating the effectiveness of early childhood classroom practices for all children. Although there have been several iterations since its conception, its primary focus centers on an ages and stages approach through which development is assessed according to norms for developmental milestones (Bredekamp, 1997). The problem with this approach is that these norms are rooted in societal assumptions about childhood framed through a Eurocentric lens, thus leaving little room for cultural neutrality and undermining the importance of cultural experiences on the development of young children, which can have detrimental implications on the child's learning and development.

Culture structures various dimensions of development for children, including parenting, daily routines and environments, and child-rearing practices (Nsamenang, 2008). As such, it becomes the foundation for a child's core beliefs and understandings, and the frame of reference for how they view the world. Consequently, when early childhood educators fail to carefully consider the culture of the children they teach, they inadvertently alienate them by jeopardizing their security and sense of belonging (Modica et al., 2010). Thus, for us to truly ensure that all our children are actually well, we must reevaluate academic content and corresponding teaching practices to ensure cultural relevance for each and every child. This type of transformation requires early education programs to strive toward implementing culturally appropriate practices consisting of culturally relevant materials, culturally responsive instruction, and culturally fair assessments that eliminate bias. For early educators, this simply means acknowledging the unique cultures of the children they serve in every aspect of instruction.

CULTURALLY RESPONSIVE ANTI-BIAS EARLY EDUCATION

Although significant research emphasizes the importance of embedding culture and race-related content into the curriculum to support the developmental and academic needs of culturally diverse children, there continues to be an obvious gap between knowledge and practice as teachers continue to rely on traditional pedagogical practices rooted in whiteness. In fact, many teachers justify the lack of race-related content in their classrooms by emphasizing that it is not currently a required curriculum component (Vittrup, 2016). In addition, some teachers have expressed feelings that discussing race was unnecessary because they perceived young children to be color blind. This is not only a gross misconception, but it is also an unfortunate missed opportunity to intentionally address the needs of culturally diverse children.

The reality is that children begin to conceptualize race very early in life. In fact, it starts as early as 3 months of age. In addition, they begin to identify their own race as well as make racial preference by preschool (Sturdivant & Alanis, 2021). This is also the age where they begin to internalize messages about race as either positive or negative. Unfortunately, for Black children these messages are often negative as is evident by the fact that several social experiences have revealed a more negative self-perception than their White counterparts (Clark & Clark, 1947; Jarrett, 2016; Spencer & Markstrom-Adams, 1990). Furthermore, Boutte and colleagues (2011) suggested that when young children are not provided with strategies for interpreting racial messages, they may internalize negative stereotypes, believe in the superiority of one race over another, or believe that discussing race is taboo. This reinforces the importance of culturally responsive pedagogy that positively supports the identities of culturally diverse children. When culturally diverse children are affirmed in their cultural identities, they gain confidence and can fully engage in the school culture by negotiating issues that are contradictory to their home culture (Chen et al., 2009). Thus, they are empowered as active participants in the educational process.

However, it must be noted that although such transformative pedagogy was developed to address the needs of Black people and other minority children, all children can benefit from a culturally responsive environment. Dominant ethnic groups can learn security without the need to feel superior, whereas minorities can become secure in their identity, navigate between home and dominant culture, and learn how to defend themselves against injustice (Flores et al., 2011). Culturally responsive anti-bias pedagogy is a collective approach to education with the capacity to empower and promote a tradition of academic excellence for all. Its implementation must be an intentional process with several components that must be considered and addressed. These components include curriculum design, the role of the educator, and family engagement.

CURRICULUM

Banks (2008) identifies four levels of incorporating multicultural content into curriculum and classroom practices:

1. The *contributions level* is the lowest and most superficial level because it focuses solely on perceived visual cultural symbols such as food, clothing, and traditions. This level is problematic because it tends to reinforce stereotypes and dehumanizes culturally diverse children and families.

2. The *additive level* is a bit more involved than the contributions level, but it still fails to intentionally embed the culture of racially and ethnically diverse

children into the curriculum regularly. Instead, this level includes multicultural content as an add-on. For example, teachers at this level may incorporate literature of historical figures during Black history or Hispanic heritage months.

3. The *transformation level* is where teachers truly begin to be intentional about integrating the lived experiences of culturally diverse children. Thus, controversial topics and social inequities are addressed directly, and children are exposed to multiple perspectives. Furthermore, children are encouraged to critically analyze all content that is presented.

4. The *social action level* is the highest level because learning is centered around empowering children to become change agents and active participants in improving the lives of themselves and others.

Although it would be ideal to have all early educators at the social action level, the most immediate goal should be for early educators to be at least at the transformation level. To date, several pedagogical resources, educational frameworks, and curricula have been developed to support teachers in doing so. These curricula were intentionally designed to address the cultural needs and dispositions of diverse learners while simultaneously addressing issues of racial bias and inequities to various degrees. There are three that I would like to highlight because they are instrumental in creating culturally responsive anti-bias classrooms; among these are developmentally and culturally responsive practices, anti-bias early education, and anti-racist education.

Developmentally and Culturally Responsive Practices

Developmentally and culturally appropriate practices (DCAP) are a set of culturally centered teaching strategies developed by Hyun and colleagues (1995) in response to the cultural limitations of DAP. As such, this approach focuses on providing age-appropriate, culturally infused, and child-centered activities to enhance the educational and developmental experiences of young children. In addition, it encourages cultural pride and celebrates diversity while simultaneously confronting pervasive stereotypes surrounding the process of learning and development. Hyun et al. (1995) founded DCAP on four core pedagogical approaches:

- *DAP:* Focuses on the developmental needs of children to determine the content that is taught and the most beneficial and effective way to teach it.

- *Multicultural education:* Emphasizes empowerment and equal opportunity by encouraging children to embrace their own cultures while exposing them to other cultures as well.

- *Culturally congruent critical pedagogy:* Utilizes the cultural identities and personal experiences of the children as the catalysts for learning, making children active participants in their own education.

- *Anti-bias curriculum:* Challenges inequalities by confronting pervasive stereotypes while supporting the development of positive self-identity and promoting critical thinking and advocacy skills.

Anti-Bias Early Education

NAEYC's *Anti-Bias Curriculum: Tools for Empowering Young Children* (Derman-Sparks, 1989) is one of the most foundational resources for addressing issues of cultural and racial inequities in the early childhood classroom. This curriculum provides a practical guide to teaching principles to encourage fairness, support identity development, embrace differences, and facilitate unbiased cross-cultural interactions in the classroom. Since its conception, it has been the standard for multicultural education in the field and was recently revised to better align with current research on equity and diversity. In addition, this curriculum has been used as an anchor for other scholarships seeking to enhance the educational experiences of children traditionally marginalized in the schooling process. It is founded on four key goals (Derman-Sparks, 1989):

Goal 1: Each child will demonstrate self-awareness, confidence, family pride, and positive social identities.

Goal 2: Each child will express comfort and joy with human diversity; accurate language for human differences; and deep, caring human connections.

Goal 3: Each child will increasingly recognize unfairness, have language to describe unfairness, and understand that unfairness hurts.

Goal 4: Each child will demonstrate empowerment and the skills to act, with others or alone, against prejudice and/or discriminatory actions.

Most recently, the anti-bias curriculum has been adapted into a framework for teaching young children about race. This framework acknowledges that anti-bias education is a continuous cycle of observation, critical reflection, and action that centers on collaborative learning among educators, children, and families (Beneke et al., 2019). It focuses on educators intentionally using natural occurrences surrounding race as entry points for implementation of lessons related to fairness and diversity. This approach is beneficial to fostering culturally responsive environments because confronting issues of race and equity becomes a natural component of instruction.

Anti-Racist Education

Although anti-bias education is progress toward creating culturally responsive anti-bias learning environments, it has not gone without criticism, very similar to DAP. Critics have challenged its ability to create counternarratives to pervasive understandings in early childhood education that are rooted in whiteness (Escayg, 2018). For example, Pacini-Ketchabaw and Bernard (2012) assert that anti-bias education reinforces individualism as its focal point in children's perceptions of themselves and others. Individualism is a characteristic of White middle-class culture that often contradicts with the collectivist and collaborative nature of those of culturally and linguistically diverse children (Penn, 2002). Anti-racist education strategically centers race, privilege, and power and creates space for the intersectionality of perspectives (Dei, 2011).

Furthermore, anti-racist education interrogates anti-bias education's dependency on the implementation of DAPs to meet the needs of all children. As discussed previously, there are some obvious cultural limitations to DAP that inherently place a premium on Eurocentric values and beliefs. Consequently, proponents of anti-racist education argue that anti-bias education's failure to dismantle White supremacy is the perpetuation of racist ideologies and systemic racism, rooted in oppression and discrimination (Escayg, 2018). Thus, anti-racist education builds on the foundation of anti-bias education to center racially marginalized groups in positions of agency and power. It pushes the importance of promoting racial pride and critical consciousness (Dei, 2017). Young children should be made aware of how race, particularly their race, is explicitly connected to how they are treated and perceived. Thus, the anti-racist approach is truly representative of Banks's (2008) transformative level of multicultural education as it moves beyond simple integration to authentic understanding.

Environment

Curriculum and classroom environment are inextricably linked. In fact, the environment should be considered as an instructional strategy in and of itself. Its appearance is indicative of the first impression you make about children and families you serve because it sends clear messages about who and what your program values. Don't believe me? Just take a moment and look at the pictures hanging on the walls in the lobby, hallways, and classroom of your program. Next, ask yourself who is represented and who is not. Can the families you serve easily relate to what they are seeing and hearing? Are the visuals presented representative of their lived experiences? Likewise, the exact same questions should be applied to the instructional and play materials present in your classroom environment. Unfortunately, an honest assessment of your classroom based on those questions will often reveal that your environment unintentionally affirms some groups while unintentionally excluding others. For example, a program may have several displays of families that capture two-parent households but none that reflect the single-parent or same-sex parents they also serve. Although subtle, these types of situations convey powerful messages that in some cases have long-lasting effects. For this reason, any program committed to promoting equity must critically examine all of their displays and materials. To avoid issues of bias and exclusion in your environment, here are a few things you should look for:

- Opportunities to display photographs of the children and families you serve both inside and outside of the program. For example, you can use pictures of the children showing different emotions to make a poster about feelings, or use family photos to make a family tree in the classroom.

- Instructional and play materials with realistic images that depict the represented groups in various roles and professions, particularly in those in which they would not commonly be presented; for example, a Black man working as an early childhood teacher or a Hispanic woman working as a lawyer.

- Instructional and play materials written and recorded in the home languages of the various cultural/ethnic groups of the children and families you serve.

- Art materials and play materials that represent the various skin tones of the children.

- Books in which the main characters are positively portrayed and culturally similar, have familiar life experiences, or emphasize prominent members of the cultural communities of the children.

The incorporation of these types of materials counters negative stereotypes and promotes cultural pride, both of which are critical in the creation of equitable and inclusive high-quality early learning programs. Although beneficial for all children, this is exceptionally important for children of color. They are constantly receiving messages, both directly and indirectly, through mainstream cultural and societal practices about who they are and where they come from. By the time Black children enter kindergarten, they have already been exposed to an abundance of media images depicting negative stereotypes about them and their communities. Unfortunately, these messages are only reinforced by school resources such as books and curriculum. Children's literature often portrays African Americans negatively but are often overlooked by most readers because of the assumed innocence of children's books. For example, Black children are often characterized as the class clown or the mischievous sidekick disguised as comic relief. The perpetuation of such negative stereotypes can have detrimental effects on the psyche of Black children by negatively affecting their motivation, engagement, and academic achievement (Seaton, 2010). Consequently, it is important for teachers to confront social injustices and negative perceptions of their children of color instead of pretending they do not exist.

Role of the Educator

Educators play a critical role in creating culturally responsive anti-bias/anti-racist early education environments. In her research on teachers' approaches to multicultural education, Vittrup (2016) classifies teachers into two categories: *color-conscious* (those who intentionally address race-related issues) and *color-mute* (those who intentionally avoid race-related issues). Unsurprisingly, she found that there was a much greater percentage of color-mute than color-conscious teachers. However, it still speaks volumes about the current challenges present in the inequitable treatment of Black children in education environments across the U.S. Whether or not they realize it, color-mute teachers are equally responsible for the perpetuation of White privilege and power as is a professed racist. By intentionally avoiding race, educators are choosing to operate from a color-blind discourse, dismissing the detrimental effects of historical injustices on the current lived experience of the children and families they serve (Leonardo, 2004). The reality is that Black children and families are still plagued by the ramifications of slavery and segregation daily. Hence, teachers need to be intentional about creating culturally affirming environments that foster positive racial identities, serving as a key protective factor from discrimination as well as a buffer against negative stereotypes (Seaton, 2010).

Unfortunately, many teachers are ill-equipped to construct these types of environments because they are grounded in their own cultural, racial, and linguistic identities. Terrill and Mark (2000) referred to this notion as teachers being culture bound. They suggest that if teachers are unfamiliar with the culture of their children, then there are limitations on their ability to effectively interact with them. Likewise, Boutte (2012) argued that one of the biggest challenges in altering the educational experiences of Black children is preparing a White workforce that can effectively educate culturally and linguistically diverse students. Many White teachers feel that teaching is culturally neutral and thus feel little need to alter their teaching styles or adjust their expectations (Sanders & Downer, 2012). However, Boutte and Strickland (2008) argued that the field of education and the process of teaching are anything but equal. In fact, to meet the developmental and cultural needs of Black children, teachers must acknowledge the sociocultural realities of being non-White in the United States and how they affect the schooling experience.

Correspondingly, Boykin and Toms (1985) described these realities as a negotiation of three different experiences simultaneously, including the mainstream, the minority, and the Black cultural experiences. Each of these experiences possesses its own unique set of requirements that these children must address. The mainstream experience refers to adhering to White middle-class values and personal achievement; the minority experience encompasses the recognition of discrimination and the acceptance of being Black; and the Black cultural experience addresses racial pride and tradition. Boutte and Strickland (2008) expressed the same sentiment by affirming that Black children must be viewed through an Afrocentric lens, including acknowledging the sociocultural realities of being Black in the United States and how that impacts their schooling experiences and behaviors.

The acknowledgment of these multiple realities exemplifies the views of postmodernism, which emphasizes that all knowledge must be contested, and that knowledge must be deconstructed to identify truths. One of the ways in which this can be done is by breaking down grand narratives to create spaces for multiple realities and truths, rather than institutional regulation of human thinking. For that reason, it is important that all teachers are reflective of their practices and intentional in honoring the ethnic identity and heritage of their children through culturally sustaining pedagogy (Sanders & Downer, 2012). Teachers, regardless of culture and economic status, must be willing to do honest and in-depth introspection. Han and Thomas (2010) suggested that to become culturally effective and responsive, teachers must be aware of their own personal biases and assumptions, be knowledgeable about the children they serve, and be able to implement culturally appropriate practices consistently. However, awareness is only the first step. Teachers must also be willing to interrogate those biases in a way that confronts and uproots them, which is a continuous and intentional process. It is only when this is done that teachers can begin to form authentic relationships with the Black children they teach.

Research on Black children consistently highlights the importance of positive nurturing relationships for student achievement and engagement in schools (Tobin & Vincent, 2011). Through the establishment of trusting relationships, educators can easily create and maintain culturally sensitive learning environments that foster racial identity and challenge racial biases. In fact, Noguera (2008) asserted that establishing these types of relationships is a continuous process in teaching and learning that requires teachers to commit to getting to know about their children in a way that defies stereotypes. By taking this approach to relationship building, all children are treated as equals and valued as individuals. This is extremely important for culturally diverse children because educators can influence the level of protection they feel as well as promote resiliency when they have formed strong bonds. Accordingly, positive interventions at critical moments can neutralize negative repercussions of external life events that they may experience (Evans-Winters, 2005).

FROM THEORY TO PRACTICE:
CULTURALLY RESPONSIVE ANTI-BIAS EDUCATION

I am a firm believer that the best advice comes from lived experiences. It is only through shared experiences that one person can genuinely understand and effectively guide another person. Hence, I have always struggled with the top-down approach to early education reform, particularly when the decisions are being made by individuals who have never held the responsibility of managing a classroom full of eager young minds with varying developmental needs, family backgrounds, and personal dispositions. It is easy to make assumptions and critiques about an educator's classroom management and teaching practices from the outside looking in, but the reality is that unless you have been in the trenches as a classroom educator yourself, you have no idea. It is for this

reason that I want to end this chapter with an overview of my own experiences with implementing culturally responsive anti-bias education and a practical framework I developed to support early childhood educators in consistently meeting the needs of culturally diverse children.

Early Childhood Framework for Culturally Engaging Practices

Drawing from a strengths-based approach, the Early Childhood Framework for Culturally Engaging Practices (ECCEP) capitalizes on the shared culture already prominent in the early childhood setting (Ardrey, 2020). Although easily adapted to any culture, it was strategically built on the Afro-cultural capital that the Black children were already bringing into the classroom environment. It was designed to be a practical framework to guide my teachers in consistently embedding culturally responsive practices into their classrooms daily. This framework is governed by four guiding principles:

1. *The fostering of a school culture of unity.* The creation of a collaborative community of scholars that values and depends on the individual contributions of each one of them to work effectively and efficiently.

2. *The development of scholarly identity.* Scholarly identity refers to the identification of oneself as an intelligent and competent learner in the schooling environment (Whiting, 2006). This is an important aspect to academic achievement because it directly relates to an individual's belief in their ability to achieve and succeed in the school. The primary strategies we used were daily affirmations and the study of scholars whose cultures reflect those of the teachers and children represented in the program.

3. *An emphasis on school readiness through the reinforcement of essential academic skills.* With this, we worked to ensure that our scholars would acquire all the essential school readiness skills necessary for academic success, including effective communication, excitement about learning, recognition of the alphabet, counting, and knowing basic concepts (Wesley & Buysse, 2003). Nevertheless, I knew that to effectively do so, we had to use pedagogical strategies that would cater to the Afro-cultural characteristics, strengths, and qualities the children already possess.

4. *The inclusion of culturally consonant character education.* This component challenges traditional views of character education grounded in Western views of morality and good citizenship, perpetuating assimilation. In juxtaposition, culturally consonant education does the exact opposite. Instead, it strives to inclusively foster a sense of connectedness while respecting cultural differences and identities (Johnson & Hinton, 2018).

In the next section, I highlight some of the activities and strategies that we used to address each of these principles in our program.

The Fostering of a Culture of Unity

Ubuntu   Ubuntu was the name of the morning assembly we had each morning. It served dual roles in the program. It set the tone of academic excellence for the day and served as a powerful teaching tool for our children. The characteristic of communalism, a key characteristic of Black culture, emphasizes the connectedness to and humanity toward others, reinforcing that simply being a scholar is not enough. It was

imperative to us that the children understood that they had to be accountable for how their words and actions impacted not only themselves but everyone around them as well, be it positive or negative. Considering the overwhelming disproportionate expulsion rates of Black preschoolers (Gilliam, 2005a, 2005b), the goal was for the children to begin to develop empathy. During this time, children participated in culturally affirming music and movement activities, special theme-related presentations, and interactive content review.

Music and Movement   Music and movement were another essential element for the creation of the culture of unity and the spirit of communalism. Without question, music is inextricable from Black culture. Throughout history it has been a vehicle of expression and continues to be just as relevant today, hence its incorporation into Ubuntu each morning. During this time, we would sing and dance to a variety of songs, ranging from songs of affirmation about the brilliance and beauty within ourselves to those exploring letters and numbers. The songs we sang with the children had melodies that included rhythms and beats reflective of the music that the children heard in their homes, communities, and churches. For these children, this connection was critical because it eliminated the potential for cultural discontinuity within the learning process.

The Development of Scholarly Identity

Daily Affirmation   Keeping with the oral tradition of Black culture, children were encouraged to verbally proclaim their worth as individuals and scholars. Children not only recited the affirmation at school, but copies were sent home for them to implement as well. In accordance with the tenets of culturally relevant teaching, this affirmation challenged deficit ideologies by presenting a counternarrative to pervasive negative perceptions of Black children (Ladson-Billings, 1995). As opposed to letting others dictate their identities and abilities, they were empowered to proclaim powerful counternarratives for themselves and each other. This affirmation asserted their value as competent individuals capable of achieving goals and positively impacting the world.

Emphasis on Black Scholars   Each week, the children learned about a Black scholar related to the theme of study, whose life's work positively impacted the lives of all of us. Exposing our children to these positive scholarly role models, representative of their own racial and cultural backgrounds, allowed them to make a personal connection by immersing them into the richness of their past but also giving them a glimpse of multiple possibilities for their future (Akua, 2020). Aligned with anti-bias education and with the DCAP framework, the presentation of Black individuals in unfamiliar or underrepresented professions challenged pervasive stereotypes about career paths, opening children to a world of options (Hyun et al., 1995).

The Emphasis on School Readiness

The KWL Chart   The KWL (*What I know, What I want to know, What I learned*) chart is an invaluable tool for empowering children to become active participants in the education process by activating their prior knowledge as a foundation for future knowledge. We used it at the beginning of each unit of study. Through it, children were given a degree of ownership for the planning of their learning experiences for each theme. Reinforcing the quality of orality, children were encouraged to vocalize what they already knew about the theme and had the opportunity to determine what they wanted to learn next. Ultimately, the children were empowered as stakeholders in their own education, which exemplifies the practice of engaged pedagogy.

Learning Through Simulation   The pinnacle of our school readiness strategy was the creation of interactive lifelike experiences that enhanced student learning by positioning them as active and engaged participants. This was particularly important for our children because it catered to several of the essential Afro-cultural qualities such as verve (the tendency to address several concerns at once to keep oneself stimulated), orality (partiality to oral communication), and expressive movement as children were encouraged to actively engage in multiple experiences and discussion simultaneously. The teachers not only embraced this teaching strategy, but also they implemented it with a high level of proficiency. Classrooms were transformed into faraway lands and simulated practical experiences such as visiting the airport and flying on an airplane, complete with the passport process and a doctor's visit to receive travel vaccines.

The richness of this experience for our children was undeniable and proved to be a memorable experience for everyone involved. Crucially, the innumerable teachable moments thoroughly addressed skills pertinent to school readiness. The intentionally planned activities targeted academic skills such as literacy, numeracy, sequencing, fine motor development, and critical thinking. In addition, they addressed social skills such as following directions, attentiveness, collaboration, and turn taking. Most important, it was all done in a way that acknowledged and celebrated who the children were and what they knew.

Culturally Consonant Character Education

Service Projects   The purpose of the service projects was to reinforce the cultural characteristic of communalism by emphasizing the importance of service and showing kindness to others. It consisted of activities such as making get-well cards for children in the hospital or collecting canned goods to donate to the food bank. These intentional types of service projects not only reinforced the designated character traits but also enhanced the learning experiences of the children. In fact, research suggests that children who engage in civic engagement opportunities gain more academic knowledge, have higher levels of critical thinking and communication, and have increased emotional intelligence and community advocacy (Johnson & Hinton, 2018).

Field Trips   Each field trip was selected with the intention of enhancing the children's understanding of the field of study or of the scholar of focus. For example, while discussing the field of aviation, we visited the aviation museum. In addition, when we discussed a popular artist, we visited a park that was named after him where children completed their own paintings. Character education was embedded through discussion on what character traits would be necessary for the related scholars to be successful in their designated field.

CONCLUSION

Without question, the implementation of the ECCEP framework transformed the overall early education experience for everyone involved. The children were excited to come to school and their level of engagement increased tremendously as they became active participants in the planning and implementation of daily activities. Families were eager to support the mission and goals of our program through sharing their expertise about

certain topics, volunteering when possible, and making connections to various resources in the community. The teachers became more confident in their abilities to effectively facilitate culturally responsive and anti-bias education strategies and displayed excitement about co-constructing new knowledge with the children about their own cultural backgrounds and identities in the early learning classroom. Indeed, if someone were to ask me how the children were during that time, without hesitation I would look them directly in the eyes and confidently proclaim, "The children are very well. In fact, they are thriving and the future looks bright!"

8

Culturally Responsive Family Engagement

Ebonyse Mead

Contemporary families consist of blended families, same-gender-loving families, single-parent households, adoptive families, grandparents raising grandchildren, and so on. Regardless of the family composition or structure, family engagement plays a central and mediating role in children's academic success. Because today's families are diverse in terms of race, socioeconomic status, ethnicity, sexual orientation, religion, language and so forth, educators are asked to develop the knowledge and skills to effectively engage with all families. Although schools and early childhood programs understand the importance of family engagement, many early childhood professionals struggle to effectively engage culturally diverse families. Traditional methods of family engagement such as volunteering in the classroom are not sufficient strategies to engage culturally diverse families. Traditional engagement practices are often rooted in a White, middle-class worldview that is very different from the cultural perspectives and frame of references of families and children of color. Because the White, middle-class standard of family engagement (i.e., parent-teacher conferences or back to school nights) is seen as the norm, the ways families of color engage with their children is often not respected or is pathologized because their practices do not align with how schools believe families should be engaged (Kubota & Lin, 2009).

This one-size-fits-all ideology of family engagement is not only problematic for families of color but impairs the potential for positive family-school partnerships. For example, research shows that teachers are more likely to contact Black and Latine families when children have behavioral issues, rather than contacting families to report something positive about the child (Cherng, 2016). If families only hear from the teacher when there are behavioral issues, this impedes the potential to build authentic and trusting relationships as families can interpret the message that they are doing something "wrong" in their parenting. Research also showed that many racially and ethnically diverse families feel they are ignored or dismissed because they already have a label as being a "problem" when they bring up concerns (Ishimaru, 2017).

BARRIERS TO ENGAGING RACIALLY AND ETHNICALLY DIVERSE FAMILIES

Transportation, time, and child care are just a few of the barriers to engaging families. However, culturally and linguistically diverse families experience other barriers, such as the cultural disconnect between home and school, implicit racial bias rooted in anti-Blackness (see Chapter 10 for a discussion on anti-Blackness), and cultural mistrust. The following paragraphs will discuss common barriers to engaging racially and ethnically diverse families.

Cultural Disconnect Between Home and School

While culturally diverse students are increasingly attending early childhood programs, the demographic of the educational workforce remains constant. Teachers, specifically in the K–3 grades, are White, non-Hispanic, monolingual, and middle class (Banks & Banks, 2001; Saluja et al., 2002). In addition, they often lack experience and exposure to children from culturally, linguistically, and socioeconomically diverse backgrounds (Hollins & Guzman, 2005). Because the cultural experiences of these teachers are uniquely different from the culturally diverse students in their care, it is crucial that teachers develop the knowledge and the skills to establish authentic and meaningful relationships with families of color built on trust and mutual respect.

Implicit Racial Biases

None of us are immune to implicit racial bias. Our biases can adversely influence our responses and interactions with others. Because racism and white supremacy are enmeshed within American institutions, including education, addressing teachers' implicit racial bias is imperative. Implicit racial bias is rooted in anti-Blackness. Anti-Blackness is a form of racism that devalues and dehumanizes Black people. This form of racism systematically produces inequities in education, health care, housing, criminal justice, and other aspects of social life for Black Americans. Since racism is built into the core of American society, many people internalized both positive and negative racialized messages about other racial and ethnic groups. These internalized messages affect our views and opinions of others, thus influencing how we respond and interact with people, especially people of different backgrounds than our own.

Data collected by the U.S. Department of Education, Office of Civil Rights reported that Black preschool children are 3.6 times more likely to be suspended than their White peers (U.S. Department of Education, 2016). Research findings by Walter Gilliam, Yale University professor, support this data. In his study, Gilliam (2016) found that preschool teachers tend to watch more closely Black children and Black boys in particular. Other research suggests that Black children are often criminalized, dehumanized, viewed as less innocent or "childlike," and treated more harshly than their White peers (Goff et al., 2014). Recently, the *Georgetown Law Review* found that Black girls as young as 5 are viewed as needing less nurturing and protection than other girls their age. The adultification of Black children is rooted in anti-Blackness concepts (i.e., unworthy, problematic, unable to learn) that must be thoroughly examined and thoughtfully addressed to create learning environments where children of color can thrive and be successful in their own skin. Educators must explore their own cultural identities and examine how their identities show up when they are interacting with students and families of different cultural, linguistic, and socioeconomic backgrounds.

PRACTICES TO SUPPORT THE DEVELOPMENT
OF AUTHENTIC PARTNERSHIPS WITH FAMILIES

The use of culturally responsive practices will help to build authentic and meaningful partnerships with culturally and linguistically diverse families. According to Grant and Ray (2013), culturally responsive family engagement includes practices that respect and acknowledge the cultural uniqueness, life experiences, and viewpoints of families, while also drawing on those experiences to establish authentic and respectful partnerships with families. When educators understand aspects of the family's culture, it helps them not only understand children's learning and development, but also build true partnerships with families. As early childhood classrooms become more culturally diverse, creating a culture of inclusion and belonging is crucial. The following strategies are offered to help early childhood programs engage all families, particularly those from culturally, linguistically, and socioeconomically diverse backgrounds.

- *Conduct a cultural audit of your classroom.* Grant and Ray (2013) suggest conducting a classroom cultural audit that involves reviewing classroom displays to ensure that there is diversity throughout the classroom environment (e.g., age, gender, ability, race, ethnic, religion, social class). The goal is to make all children and families feel both included and welcomed.

- *Understand families within the context of their culture.* Culture influences who we are as racial beings, dictates our parenting practices, impacts the way we respond to others, and shapes our way of life. For Black families it is important for teachers and other school personnel to understand that Black cultural values are deeply rooted in West African traditions and beliefs (Baugh & Rajaei, 2022). Cultural values, such as extended family networks, communalism, and spirituality, impact the way of life for many Black families. These cultural values contribute to resiliency in the Black family. When teachers and other staff understand families within the context of their culture, they are more likely to create and design family engagement efforts that are culturally responsive.

- *Acknowledge and interrupt implicit racial biases rooted in anti-Blackness.* Taking the Implicit Bias Association Test will help teachers become aware of the biases they hold and reflect on ways to challenge them. It is also imperative to understand the ways in which anti-Blackness shows up in the early learning environment through subtle messages including books, classroom displays, or the curriculum. A thorough understanding of anti-Blackness is essential for creating equitable learning environments.

- *Develop authentic, trusting relationships with families by conducting regular home visits.* Conducting home visits with families provides teachers the opportunity to see families in their natural environment. Visiting families at home sends the message that teachers are genuine in their efforts to collaborate with families and build strong school-family partnerships. Additionally, teachers gain a better understanding of the family dynamics and a deeper understanding of a family's funds of knowledge. A family fund of knowledge can include the cultural capital of the family and their ways of knowing and being, which influence how the family functions as a unit.

- *Host a cultural night at the school and invite parents to share their family's cultural heritage and background.* Families can share artifacts, food, or other items representative of their culture.

- *Attend a neighborhood or community event.* Many families are deeply connected and involved in their community. Often, the community serves as an extended part of the family. Having a better understanding of the family's neighborhood/community can help teachers make meaningful connections with families.

- *Host school events in the community.* Transportation can be a barrier for many families. Hosting events in the community not only addresses the transportation barrier but also lets families know the school is invested in getting to know the family and the community on a deeper level.

- *Implement family-teacher café conversations.* Some families have had their own negative experiences with school and often feel intimidated meeting with teachers and other school personnel. Having conversations with families that are less formal in nature gives families the opportunity to relax and connect with teachers in a meaningful way without feeling fearful and/or judged.

REFLECTIVE THOUGHT

1. Do you see families as assets to the school or program? Why or why not?

2. Which strategy above resonates with you the most and why?

3. In what ways are you creating a culture of inclusion in your classroom now?

4. How might you engage culturally and linguistically diverse families in the program to make them feel valued, welcomed, and respected?

MOVING FORWARD

Because families are dynamic, the types and levels of engagement will vary for each. Early childhood programs should expect family engagement to look different for every family based on their cultural needs, preferences, beliefs, and life circumstances. Acknowledging and respecting the cultural differences in students and their families positions the school to develop engagement strategies that are conducive to the family's life circumstances and are culturally responsive. Because the goal of family engagement is to partner with all families, early childhood programs can serve as a welcoming place where all families feel connected, supported, valued, and respected. Teachers and early childhood leaders must implement culturally responsive family engagement strategies that consider the funds of knowledge that families possess, including their ways of knowing and ways of being, especially those that are different from the White, middle-class worldview. Family engagement in early childhood programs is more than parents volunteering in the classroom. It is about creating opportunities where families are seen as equal partners and are integral in actively supporting the learning and development of their young children.

9

Equity-Aligned Uses of Data Collection and Data Systems in Early Childhood Education

Doré R. LaForett and Iheoma U. Iruka

Early childhood education (ECE) programs and systems are increasingly using data collection and data systems in myriad ways to gather information about children, families, and the ECE workforce; to understand and improve program quality; and to make decisions about ECE practices and policies. With increasing attention to advancing equity goals in ECE (National Association for the Education of Young Children, 2019), there are many opportunities to use data and data systems to go beyond identifying disparities in ECE and address them. However, in this chapter we argue that current uses of data collection and data systems within ECE are instead exacerbating inequities, largely because they typically are not designed using equity-aligned approaches and goals from inception, or because the users are conditioned to adhere to the status quo rather than challenge how it reinforces inequities. Thus, current practices lead to missing, misused, and incomplete data—especially when they do not consider the cultural wealth of children, families, and communities—which subsequently undermine equity goals and lead to ill-informed decision making about practices and policies.

In this chapter, we aim to describe (1) commonly used data collection efforts and systems in ECE, (2) how misuses of data collection efforts and systems exacerbate inequities within ECE, and (3) how an equity-aligned use of data and data systems can avoid misuses that exacerbate inequities and instead dismantle inequities within the ECE field. To accomplish these goals, we first provide an orientation to using a racial equity approach in data collection, data systems, and research more broadly. In covering each of the goals for the chapter, we take a multilevel and ecological perspective to examine the intersection with and implications of ECE data systems for children, families, the ECE workforce, ECE programs, and communities. We conclude with a brief discussion of how an equity-aligned approach to data and data systems has the potential to bring transformative change in ECE practices and policies. Overall, we endeavor for the reader of this chapter to challenge their own assumptions and practices when it comes to data-driven efforts in the context of ECE.

A BRIEF PRIMER IN USING A RACIAL EQUITY APPROACH IN DATA, DATA SYSTEMS, AND RESEARCH

Concurrent with the recent (re)awakening in the United States and globally to the persistent realities of racism and its manifold consequences, a confluence of guidance across different contexts is emerging for using a racial equity approach in data, data systems, and research (Andrews et al., 2019; Christopher et al., 2021; Hawn Nelson et al., 2020; King et al., 2021). A racial and ethnic equity perspective in research and evaluation is one that

> adapts the research process by applying tools and practices needed to recognize people of color's experiences with unequal power differentials and access to resources and opportunity, while considering historical and current lived realities, including structural racism. (Andrews et al., 2019, p. 4)

Further, a racial equity perspective sheds light on the serious harms communities of color have endured due to racism and discrimination, while it also questions who is being elevated, centered, and excluded in the data, data systems, and research efforts (Christopher et al., 2021). Finally, racial equity is both a process and an outcome (Andrews et al., 2019).

An in-depth look at the many nuanced issues in promoting and implementing data-driven endeavors in ways that promote, rather than undermine, an equity perspective

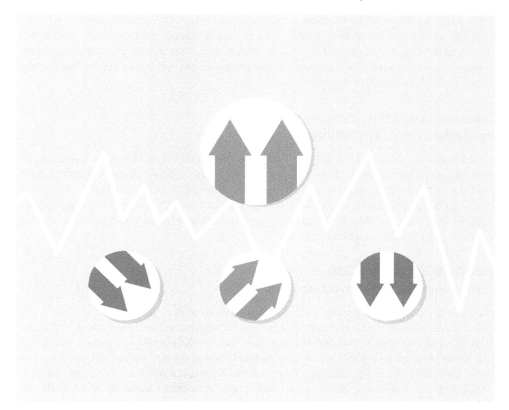

and related goals is beyond the scope of this chapter. Nonetheless, to consider the intersection between racial equity as a process and an outcome with ECE data and data systems, we draw from the following principles as points where there appears to be consensus from emerging guidance:

Data collection and data systems must lead with the voice and priorities of the communities affected by these efforts. Paramount in this point is the idea of authentic engagement with community members as equal partners. This principle is often reflected in the saying, "Nothing about us without us." Further, this notion is aligned with community-based, participatory research practices (Wallerstein et al., 2017).

Disaggregating data is a necessary, but not sufficient, practice to understand the strengths and needs within and across different groups. Collecting demographic information is a minimum requisite to examine data for different groups. However, relying on demographic markers is an overly simplistic approach that can undermine a racial equity perspective. In contrast, rich and nuanced indicators of community members' lived experiences better capture groups' strengths and needs, and these indicators also illustrate the heterogeneity within groups.

Continuous checking of the assumptions guiding all aspects and stages of data-driven endeavors is needed to identify and distinguish causal factors versus root causes, minimize deficit-based thinking, and challenge a status quo that reinforces structural racism. Data-driven efforts are not bias free or race neutral. Bias is entrenched in the experiences of those carrying out data-driven efforts, and in the assumptions underlying theories, what is "known" from research, data collection tools, interpretation, and the actions based on data-driven efforts. That White populations are the normative standard and those outcomes are primarily driven by individual factors are examples of such persistent assumptions.

Commonly Used Data Collection Efforts and Systems in Early Childhood Education

Even though it is beyond the scope of this chapter to detail all the data collection efforts and systems within ECE, we highlight two commonly used processes. At the child level, we consider processes to collect data about children and their families to make decisions about children's opportunities to participate in ECE settings. At the program level, we consider the ripple effects of the decisions made based on Quality Rating and Improvement Systems (QRIS) data.

Data Collection Efforts Affecting Children's Participation in Early Childhood Education

Multiple processes within the ECE system seek to collect data about children and their families for which a primary purpose is for teachers, administrators, and other ECE professionals to make decisions about, for, or on behalf of children and families; these decisions determine the extent and types of opportunities children have to participate in ECE programming. Four critical examples of these decisions include (1) during the eligibility, recruitment, selection, and enrollment process to decide which children gain entry to ECE programming; (2) about children's early learning skills and development to inform instructional practice; (3) about children's early learning skills and development to determine eligibility for special education services; and (4) about children's behavior to make decisions that can exclude children from ECE programming.

Decisions Related to Early Childhood Education Enrollment   At a community level, needs assessments are data collection efforts that aim to ensure that ECE programs respond to the needs of the community and that their services are well matched to families who are seeking enrollment. In addition to this goal, Head Start's community assessment involves gathering data about the community's history, economic and political landscape, and strengths and challenges as well as getting the opinions about community needs from parents, community leaders and institutions, and Head Start staff (National Center on Program Management and Fiscal Operations, n.d.). As such, a community needs assessment is aligned with the equity principle of authentic engagement with community members as equal partners. Still, not all ECE programs have the capacity to do this.

At the child and family levels, the data collected and processes involved in recruitment activities reveal access barriers that could limit families' opportunities to apply for and enroll their child in ECE programs. Studies of state pre-K programs indicate data systems barriers such as limited application submission options (on-site vs. remote), confusion about the application process or instructions, the application format and number of forms, and limited materials and supports in families' home languages (Peisner-Feinberg et al., 2013, 2018). Whereas ECE programs jointly engage in the application process (Peisner-Feinberg et al., 2018), universal applications (e.g., NC Early Childhood Foundation, 2019) may promote equity by attenuating access burdens. Still, programs may nonetheless rely on static application form data, a practice that is less equity-aligned than family intake interviews that center families' voices, experiences, and priorities. Although interviews present a heavier administrative burden and programs vary in whether they are required (Peisner-Feinberg et al., 2013), family interviews may help programs anticipate needs that could later prompt families to seek care elsewhere if those needs are not met (e.g., D'Elio et al., 2001). For example, parents of children with disabilities report leaving programs when their needs are not met (Ceglowski et al., 2009; Glenn-Applegate et al., 2011; NACCRRA, 2008), and parents have expressed wanting ECE programs that offer evening and weekend hours, serve infants and toddlers, and are responsive to their cultural and linguistic needs (Franco et al., 2020). The idea of families' "fit" with programs, versus structuring programs to fit families' needs, can be better understood with more family-centered data during the recruitment and application process and can challenge assumptions that ECE programs know what families need.

To select and enroll children, programs range from using "first come, first served" to methods that consider family and program factors. For example, Head Start programs use predetermined eligibility criteria to assign point values for a family "risk score" typically accounting for child age, family income, child disability, single parent or child living with grandparents or in foster care, or agency referral (D'Elio et al., 2001). Individual Head Start staff or committees make selection decisions, although staff have reported limited success targeting the neediest of families and bending the rules to serve needy families not meeting eligibility criteria (D'Elio et al., 2001). Yet, it is not clear if programs document and analyze such decisions to know if they promote or hinder equity efforts. Indeed, the Center for Law and Social Policy (Schmit & Walker, 2016) found that Head Start only served 43% of income-eligible children, and NC Pre-K Program administrators estimated missing 5%–50% of eligible families (Peisner-Feinberg et al., 2018). Disaggregated enrollment data show patterns in family factors such as fewer employment constraints on child-care needs (i.e., part-time work), fewer specific care needs, higher education, dual language learner status, no prior ECE connections, no transportation, race and ethnicity, low-income status, or transiency (e.g., moved, homeless) (Crosnoe et al., 2016; Peisner-Feinberg et al., 2018; Shapiro et al., 2019). Disaggregation, particularly at the program level, is needed to identify disparities and consider equity of opportunity for specific groups.

Decisions Related to Children's Early Childhood Education Experiences

Data processes used to make decisions related to child eligibility for special education services, instructional practices, and whether to exclude a child from an ECE program involve gathering information about a child's school readiness skills, development, and/or behavior—which are dynamic and mutable. Such data collection practices can range from using norm-referenced or formative assessments, teacher and parent rating forms, and observations of the child's behavior. Further, these data collection practices—and the decisions about instruction, eligibility, and exclusion—vary in the extent to which they lead with families' voices. Inclusion of families' voices is most explicitly addressed in the process of determining children's eligibility for special education services under the Individuals with Disabilities Education Act (IDEA, 2004) as required by law; yet families have also experienced barriers preventing them from advocating for their child, ranging from the data collected, to services provided, to decisions made (e.g., Hess et al., 2006).

In addition, ECE systems seem to be increasingly seeking and utilizing parents' voices and knowledge about their child to support instructional practice. For example, North Carolina has a pilot program for pre-K teachers to include parents' input when sharing data on children's end-of-year skills and development with the child's kindergarten teacher to help inform instruction (NC DHHS, 2018). Still, it is important to consider the assumptions embedded in different assessment types and their utility for informing practice. Standardized assessments that compare a child's performance may be helpful in certain contexts (e.g., program evaluation) but have limited utility to inform instruction and help teachers understand how children compare to their peers. In contrast, formative assessment methods, which include universal screening and progress monitoring, are more appropriate for informing instructional planning as they involve teachers continually gathering evidence of children's learning and skill development during the regular course of classroom activities with the express purpose of informing instruction (Buysse & Peisner-Feinberg, 2013). Formative assessment can also produce local, rather than national, norms to help teachers understand how a child compares to classroom peers. This may be particularly important for children from underresourced communities, children who are dual language learners, or other groups for whom comparisons to national norms may exacerbate deficit-based assumptions and ignore children's strengths (Mendez & LaForett, 2020).

Regarding exclusionary practices, Gilliam and colleagues' (2005a, 2005b; 2016a, 2016b; see Chapter 6) efforts to disaggregate data helped expose the disproportionate use of exclusionary discipline practices toward children of color in ECE programs, a practice that was exacerbating inequities especially for Black boys. This work challenged assumptions about the root causes of these disparities, which held an underlying assumption that certain children are not worthy of experiencing ECE. Without examination of potential root causes, using data to reveal racial disparities risks reinforcing dangerous assumptions about which children are worthy of, or "a good fit" for, participating in ECE. By challenging the assumption that discipline disparities result from deficits within the child, Gilliam's team tested and found support for the hypothesis that these disparities could be implicated by teachers' racially biased expectations of children of color. Continuing work to reduce racially disparate discipline practices will involve reconsidering practices that have placed less value on the child's experience and failed to center the knowledge, experience, values, and voice of the child's family. Indeed, certain children are often labeled as "not a good fit" and are villainized, where programs often prioritize data about how that child's behavior affects other children, the teacher, and the classroom to justify exclusionary practices. Thus, such practices that do not center the child and family can subsequently fail to consider data from families about a child's strengths and also what opportunities this child would be denied if they cannot attend their ECE program.

Program Quality Assessments and QRIS   QRIS is a primary data collection system that chiefly aims "to assess, improve, and communicate the level of quality" at the program level through the alignment and coordination of systemwide initiatives (National Center on Early Childhood Quality Assurance [NCECQA], n.d.). Implemented at the state level, a QRIS awards quality ratings to programs that meet a set of defined program standards, typically linked to their state's program standards. Potential benefits of a QRIS include (1) increase in quality of early care and education services; (2) increase in parents' understanding and demand for higher-quality early care and education; (3) increase in professional development (PD) opportunities, benchmarks, and rewards for a range of ECE practitioners and providers; (4) creation of a cross-sector framework that can link standards, technical assistance, monitoring, finance, and consumer engagement for programs in a range of program settings; and (5) development of a roadmap to align the many pieces of the ECE system (e.g., licensing, program oversight, national program accreditation, early learning guidelines, subsidies, T/TA, quality initiatives, PD systems). According to the NCECQA (2017), among the 42 QRIS in the U.S., they used them for reporting and monitoring functions (93%), for evaluation purposes (86%), to make quality ratings (86%), to guide program implementation activities (70%), and for other purposes such as providing technical assistance and disbursing financial incentives (30%). Relatedly, the most common data elements collected by these QRIS included overall ratings (89%), indicator scores (80%), observational scores (77%), licensing status (73%), case management (64%), subsidy program participation (61%), PD (55%), and distribution of financial incentives (50%).

A primary assumption within QRIS and other quality initiatives is that by incentivizing quality, such as through tiered reimbursement for programs based on their quality ratings that will result in receiving higher subsidy rates, programs will engage in practices that are emblematic of high-quality ECE. However, the metric and indicators used to gauge quality have been criticized as inherently biased against programs serving children from low-income households and communities, especially communities of color (Dale, 2020). Specifically, programs serving more advantaged communities, including predominantly White and higher-income households, are likely to have the resources to meet QRIS standards. Thus, programs in advantaged communities are more likely to receive incentives tied to quality ratings, resulting in the "rich getting richer." Consequently, providers serving children and families who face social and economic challenges thereby receive fewer economic resources and supports, further undermining programs' abilities to meet the QRIS-designated quality metrics. For example, providers who are serving families who are socially and economically disadvantaged likely need access to more comprehensive services.

Multiple lines of evidence show that children from low-income households and children of color are likely to experience adverse childhood experiences and community environments compared to families from higher income and White households (Mersky et al., 2021; Slopen et al., 2016). Yet, when programs from less advantaged communities do not have the resources to meet QRIS metrics, they have inequitable access to the incentives that would help them attain the resources needed to meet QRIS metrics. Programs' inequitable access to these resources results in inequitable access to services for children and families. Disregarding the economic and contextual factors affecting whether programs can reach designated quality metrics leads to assuming that QRISs in ECE are measuring quality, when instead they are likely assessing privilege or disadvantage, further compounding inequities.

In addition, the ways in which QRIS data are structured and used reveal other assumptions that exacerbate inequities. Specifically, the practice of aggregating multiple indicators into a binary number aims to communicate whether one program is good quality or "bad" quality, but it leaves little space for nuance. For example, a four-star program in a five-star system could reach four stars because it may get most of its points from one of the standards (e.g., education, access to learning materials), but it does not necessarily mean it has the best teachers, classroom quality, or resources. This number is purported to distill a lot of information about the structure and process of a classroom, which is complex and diverse, especially when many QRIS weigh classroom observation heavily, which is often done through a short visit and for less than a third of classrooms. This rating assumes that all QRIS indicators are reliable, valid, and culturally meaningful. That is, it is assumed that a provider or teacher with a higher education will carry out higher-quality programming for children compared to a 30-year education veteran without a college degree. This suggests that education is treated as the more valuable commodity, a tool often out of reach for members of historically marginalized communities, and does not connote the same benefit across racial/ethnic groups (Hamilton & Darity, 2017). Thus, assumptions about QRIS indicators and the summative information they communicate ignore the valuable experience and realities of providers, especially those who are from less-advantaged communities or care for and teach children from low-income households.

Applying an equity lens to program quality assessment and QRIS specifically would require a paradigm shift that attends to how data can be used to address historical injustices and create fairness of opportunities, access, and experiences. The QRIS primarily examines present-day structures and processes including education level of providers, teachers, and staff; available resources and supports; enriching learning opportunities; and, in some instances, engagement and support of families. However, these metrics rarely consider the sociocultural context of programs and schools, including segregation from (or access to) economic, health, and social resources; disinvestment/underinvestment of communities; and other community metrics. For example, the Centers for Disease Control and Prevention (CDC, n.d.) created a social vulnerability index that assesses a number of factors including poverty, lack of access to transportation, and crowded housing, which may weaken a community's ability to prevent human suffering and financial loss in a disaster. This index would help communities prepare for and respond to hazardous events, whether due to a natural disaster like a tornado or disease outbreak, or a human-made event such as a harmful chemical spill.

In parallel to QRIS and program assessment systems, there is a need to capture the social vulnerability index of a program to examine its capacity to provide culturally grounded, high-quality, continuous, and equitable learning for children and families. That is, there is a need to consider the social ecosystems that programs are part of that may promote or hinder their ability to provide quality of care. Furthermore, there should be attention to the cultural assets of programs (Yosso, 2005), including their *social* (i.e., network of people and community resources that provide support), *linguistic* (i.e., skill to effectively communicate in more than one language and/or style), *navigational* (i.e., skill to navigate through social institutions), and *aspirational* (i.e., maintain hopes and dreams for a better future even when faced with barriers) capital. The compilation of the vulnerability and assets of programs would consider historical and contemporary inequities and make adjustments that ensure fair opportunities, resources, and supports to meet standards and expectations. That is, there is a need to examine the ability for programs to meet the quality guidelines through a wholistic lens that acknowledges historical and current inequities while rewarding the knowledge and assets providers and educator engage in to move beyond systemic barriers. When this happens, quality efforts in ECE—and the underlying assumptions undergirding them—will be more family and community centered.

BRINGING TRANSFORMATIONAL CHANGE TO EARLY CHILDHOOD EDUCATION THROUGH EQUITY-ALIGNED APPROACHES TO DATA AND DATA SYSTEMS

In this chapter, we argued that an equity-aligned approach to ECE data and data systems must intentionally adhere to racial equity principles that include centering family and community voices, examining the nuanced experiences of different groups, and challenging underlying assumptions. We highlighted commonly used data collection efforts and systems within ECE—those that affect children's ability to participate in ECE and those embedded within program quality assessment systems—to consider the extent to which current processes and practices may exacerbate inequities. We suggest that although some aspects of these data collection efforts and systems are equity aligned, overall there remains much work to be done to create the transformational changes needed to counteract current practices that contribute to inequities. Per the three equity principles anchoring this chapter, we conclude that

1. *There remain multiple avenues for active, meaningful inclusion of family and community voice in ECE data collection and data systems across a range of ECE processes.* Positive shifts to create transformational change include practices such as community needs assessments and more movement toward getting and utilizing parents' input on children's skills and development. Greater changes are possible when prioritizing the perspectives of those who are being marginalized or excluded (e.g., a child villainized for showing challenging behaviors, programs deemed as low-quality), and gathering information that can be used to their benefit.

2. *Disaggregating data has uncovered evidence of inequities and disparities within early childhood, but more nuanced information about the strengths and needs within and across different groups and communities is still lacking.* Research on discipline disparities showed how disaggregated data can spur nuanced explanations of ECE processes, practices, and outcomes. Still, the multitude of diversities at the child, family, program, and community levels—and the contexts that surround them—can be better understood when data collection systems and methods are more accessible and structured to understand nuances that reveal strengths and contextual factors.

3. *Decisions about and affecting individual children, families, programs, and communities hinge on assumptions that often fail to identify and distinguish causal factors versus root causes, minimize deficit-based thinking, and challenge a status quo that reinforces inequities in ECE.* There is significant need to reevaluate many of the assumptions embedded in ECE data collection and data systems. Among those noted in this chapter, these include assumptions about how program quality is defined and assumptions made about programs that do not meet quality standards. For children and families, such assumptions include those embedded processes that use data and data systems to offer (e.g., recruitment, selection, enrollment) or deny (e.g., exclusion) children opportunities to participate in ECE. Of the three equity principles featured in this chapter, we suggest that challenging assumptions has the greatest potential to create transformational change, because the other two principles are often constrained by the assumptions undergirding data and data systems efforts.

A common saying among those who use data is "garbage in, garbage out." When data and data systems fail to adhere to equity principles, the decisions made based on these data and systems will inevitably reinforce or exacerbate inequities. Thus, the data collection and data systems that ECE programs use should be held to a moral imperative that consists of engaging in an equity-aligned approach to bring forth valid and meaningful data that can equitably and positively benefit the children, families, programs, and communities they serve.

10

Positive Racial Identity Development

Aisha White and Ebonyse Mead

Some would argue that racism did not kill George Floyd but anti-Black racism did. In the discourse on race and racism, anti-Black racism is often left out. Anti-Black racism is a form of racism that dehumanizes and devalues Blackness and systematically marginalizes Black people. Anti-Black racism is prejudice, attitudes, beliefs, stereotyping, or discrimination that is directed at people of African descent and is rooted in their unique history and experience of enslavement and colonization. It is a specific kind of racial prejudice directed toward Black people that involves the disregard of Black institutions as well as the Black experience.

The manifestations of anti-Black racism can be seen in every aspect of Black life and across institutions, such as inadequate health care, poor housing, lack of access to nutritious and healthy foods, mass incarceration of Black men, disproportionate imprisonment of Black women, and inequities in education. Because Black people have been devalued and maligned across the globe, understanding anti-Black racism must be a central part of the discourse on race and racism to address the specific ways racism disproportionately impacts various peoples of color.

As educators engage in thinking through ways to create inclusive and equitable learning environments, deconstructing anti-Black racism is imperative. Educators must reflect on the ways anti-Black racism shows up in the curriculum, in the interactions between teachers and children, in children's peer-to-peer interactions, in their play, and in children's books. Too often, Black children are bombarded with daily messages from individuals and institutions that tell them they are not good enough, not as smart, or not as beautiful as White children (White & Wanless, 2019). In school, far too many Black children have experiences that devalue their Blackness, thus impacting their sense of self and self-esteem. Barbarin and Crawford (2006) concluded that the labeling of preschool-age Black boys as "bad" or troublemakers" negatively impacts their self-worth. When a teacher constantly mispronounces a Black student's name or shortens a name because they cannot pronounce it, that sends the message that a child is not important enough to the teacher for them to learn to correctly pronounce that child's name. Other microaggressions, including statements such as "You're pretty for a Black girl" or "You speak so well" are constant reminders to Black children and other children of color that they are different from the dominant group or somehow don't really belong.

Black people have the arduous task of trying to navigate who they are as racialized Black people in a society that devalues their very essence. W.E.B. DuBois referred to this concept as the "double consciousness," arguing that a double consciousness is the challenge African Americans experience in "always looking at oneself through the eyes of a racist white society," and "measuring oneself by the means of a nation that looked back in contempt" (DuBois, 1903, p. 4). This double consciousness contributes to the internalized racial oppression that can begin to grow and develop in young Black children and illustrates the need to support these children in developing a positive racial identity. Race plays a significant role in how we see ourselves as racial beings. So much of a child's identity is shaped by their racial and ethnic culture and greatly influences their sense of self and self-efficacy. The adult caregivers in the lives of young children have a responsibility to help build a positive racial identity in them as they learn to navigate a racist society. Developing a positive sense of self and identity is a journey for Black children and this journey starts in early childhood.

WHAT IS POSITIVE RACIAL IDENTITY?

When children have a positive racial identity, it means they have a positive attitude and hold affirming beliefs about themselves and their racial group. Those attitudes and beliefs are connected more narrowly to ideas about themselves as racial beings—their skin color, their hair texture, or their facial features for example. Having a positive racial identity proposes that they accept and ideally embrace how they look. This personal racial identity is internally constructed, causing one to ask, "How do I identify myself?" However, it is also externally imposed, causing one to ask, "How do others perceive me?"

As such, positive racial identity is also connected to how individuals define themselves more broadly with respect to race. Sellers et al. (1998) defined racial identity as the personal significance and meaning of race to one's self-concept. This means that even though having a positive racial identity suggests having good feelings about one's physical appearance, it goes beyond that. Feeling good about one's race also involves welcoming and accepting the cultural practices, history, and heritage connected to one's racial group.

Having a positive racial identity also entails—in the case of Black people—acceptance of all aspects of Blackness, including Black language, and all other Black "ways of being." Given that most attributes or ways of being that can be described as Black, from hair, to speech, to dance, have at some point in American history been ridiculed or denigrated, the ability to accept and love what it means to be Black in many cases is something that requires consistent, persistent work. Related to that, one of the ways racial identity has been defined is in terms of the psychological process of healing from the wounds of racism. With young children, whose cognitive development may sometimes prevent them from fully understanding, internalizing, or being immediately affected by negative racial messages, the goal is to help them begin to develop awareness, understandings, and strategies that will stand in opposition to any forms of racism they may encounter.

POSITIVE RACIAL IDENTITY: WHY IT IS IMPORTANT

Having a positive racial identity has been linked to myriad beneficial outcomes for Black children and other children of color (Wakefield & Hudley, 2009). Research has also shown that African American, Latine, Asian/Pacific Islander, and Native American children learn best when they have strong positive racial identities—that is, positive attitudes and beliefs about their racial group (Stone & Noblit, 2009). Although these findings have been noted in studies with children from late elementary through college, there are also unique outcomes among children 6 and younger, including better recall of information, improved behavior, and better problem-solving skills (Caughy et al., 2003).

Because of the negative impact of racism, being able to resist messages that might lead to internalized racial inferiority early on (i.e., the acceptance and acting out of an inferior definition of self, rooted in the historical designation of one's race) could potentially result in healthier adult outcomes for Black children who have a positive racial identity. Research has shown that Black children who experience racial discrimination can develop feelings of inferiority and, more disturbingly, develop suicidal ideation—that is, ideas of not wanting to continue living. Development of a positive racial identity does not just happen, however. It must be cultivated. In a society that emphasizes race but often denigrates the Black race, a strong racial identity enables a Black child's self-esteem to cushion the messages of inferiority they may receive from others.

HOW IDENTITY DEVELOPS

Identity includes the qualities, beliefs, personality, looks, and/or expressions that make up a person or group. It encompasses the memories, experiences, relationships, and values that create one's sense of self and is an amalgamation that creates a steady sense of who one is over time. Racial identity, on the other hand, describes a person's identification with membership in a racial group as well as one's attitude about their race. That identification is affected or influenced through the interactions children have with other individuals and through their relationship with the broader society.

To illustrate this, using Bronfenbrenner's ecological systems theory (Figure 10.1), we can see the many levels at which children's identity can be and often is impacted by race. For example, at the microsystem level, children can be affected by the ideas and attitudes the people in the closest proximity to them have about race. At the mesosystem level, children's identities can be impacted by the racialized experiences their parents have with individuals in the educational system. At the exosystem level, identity can be affected by the racialized experiences their parents have at work or in other social arenas. At the macrosystem level, they can be impacted by messages about race in mass media (e.g., noticing or being made aware of their invisibility). At the chronosystem level, their identity can be affected by the historical treatment of their racial group.

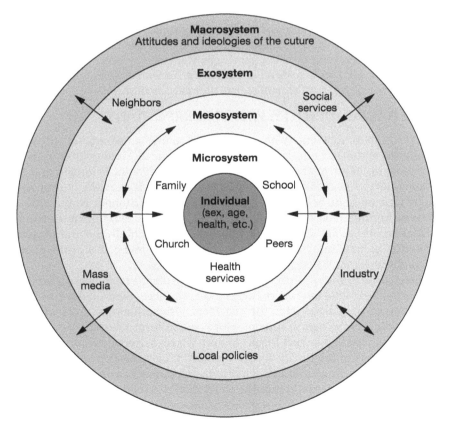

Figure 10.1.   Bronfenbrenner's ecological systems.

Development of these ideas about identity and views of self begins early, and the messages children receive about themselves and their racial group at each of these levels can have a major effect on their sense of personhood. Developing identity begins with asking and answering the question, "Who am I?"—an aspect of being human that begins as early as infancy. Because very young children are so sensory driven, one of the earliest facets of their identity is to develop an awareness of their own body, which begins in toddlerhood. Later, seeing their own image, in a mirror for example, becomes more interesting, as babies come to understand that the image they see is themselves. By 2 years of age, children have gathered enough information about their physical selves that they can identify themselves in photographs.

Identity is also greatly influenced by one's sense of efficacy. Young children quickly notice the enthusiasm and pleasure familiar adults express when they begin to achieve early physical milestones. Those adult actions and reactions can affect children's views of themselves. Even older preschoolers, when asked to talk about themselves, focus almost exclusively on what they look like, what they like to play with, and what they physically can do.

The ways we characterize children's behavior are also quite important. When adults make comments to or about children that are positive, negative, or neutral—that provides data that are added to children's mental structures of who they are. If repeated enough, adults' descriptions or labels of children's traits become part of their self-image and can become increasingly ingrained over time. Therefore, messages that support positive identity and that support the development of a positive racial identity, specifically, are especially important. One reason for that is the ways in which children of color must manage dual messages, again related to how they see themselves and how others see them: "This is what I see when I look at myself. This is what society is telling me about people who look like me."

Role models and the quality of the relationships in a child's world (e.g., family, school, society, media) also can affect identity development. Children who are from the dominant group (i.e., the group that has power and status) begin forming their identities by (a) observing what group is in power, (b) determining that the members of the group in power are themselves, (c) assuming that they are like the group in power, and (d) understanding they have the same rights and will achieve similar accomplishments as members of that group. The result of that child's identity is a sense of positive self-esteem, self-confidence, self-worth, entitlement, and goals. Children who are not part of the majority group begin their identity formation by engaging in the same process and assuming that because they are like members in the group that is not in power, they have limited rights, they can only achieve the same accomplishments and status as similar group members, and members of his group are not as good as those in power (Crumbley, 1999).

As a result of these observations and the internalization of those messages, children begin to develop their own partialities that reflect the dominant society. Research by Katz and Kofkin (1997) showed that at 2.5 years of age, when asked to choose a potential playmate from among photos of unfamiliar White and Black boys and girls, all the children expressed an in-group bias by choosing a same-race playmate. However, by 36 months (3 years), both Black and White children chose mostly White children as playmates (Winkler, 2009). The Black children had internalized messages about which race was preferred. This, among other reasons, is why it is important for Black parents and parents of children of color to engage their children in rituals of affirmation and other practices that help them feel good about themselves, feel equal to others, embrace their heritage, and develop self-confidence and agency.

Another way young children learn to think about themselves is through the memories others share with them, called "the remembered self." These memories help children build a narrative—a story of who they are within the context of family. When parents create these memories and share them with schools, educators can work to sustain and share that narrative. The process of engaging children in experiences that allow them to consider the remembered self are also great opportunities to help children build positive ideas about themselves, their family, their extended family, and their race. Within this framework of identity formation, the question becomes: how can parents and educators use their understanding of children's experiences and development to support them in building a positive racial identity? There are, in fact, a range of things parents and the other important people in children's lives can do to help them develop and maintain positive ideas about who they are.

RACIAL SOCIALIZATION

Because young Black children and other children of color can be negatively affected by the identity that society imposes upon them, it is critical that they hear positive messages about both appearance and ability in order to promote positive racial identity development. Adult behaviors that support the development of a positive racial identity are called racial socialization practices. Racial socialization is the process by which parents transmit or pass on race-related messages about the meaning of race and racism to their children (Neblett et al., 2008). Many believe it is one of the most critical developmental processes for African American youth (García Coll et al., 1996; Neblett et al., 2012).

Racial socialization consists of several different kinds of messages parents send; activities parents engage in with their children; and behaviors parents practice (Bowman & Howard, 1985; Boykin & Toms, 1985; Hughes et al., 2006; Stevenson, 1994). These practices can be grouped into four types: (1) *cultural socialization* (teaching children about racial or ethnic heritage and history, (2) *egalitarianism* (encouraging children to value individual qualities over racial group membership or avoid any mention of race), (3) *preparation for bias* (engaging in efforts to promote children's awareness of discrimination and prepare them to cope with it), and (4) *promotion of mistrust* (engaging in practices that emphasize the need for wariness and distrust of interracial interactions). For example, some of the most common messages utilized are ones that teach children about their racial–ethnic heritage and history and that promote racial pride. Parents also involve their children in race-related activities and behaviors such as buying African American books, toys, and artwork for the home (*racial/cultural socialization*). Further messages highlight inequalities between groups and prepare young people to better deal with discrimination (*preparation for bias*). Other practices emphasize individual character traits such as challenging work (*egalitarianism*) and focus on the need for children to aim for individual excellence and ongoing self-development. Still other practices involve conveying messages of distrust in interracial communications (*promotion of mistrust*) (Hughes et al., 2006; Lesane-Brown et al., 2006; Neblett et al., 2012).

Together, these various racial socialization practices provide Black and other children of color with an understanding of both the significance and meaning of race (and ethnicity) in U.S. society. When parents practice racial socialization, they are helping children have a positive racial identity by providing them with an affirmative awareness of their racial heritage, ethnic heritage, and history. In doing so, parents help them understand that the characteristics they share with their biological family extend to people who make up their larger "racial" family, and that many of their "group" experiences are similar.

Parents' racial socialization practices have been found to be grounded in their own beliefs and attitudes about ethnicity and race. This is particularly true among Black mothers with higher levels of education (White-Johnson et al., 2010) as well as with parents who have a strong sense of their own racial and cultural identities (Romero et al., 2000; Scottham & Smalls, 2009). In a study of middle-class Black mothers and fathers, researchers found that parents' internalization of their own racial identity was positively associated with their use of racial socialization practices (Thomas & Speight, 1999). Nearly all parents in the study felt it was important to engage in racial socialization practices with their children. A primary goal of the Positive Racial Identity Development in Early Education (P.R.I.D.E.) program is to support adults in learning and understanding issues of race and identity so that they can in turn support young children.

THE P.R.I.D.E. PROGRAM

The P.R.I.D.E. program, located in the Office of Child Development at the University of Pittsburgh School of Education, is an early childhood effort designed to help the important adults in children's lives (e.g., parents, caregivers, teachers, community members) build knowledge and skills, as well as gain access to resources needed to support young Black children in developing a positive racial identity. Both the acronym and the concept aim to draw attention to the need for family practices, school and community programs, and increased research focusing on racial identity as it relates to Black children 0–8 years old. The P.R.I.D.E. program has three goals, four guiding principles, and five strategies.

P.R.I.D.E. Goals

First, the P.R.I.D.E. program is designed to help young Black children from birth to age 8 develop positive attitudes and feelings toward themselves as individuals and their connection to Black people as a racial group. Because children at this age are dependent on the adults closest to them to provide love, support, and nurturing, the second goal of the program is to help those adults learn more about race and how it relates specifically to young children, and to understand ways to engage with children so that they receive messages and have experiences that counter feelings of invisibility or messages of inferiority they may receive from the broader mainstream society. Finally, the program works to elevate knowledge levels in the broader community about the ways race impacts all young children. As educators consider their role in helping all children meet their developmental needs, it is important for them to become attuned to the ways race enters the classroom and to keep in mind the significance of helping all children know about, understand, and celebrate their race and culture, all goals of the P.R.I.D.E. program.

P.R.I.D.E. Guiding Principles

At the start of the program, the P.R.I.D.E. team saw a need for principles that would assist in keeping the program's work focused on young children and that would counter prevailing views about race and young children that tended to place learning about race on the margins. In addition, there was an emphasis on encouraging team learning.

Principle 1: Race Is Central   The primary focus of the P.R.I.D.E. program is race. Our work is most effective when we help families, educators, and communities (a) develop an understanding of how race affects them, (b) cultivate a full appreciation for the significance of race in the lives of children, and (c) build the skills needed for them to support young children in developing P.R.I.D.E.

Principle 2: Pride Is Crucial to Children's Healthy Growth and Development
The P.R.I.D.E. work emanates from a desire to see young children grow, develop, and learn in ways that are healthy and in environments that are supportive of all their needs—including those related to race. Young Black children exposed to multiple and continuous P.R.I.D.E.-rich settings will have long-term gains and encouraging outcomes, including social-emotional and academic benefits. Our approach is preventive, proactive, and protective, all key aspects of whole-child education and development.

Principle 3: A Comprehensive Project Approach Is Most Effective   P.R.I.D.E. strategies are best developed by taking an approach that includes parents and others with expertise in topics such as, but not limited to, racial identity, child development, early education (pre-K–third grade), social-emotional development, and Africana history/arts/literature/culture. We will be most successful working with the primary adults in young children's lives so that they view their race with pride and understand how having a positive racial identity can impact their own life. Our approach also embraces a commitment to being accountable to each other and to children, parents, families, educators, and the community at large, incorporating honesty, dependability, and conscientiousness in all P.R.I.D.E. work.

Principle 4: Ongoing Learning and Information Sharing   As a team, we are obliged to maintain continuous learning, dialogue, education, and skill building around race and as it applies to young children to inform our work and to move the field forward. We will remain committed to being abreast of the issues connected to this work so that the field continues to advance in knowledge and practice. As a result, the adults will acquire P.R.I.D.E. skills and strategies informed by the literature and will have a positive impact on the outcomes of young African American children.

P.R.I.D.E. Guiding Principles: Research to Practice

Each of these guiding principles applies to and is easily transferable to the early care and education setting. Starting with Principle 1, although some educators may not fully agree that race is central in early education, they should at a minimum understand that race has affected all aspects of American life, including the institution of education. From pre-K through higher education, race has influenced such things as theories that guide practice, the racial makeup of the education workforce, attitudes toward children's abilities and capacities, and the curricula.

      If one agrees that a racialized or racist society is an unhealthy one, it does not require a stretch of the imagination to accept that helping children grow in healthy ways requires engaging them in learning that will undo the racial harm that exists in such a society. For educators, P.R.I.D.E. Principle 4 mirrors the need for school–family connections that replicate efforts to give children positive racial experiences in all the environments most important to them—in this case, school and home. This principle also models for teachers a commitment to ongoing—ideally lifelong—learning as a professional aspiration.

P.R.I.D.E. Strategies

P.R.I.D.E. strategies encompass work—with parents, the arts, professional development (PD), a speaker series, and evaluation and research. All P.R.I.D.E. strategies emerged from the P.R.I.D.E. report (University of Pittsburgh, 2016) that launched the program. In the report, the research team, which included Office of Child Development staff and colleagues from the University of Pittsburgh School of Education Center for Urban Education, identified needs for parent education, teacher training, more research, implementation of the arts, and opportunities for ongoing communitywide education around race and young children.

Parent Village   Named in recognition of feedback from a parent involved in P.R.I.D.E. focus groups, Parent Village is a six-session curriculum designed to help parents of young Black children gain skills and have experiences that support the P.R.I.D.E. goals.

The curriculum modules include (1) *Happy in My Skin,* which addresses skin color issues; (2) *Black Hair, Beautiful Hair,* which focuses on celebrating Black hair; and (3) *Using Words and Working Together,* which addresses racial bullying. The other three modules cover learning about (a) Africa: *Learning About My Roots/My People*; (b) the African diaspora: *The Diaspora—The World*; and (c) learning to resist, particularly in the context of education: *Striving for Fairness—Learning About Resistance.* Parent Village sessions include interactive games and competitions, presentation of historical information, and picture book reading. Each session also provides take-home activities for parents to complete with their children to bring back and share with the group.

P.R.I.D.E. Pop Up Mini Art Festivals   A combination of cultural festival and block party, P.R.I.D.E. Pop Up Mini Art Festivals are uniquely designed community events constructed to immerse young children and their families in an Africana experience. Festivals include live music, a disc jockey, free food, physical activities, face painting, and giant bubble making. Most important are the hands-on art activity stations manned by an artist and early educator, which allow children and their parents to

Lakhia

I love your beautiful caramel brown skin!

I love your beautiful dark brown eyes that look like mine!

My baby girl yearns for straight hair but I LOVE your thick, bushy, natural hair, just like mine!

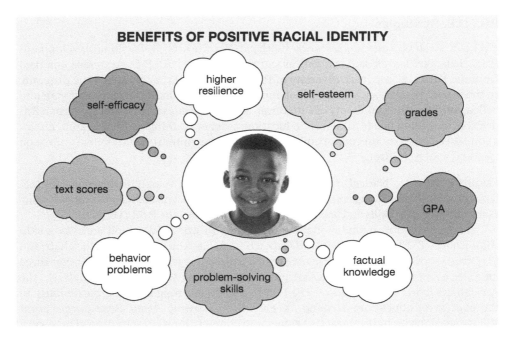

create take-away products that support children's positive racial identity development. Art activities have ranged from making mini-Ndebele (South African) homes to crowns and Africana dolls.

Professional Development   To date, the P.R.I.D.E. program has invested hundreds of hours helping educators and other professionals understand the significance of positive racial identity. Among the many powerful bits of information shared in the trainings, one PowerPoint slide stands out because of the message it carries about the benefits of having a positive racial identity.

The P.R.I.D.E. PD strategy, which is a fee-for-service training model, is unique in that it covers not only content that addresses individual racial and equity work, but it also delves into other topics not typically covered in PD designed for early educators. Encompassing five separate learning components, the model is quite comprehensive. The modules include (a) doing internal work, (b) the history of race and racism in America, (c) the history of race and racism in the profession, (d) young children and race, and (e) pulling it all together. Sessions are designed to be 3 hours long and include opportunities for dialogue, hands-on "making," games, and lecture/presentation. The PD strategy also engages teachers through the P.R.I.D.E. teacher cohort program, which recruits early educators who meet monthly to learn about and discuss issues important to race and early learning, as well as create a final classroom project.

Speaker Series   Even though awareness of the ways race impacts young children has grown significantly over the past few years, there still remains a need to reach early educators and other professionals, as well as community members who are not yet convinced that race is an important topic of discussion for the program's target age range. P.R.I.D.E. works to help the broader community better understand how race impacts young children and the ways in which their understanding of race should develop.

Speaking events are free and open to the public, and speakers have included scholars, educators, and community leaders. The speaker series is a space where educators, community members, and parents can all learn from experts in the field about the ways children learn about race by helping them understand when these ideas develop, how they develop, and ways to uncover and respond to them.

Evaluation and Research   To assess the effectiveness of program components the P.R.I.D.E. team works closely with the Office of Child Development evaluation and research division to develop data collection and assessment tools and strategies. For example, each P.R.I.D.E. training series and Parent Village series utilizes pre- and post-surveys to measure knowledge gained. The program is also currently wrapping up a separate study of preservice teacher responses to picture books that address racial bullying and skin color.

P.R.I.D.E. Strategies: Research to Practice

Like the P.R.I.D.E. guiding principles, P.R.I.D.E. strategies are also easily transferable to early education settings. For example, the Parent Village program not only models how to build common knowledge among educators and parents, it also emphasizes aspects of the curriculum that can be utilized with groups of young children such as (a) using picture books during circle or story time to talk about skin color differences, why they exist, and how to celebrate them (e.g., *Happy in My Skin*) and (b) exploring textures from the natural world (e.g., corn silk, lamb's wool, cotton rope) to discuss different hair textures (e.g., *Black Hair, Beautiful Hair*). The same creative approach could also be applied to the other four Parent Village topic areas.

In line with the P.R.I.D.E. guiding principle of ongoing learning, early childhood educators should see themselves as professionals always in pursuit of new knowledge. The P.R.I.D.E. PD and Speaker Series strategies are both designed with the idea that there will always be more to learn about early education in general and children and race specifically. By taking advantage of the wealth of free PD and webinar programs being offered by organizations such as *Early Childhood Investigations* and *EmbraceRace,* teachers can stay abreast of the latest learning, which has begun to focus increasingly on race and early education.

Early childhood educators must reframe the way they view professionalism and commit to the idea that professionalism is a lifelong process. As such, teachers should also consider themselves practicing researchers. When educators spend time at the end of the day assessing how things went for children, what strategies were introduced successfully, which ones did not work and why, and how to improve their teaching, they are engaging in their own evaluation and action research. Finally, many aspects of the P.R.I.D.E. Pop Up Mini Art Festivals can be replicated with little effort in the classroom setting from storytelling, to making, drumming, and dancing. However, for those educators who want to delve a bit deeper into using the arts to support positive racial identity, exploring the visual arts may be a specific strategy to consider.

POSITIVE RACIAL IDENTITY AND THE VISUAL ARTS

In a speech given in 2017 for a local "Unconference" focusing on the arts and creativity, Pittsburgh artist Vanessa German described her work with young Black children at *Art House*, her former home in the Pittsburgh neighborhood of Homewood that also doubled as a place where kids could go to become artists. In her presentation, German described how children repeatedly asked her why some of the dolls she created—her art pieces—were "so dark." The question implied that the dolls were in fact "too dark." It also revealed the ways dark skin is often questioned, seen as unusual, and considered undesirable, even by children of African descent.

Like the work of artist Kehinde Wiley (an American painter known for his naturalistic paintings of Black people, which frequently reference the work of Old Master paintings), Vanessa's art celebrates the adorned, the intricate, the regal. One could easily imagine Black children learning to see, understand, embrace, and love the unique renditions of the Black image created by these two artists instead of questioning the subjects' skin tones. Giving Black children opportunities to experience beautiful pieces of art and helping them appreciate visual art can bring many benefits and is another way to support their positive racial identity development. Studies have demonstrated that under certain circumstances viewing great works of art brings about a chemical cascade like the sensation of "falling in love." By looking closely together as a class at a Picasso or a Cezanne, even 4- and 5-year-olds can learn how to observe and translate their thoughts into language and listen and respond to multiple perspectives (Frey, 2015).

The visual thinking method, an art appreciation method created 20 years ago, asks three questions of young art students: (1) What's going on in this picture? (2) What do you see that makes you say that? (3) What more can we find? Research on the method has shown that students in classes where the visual thinking program was used had a better understanding of visual images, exhibited stronger growth in math and reading, and showed better social-emotional growth than students in classes that did not use the program.

Bringing Black art to Black children can potentially produce these kinds of positive academic outcomes and at the same time experiences of joy, adoration, and love for the Black image. They also open up opportunities to learn about a range of Black experiences and counter the long history of the Black image being ridiculed and mocked, particularly during the racial apartheid Jim Crow era during which the Black body was objectified, commodified, and derided.

Asking children questions about what they see, what they notice about the way faces are drawn or expressions are presented, helps children to learn how to engage in "close readings" of these images, but it also subtly helps them think differently about what they're looking at. Asking how they feel about the image can show them that art of all forms evokes emotions that they should pay attention to as well as explore and try to better understand. Applying this method to the works of Black artists could produce rich conversation and a vastly different kind of learning for young Black children while simultaneously supporting their positive racial identity.

Ways Educators Can Use Art to Support Positive Identity Development

Increased resilience is one of the many benefits that comes with having a positive racial identity. Art (or more specifically art creation) can also support resilience. Creative endeavors such as making are not only self-rewarding, but they are also tangible moments of mastery and personal empowerment that enhance an internal locus of control. The act of making art is synonymous with creativity. When we engage our creativity, we are taking a risk. We risk failing. We risk exposing our deeper selves to others, and as we become accustomed to taking those risks, our resilience is enhanced.

Locus of control describes how strongly people believe they have control over the situations and experiences that affect their lives. When children engage in art making, they are enhancing their locus of control because they learn that they can go back and create something new—they have control over that process. That, in essence, is resilience. Every time we do it—make something, take a risk—it becomes a little bit easier, a little less scary, a little less difficult. Like learning to walk, each small failure and recovery teaches us to stand and also to be unafraid of falling in the first place. Resilience, having a strong locus of control, and taking risks are all reinforced by the positive racial identity practice of egalitarianism. There are many ways to help children feel good about who they are and help them develop a positive racial identity, and art can and should be a significant part of that process.

In an article I wrote some years ago about using art to teach Black history, I shared some of the art-based strategies that educators and parents might consider in helping children learn about Black history and culture (White, 2019).

- Use artist Jacob Lawrence's pieces in his migration series to help children understand the Black migration experience in the mid-1900s.

- Start conversations about the Black farming tradition and inequality by discussing painting and printmaking based on the iconic sharecropper images by artist Elizabeth Catlett.

- Introduce the work of artist Romare Bearden to discuss music and the northern urban environment Black people moved into after migration.

- Share works by artist Kehinde Wiley to explore the hip-hop generation in styles full of majesty and regality.

Of course, the simplest way for educators to enter this aspect of work is through picture books. Educators should not only engage in art making with children, but they should also read picture books about Black art and artists, and books with photographs and illustrations by Black photographers and illustrators. Picture books are sometimes the first entrée for young children into the world of beautiful art. By presenting books about the artists mentioned previously, educators are engaging them in an up-close experience with remarkable, professional Black art. From *Come Look With Me* to *Radiant Child,* a plethora of picture books about Black art and artists is readily available at the neighborhood library or bookstore. Works by well-known Black children's book illustrators bring authenticity and reverence to images of Africana people. Many of these books cover eras and heroes from Black history, such as these read alouds that feature Black illustrators and history:

- *We Are the Ship* is written and illustrated by Kadir Nelson, who uses oil paintings to tell the story of the gifted athletes of Negro league baseball.

- *The Cart That Carried Martin,* written by Eve Bunting and illustrated by Don Tate, uses soft colors to convey hope in depicting the funeral procession of Dr. Martin Luther King, Jr.

- *Art From Her Heart, Folk Artist Clementine Hunter,* written by Kathy Whitehead and illustrated by Shane Evans, is a picture book biography that introduces children to a self-taught artist whose paintings captured scenes of backbreaking work and joyous celebrations of southern farm life.

By now, you may be thinking, "This is all useful information but exactly how do I use it? Where is the best place to begin with the arts?" Starting may be simpler than you think. You might want begin by viewing it as a journey for you and the children with whom you work. We know that all books should be read in their entirety before introducing them to children, but having done that, look at these activities as a place for all of you to learn together. Ask some of the questions suggested earlier, as well as the following: "What shapes do you see? What stands out to you most and why? What does the picture make you think of? How do you think the artist made this—why do you think they made it?" Finally, if you are still hesitant to dive into the world of Black art with children, consider reaching out to a local Black teaching artist who can serve as a model or guide for you as you ease into things.

One thing to keep in mind is the ways in which art books open space to discuss all colors—including the color brown—in ways that are nonjudgmental and in a context that celebrates things that are light and dark and colors that are light and dark. In an article titled "Engaging Young Children in Activities and Conversations About Race and Social Class" (Lee et al., 2008), the authors found that the children's attitudes about the color brown changed in positive ways after producing self-portraits over a period of time. Many Black artists are conscious of the stigma assigned to Blackness, and their work takes an intentional, in-your-face stance that says all black is beautiful, which is an important positive racial identity message.

MOVING FORWARD

Feeling good about and comfortable with who we are is always a work in progress—something we must address throughout our lives. What happens to us when we are young, those early messages we receive, is so important to the kind of person we may grow up to be. The things the important adults in our lives do or do not do could result in children having to work hard to repair harm or could on the other hand give them the kinds of affirming messaging, joyful interactions, and rich cultural experiences that build the solid foundation young children need—a foundation that helps them be healthy, survive, and thrive in a highly racialized society. We can all help children build and maintain a positive racial identity.

11

A Transformed
Early Childhood System

Jen Neitzel and Ebonyse Mead

The goal of this book is to provide teachers, practitioners, administrators, and policy makers with a comprehensive roadmap to guide the transformation of early childhood programs, organizations, and ultimately the system itself. Throughout the book, we have covered topics that are foundational for understanding the complexities of our current issues and what is needed to promote better outcomes for Black children and families. Our vision and approach for working toward equity and justice in early childhood is grounded in healing—of adults, communities, organizations, programs, and systems, but also of our children. Deep wounds exist within our society, and they manifest themselves in our current policies and practices that directly affect the lives of young children and their future outcomes.

When we talk about a transformed early childhood system, we are talking about creating spaces of healing for all who enter—children, families, teachers, and administrators. When we commit to transforming the ways in which we provide early childhood services, we are committing to examining everything that we have done and currently do. This means that we are evaluating assessments, practices, rating scales, and the like. This will take a reckoning by many in the field, particularly those who have been the forerunners in bringing about improvements in how we provide early care and learning to young children and their families.

Those early efforts were critical for advancing the field from one that was seen as babysitting to one that is now seen as essential for later learning and development. We must build on the foundation that has been provided for us; however, those bricks and mortar will not be enough to truly advance the cause of equity and justice in early childhood. Throughout this chapter, we provide a critical examination of current practices and how we can adapt and grow to transform our early childhood system so that it brings about the change that we all want to see for our young children.

FALSE NARRATIVES OF WHITE SUPREMACY

The focus of Chapter 5 was on whiteness and white supremacy, including how it shows up in early childhood education (ECE). In this chapter, we dig a bit deeper into these constructs because they are the root causes of many of the inequities that we see in early childhood. However, before we can deconstruct white supremacy in ECE, we must have a deeper understanding of societal values that are grounded in whiteness and serve as the foundation for the worldview that was used to develop our modern-day early childhood systems.

"Affluent White" Whiteness

Deconstructing whiteness and white supremacy can be difficult for many White people because they see it as a personal affront to who they are as people. None of us wants to be called a racist, particularly progressive White people because they are the ones who traditionally support social justice initiatives on the surface. However, it is critical, especially for those of us who are working in the field of ECE, to engage in deep self-reflection about how the values of whiteness and white supremacy play out within ourselves and our daily lives. For example, whiteness places value on certain experiences within society, including social, education, financial, and so on. We get wrapped up in this false ideal of success in which we view the right house, the right neighborhood, the right schools, the right country club, the right clothes, the right body weight, or the right car as indicators that we have "made it." These ideals are wrapped up in "affluent White" whiteness, which has its roots deep within our nation's history.

It is important to understand that the whiteness and white supremacy that must be unearthed is actually patriarchal white supremacy (hooks, 2001). When we reflect on our past and the roots of current whiteness, we understand that straight, White, landowning men have created everything within our society, from our institutions to our values regarding money, appearance, and status. We have gotten so wrapped up in superficial and materialistic notions of success that we have failed to recognize we are perpetuating patriarchal falsehoods in ourselves, in our daily lives, and in our children. Affluent whiteness gets passed on to the next generation by instituting certain values regarding grades, advanced placement coursework, and elite athletics that perpetuate the ideal that "I am only successful if I am high achieving in all aspects of my life"—often at the expense of individual mental health. In their research on affluent White middle and high school students, Luthar and Sexton (2004) found that achievement pressures and isolation from adults can lead to maladjustment and mental health issues, as well in high rates of suicide and substance abuse issues. This is important to understand because these problems do not magically appear during adolescence. There is a long foundation that has its roots in early childhood when affluent White parents enroll their children in elite preschools, music, art, and athletics from a very early age.

Gender Identity Development

It may seem odd to be talking about gender in a book focused on racial equity; however, race and gender are uniquely intertwined. When we look back on the discussion regarding the social construction of whiteness, it is evident that gender roles, behaviors, physical appearance, and expectations evolved from that straight, White, wealthy male worldview. For example, as our nation was forming, White landowning men from Europe brought social structures with them to the North American continent that reproduced inequalities linked to sex, race, class, religion, ethnicity, and other "differences."

Unger (1979) described gender as characteristics and traits that are considered appropriate for males and females. A discussion about gender and gender identity is critically important when we are thinking about what a transformed early childhood system might look like. By the age of 2 or 3 years, children begin to develop their gender identity, which takes place within the context of socialization and cultural representations and expectations. A poststructuralist approach suggests that children begin to construct their gendered identities from an early age (Blaise, 2005; Francis, 2000). Our interactions with young children continuously construct and reinforce their notions of gender and what it means to be a boy or a girl within society (e.g., behavior, physical appearance, interests). In addition, Bussey and Bandura (1999) proposed that children learn through the modeling of others. Children, and specifically girls, are capable of learning gender-typed behaviors through the observation of same-sex models.

Within the United States, sociopolitical factors have created differences in the gender-role norms typically held for White women. Many of these differences grew out of the *cult of true womanhood* (Perkins, 1983; Welter, 1966), a notion of womanhood that emerged in the mid-1800s. This ideal emphasized modesty, purity, and domesticity for affluent White women and identified wife and mother as their primary and most important roles. Throughout our history, Black women have been viewed in comparison to this norm for middle-class White women. Black women have not been seen as "true" women but rather as animalistic and hypersexual, which is incongruent with the fact that many Black women throughout history have cared for affluent White children even though they were not seen as "maternal." Even today, White women are stereotyped as more nurturing, domestic, dependent, submissive, and emotional, whereas Black women are seen as hypersexual yet hyperfeminine, which further reinforces the perception that White women are the norm (Baker, 2005; Bell, 2004).

Studies with young children indicate that they begin to use gender and race as cues to status in early childhood. For example, young children expected boys to hold higher status as defined by access to resources and decision-making power (e.g., having more toys, choosing what other people play with). In addition, children expected White people to be wealthier than Black people and expected that White people were higher status (as defined by access to resources and decision-making power) (Mandalaywala et al., 2020). These findings suggest that gender and race identification, as well as the development of biases surrounding these constructs, should be addressed in ECE programs.

FALSE NARRATIVES OF WHITE SUPREMACY IN EDUCATION

Whiteness and white supremacy permeate every aspect of our society, including education. Digging deeply into our history helps us understand where we have come from, where we are now, and where we should go from here. The social construction of whiteness has done a great deal of damage to our nation's institutions and to our national psyche in general. We have always viewed education as the great equalizer; however, the current system, as it was designed, perpetuates opportunity and achievement gaps.

Whiteness has always dictated what and how children are taught. Currently, much of the curriculum in educational settings, particularly related to history, is whitewashed to provide a Eurocentric view of events throughout the trajectory of the United States. This is a huge issue that needs to be addressed because (a) we are perpetuating whiteness and entitlement in our White children and (b) we are not empowering our Black, Indigenous, and people of color youth with the truth. Instead, they are learning stories about the inferiority of their ancestors that feed into their self-worth.

Whiteness also tells us what achievement looks like. In our current educational system, we expect our children to be good at everything—every subject, sports, and so on. We promote the "one right answer" without fostering critical thinking and the ideal that there may be many different solutions to a particular problem (outside of math, of course). We measure success by grades and test scores. As those of us in early childhood know, this only provides a snapshot of what a child really knows and understands. We must provide opportunities for our children to demonstrate their knowledge and understanding of content that goes beyond multiple-choice questions and that one right answer.

Finally, whiteness dictates what behaviors are acceptable or not acceptable in school, which contributes to the disproportionate number of Black children who are suspended from early learning programs. Black children are seen as significantly less innocent, more culpable, and older than they really are (Goff et al., 2014), which may be the result of an automatic association between race and a perceived threat of aggression, even in young Black children (Todd et al., 2016). The Black–White racial gaps in suspensions and expulsions are apparent, even when controlling for racial differences in disproportionate rates of teacher referrals for misbehavior (e.g., Skiba et al., 2011). What we consider as appropriate and inappropriate behavior is intertwined with affluent White whiteness.

WHITENESS AS THE FOUNDATION
OF EARLY CHILDHOOD EDUCATION

Within education, including ECE, everything that we do is grounded in whiteness, from the way we provide instruction to promote individual achievement to how we view child development. The ways in which the education system was originally set up made it extremely difficult for Black children to receive an education. For example, in the post-slavery South, many White planters who worked on former plantations relied heavily on child labor. As such, there was great opposition from the planters to Black education. After the election of 1877, when federal troops were removed from the South, landlords and property owners regained control over Black labor, which allowed planters to establish a system of coercive labor designed to reduce wages, restrict labor mobility, and force Black people to sign repressive labor contracts. These policies, in combination with the vagrancy laws, severely limited the number of hours that Black children could attend school. For many rural Black students, the average school year was an abysmal 4 months long (Anderson, 1988).

During the early 1900s, White schools were at nearly 95% capacity; however, barely 50% of the seats were filled in Black schools because of the need for child labor to combat extreme poverty within Black families. The leftover money from Black schools was considered surplus and distributed to White schools, thus forming a system of impoverished Black education within the United States (Weinberg, 1977). Compounding this problem was the shortage of Black teachers, and White teachers, particularly in the South, refused to teach Black children (Anderson, 1988). In some schools, there were 82 Black students for each teacher, whereas the ratio for White children was 35 to 1. According to Anderson (1988), this overcrowding in Black schools led to shortened school days so that students could rotate through shifts. The combination of White school control and the prevailing inferiority mentality ensured that the roots of our current educational system set up advantages for White children at the expense of Black children.

By the mid-1940s, more than half of all Black students in key southern states had less than 5 years of formal education. In South Carolina and Louisiana, more than 60% of Black adults had not moved beyond fourth or fifth grade (Anderson, 1988). The disparities in educational attainment because of access and resources have been a key component in the disproportionate and intergenerational poverty that plagues our nation's towns and cities.

Within the current early childhood system, Black children and families have a particularly challenging time accessing high-quality early childhood programs because of location, investment, and cost. People of color are more likely to be in low-wage jobs that have erratic and unpredictable hours and are unlikely to have employment benefits such as paid time off, which makes it even more difficult to access affordable child care that offers flexible, nontraditional hours (Johnson-Staub, 2017). Although child-care subsidies are available for low-income families, only 17% of eligible families access them due to a complex maze of program rules at the state level regarding waitlists, family co-pays, and provider reimbursement rates (Dobbins et al., 2016). Children of color and their families are particularly affected by these policies (Brooks-Gunn & Duncan, 1997).

From the outset, our nation's schools and early childhood programs operated within a biased and paternalistic worldview. A widespread practice within education is to implement a standard model (often based on White, middle-class values) of practices. Young Black children and their families are expected to adapt to this model rather than the model adapting to them. Viewing early childhood from this lens will require a significant paradigm shift in how we provide instruction and services to children. This new way of thinking will mean considering learning styles and differences, specific barriers and needs within communities, and the cultural background of individual families and children.

As such, we continue to force Black children into an educational system that was not set up for them, including in early childhood. Our curricula, teaching practices, child assessments, early learning standards, and environmental rating scales have all been designed by White people within the worldview of affluent White whiteness. This is not to say that these practices and assessments do not have value; however, they are not fully inclusive of Black children and other children of color and their families. We must move into knowing that White "experts" do not have all the answers about (a) what high quality means and how to measure it, (b) how to engage families from different cultural backgrounds, (c) child development and ways to measure it (because when we talk about child development, we are really talking about White, middle-class child development), and (c) standards for learning and what it means to be "kindergarten ready." All of these issues must be addressed in a transformed early childhood system.

ENVISIONING A TRANSFORMED EARLY CHILDHOOD SYSTEM

When we begin envisioning what a transformed early childhood system should look like, the first step must be to revise our ideals for academic and life success. Whether or not we want to acknowledge it, affluent White ideals have always formed the crux of ECE. Notions of achievement, paternalism, and white saviorism provided the foundation for the current early childhood system—one in which we advance the success of White children while also saving poor Black children from their circumstances. In other words, we must deconstruct whiteness and how it shows up within our early

childhood programs. We must, as Dr. King said, have a "true revolution of values" (King, 1968).

Part of the shifting of values is to eschew the ways in which the No Child Left Behind Act of 2002 seeped into our early childhood programs and shifted the ways in which we think about child learning and development. We must move beyond the emphasis on getting children ready for kindergarten to nurturing their whole being: their mind, their body, and their spirit. When we talk about spirit, we are not using it in a spiritual or religious sense. We are talking about letting young children know that they matter simply because they exist. A transformed early childhood program is one in which young Black children can enter a classroom as their full authentic selves—one where they do not have to code switch to White English, one where they do not have to fit into White ways of being, and one where they are not singled out for behavior simply because of the color of their skin.

A transformed early childhood system is one in which little boys and girls are not forced into gender identities based on whiteness. It is one where boys who want to wear dresses and jewelry are nurtured rather than shamed, and one where boys are encouraged to have a full range of emotions, including the ability to cry when happy or sad. A transformed early childhood system is one where opinionated and strong-willed girls are not given messages that they should shrink themselves to fit into that White notion of femininity. A transformed early childhood program allows children to be free to be who they are—not what society tells them they should be.

A transformed early childhood program helps children find the beauty and awe in nature. It helps them appreciate dark, leafless branches against a bright blue sky or flowers emerging from the ground in spring. This connection to nature provides our young children with a fulfilment that is much needed in our increasingly materialistic society.

Our nation was hurting before the pandemic, even though many of us could not put our finger on it. Our shoulders were heavy from carrying our nation's false narratives for hundreds of years. Mental health must be a priority. We are all exhausted from the weight of the world and a pandemic that seems like it will never end. Our early childhood programs must be places for healing—for children, families, teachers, and staff. The workforce, in particular, is exhausted, overworked, underpaid, and undervalued. Beyond paying and respecting early childhood educators more, we also must shift out of the "this is the way things have always been done" mind-set. Space must be created for social-emotional wellness and relationship development. We must move away from individualism (only caring about me) to collectivism (caring about myself and others). This is healing in and of itself and is desperately needed right now.

Transforming our early childhood system will also require that we revise our academic/learning standards, including how we assess child learning and development. In addition, we are going to need to create new definitions of quality and ways for measuring it. This does not mean that we do away with the foundation that was created through decades of arduous work and research; however, we are going to need to include new voices and understandings about how we educate all children, particularly our Black children and other children of color. Implementing culturally responsive anti-bias practices is a key way in which we can begin to include alternative curricular approaches and how we view quality in ECE (see Chapter 7).

Revising the way teachers are educated in teacher education programs must be an integral part of transforming the early childhood system. Multicultural education has been the framework used to address culture and diversity in early childhood.

In its early years, multicultural education sought to (1) affirm issues of identity and differences and (2) assertively confront issues of power and privilege in society by challenging racism, biases, and the inequitable structures, policies, and practices of schools and society (Nieto & Bode, 2012). However, over time, multicultural education efforts have focused more on celebrating differences and affirming identity, and less attention has been given to challenging racism and inequitable structures, policies, and practices. Ideas of diversity, inclusion, equality, cultural competence, anti-bias, and culturally relevant teaching flourished in early learning settings. This is not to suggest these efforts are not important or useful in creating equitable learning environments, but they are not sufficient to address systemic inequities based on race in educational settings.

Teachers trained in multicultural education usually adopt a color-blind approach when working with culturally diverse students. Most early childhood teachers expressed statements such as "I don't care if children are Black, white, or green with polka dots, I treat all children the same" (Boutte et al., 2009) or "Kids are kids" (Meece & Wingate, 2009/2010). Some early childhood teachers think adopting a color-blind approach to cultural diversity is best practice. However, a color-blind approach is counterproductive to racial equity because it fails to highlight the unique histories, cultures, values, and experiences of children of color (Schofield, 2007). Adopting a color-blind ideology promotes the fallacy that teachers themselves do not have biases and it ignores the racial inequities in education (Neville et al., 2016).

Racial equity in early childhood is unattainable if we do not address the root causes of racial inequities in education. Addressing the root causes requires that we all move beyond examining biases and become culturally competent and implement culturally relevant teaching strategies. To achieve racial equity and create socially just programs for all children, we must address the root causes of inequities by (1) refocusing our attention on challenging racism and inequitable structures, policies, and practices; (2) deconstructing whiteness as the norm in education; (3) confronting issues of power and privilege in our society; and (4) engaging in efforts to heal from racial trauma—especially the damage to children's sense of self because of racism (York, 2016).

Revising teacher education programs is a critical component in transforming the ECE system. Many early childhood teacher education programs do not adequately prepare teachers in learning about culturally responsive instruction or anti-bias education (Derman-Sparks & Edwards, 2010); nor do they engage prospective students in opportunities to discuss race and racism and to reflect on their unconscious assumptions, prejudices, and biases (Ray et al., 2006).

Gay (2002) argued that although children from diverse cultural backgrounds are increasingly attending schools, not all teacher education preparation programs readily embrace a culturally responsive teacher education pedagogy. This is evident by the lack of coursework offered in cultural diversity, anti-bias education, and culturally responsive teaching practices in teacher education preparation programs (Sleeter, 2017). Not only is there a lack of coursework in culturally responsive instruction and anti-bias education, but the programs offering such coursework are often weak (Sleeter, 2017). In addition, Crowley and Smith (2015) found there is White resistance to talking about race and racism in teacher education programs.

Most 2- and 4-year institutions use the National Association for the Education of Young Children (NAEYC) standards to develop their teacher education programs. The 2010 NAEYC standards (2011) for advanced early childhood professional programs include (1) promoting child development and learning; (2) building family and community relationships; (3) observing, documenting, and assessing to support young children and families; (4) using developmentally effective appropriate approaches to connect with children and families; (5) using content knowledge to build meaningful curricula; (6) growing as a professional; and (7) early childhood field experiences. Some of these standards are based on White European American middle-class culture and values. For example, individualism and self-efficacy are valued in White European American culture. In early childhood, young children are taught to be independent, and autonomy is an important goal. Children learn early that they are unique individuals distinct from their families and cultures. They learn to become independent and responsible early on for their own behaviors and take responsibility for their actions (York, 2016). This is not to suggest the NAEYC standards are not valuable, but we need standards that are rooted in anti-racist education perspectives to adequately address the root causes of inequities based on race. However, it should be noted that NAEYC is moving beyond multicultural education and cultural competence to focus on anti-racist education with the publication of several resources that emphasize anti-racist perspectives and practices.

Another significant problem is the lack of faculty of color in early childhood teacher education programs. A report from the National Center for Education Statistics (2018) found that of the full-time faculty in higher education,

> 40 percent were White males; 35 percent were White females; 7 percent were Asian/ Pacific Islander males; 5 percent were Asian/Pacific Islander females; and 3 percent each were Black males, Black females, Hispanic males, and Hispanic females. Those who were American Indian/Alaska Native and those who were of two or more races each made up 1 percent or less of full-time faculty.

This lack of faculty of color is a root cause that must be addressed immediately. Early childhood researchers contend that having faculty of color may be a promising strategy to prepare culturally responsive educators (Early & Winton, 2001; Maxwell & Clifford, 2004).

In that same vein, Smith and Schonfeld (2000) argued that having racially and ethnically diverse faculty has implications on changes in course material that are more likely to incorporate courses in cultural diversity. Research by Burch (2007) showed that faculty of color are more likely to acknowledge the need for courses that focus on race, culturally responsive pedagogy, and social justice and have a desire to change the status quo. Even though having faculty of color is a critical component of transforming the early childhood system, having faculty of color with a deep understanding of the root causes, that have adopted anti-racist education perspectives, and are able to deconstruct whiteness in education is needed.

Most early childhood teacher preparation programs educate preservice teachers to work with middle-class White students (Sleeter, 2017). To achieve racial equity and justice in early learning settings, teacher education programs must prepare preservice teachers to become anti-racist educators equipped to deconstruct anti-Blackness and whiteness in early learning environments. Early and Winton (2001) argued that institutions of higher learning must be ready to respond to the increased demands for early childhood teachers to have the capacity to engage and educate a growing population of children of color. Early childhood teacher education programs must provide students with new course content and field-based experiences that are reflective of the increase in students of diverse cultural and linguistic backgrounds in early childhood programs (Early & Winton, 2001).

Course content that focuses on promoting social justice in education allows teachers to demonstrate an understanding of how bias and discrimination impact children, families, and communities; prepares teachers to examine historical roots and contemporary manifestations of racism and the implications it has on children's identity, development, and academic success; challenges policies that intentionally or unintentionally perpetuate racial inequities and disparate outcomes for children; and applies strategies to promote access, equity, and positive social change for young children and families.

As a society, many of us are uncomfortable talking about race. We cringe when the word "race" is brought up in conversations, we blame Black people for "playing the race card" when they point out racist acts, and we silence children when they inquire about race. Because talking about race and racism brings varied emotions of guilt, shame, anger, fear, and so forth, we avoid these much-needed conversations because we think they are divisive. Many people are complacent discussing diversity on a surface level and avoid diving deep into the complexities of race, racism, and white supremacy culture.

Because racism and whiteness are deeply embedded in our educational system and children as young as 4 years have racial preferences, early childhood educators, leaders, and other professionals must rethink the conventional way of preparing teachers and revise teacher education programs to include a social justice orientation with coursework that specifically focuses on race and racism as core components. Training teachers to examine and interrupt their personal biases, think critically about the impact racism has on children's identity and development, and deconstruct anti-Blackness and whiteness in the overall learning environment creates an institutional culture that not only addresses root causes of racial inequities but also seeks to create equitable policies and programs that promote optimal outcomes for all children.

STARTING THE WORK

Transforming the early childhood system will take time and intentionality on the part of educators, administrators, and policy makers. The first and most crucial step we can take to start the work is to engage in meaningful and authentic conversations with colleagues about the issues discussed in this chapter. We must peel the layers away to develop a more nuanced understanding and push us out of White patriarchal thinking. We have all internalized these notions that seep into the work that we do with young children and their families. We have said this throughout the book; however, it must be repeated: relationship building, authentic conversations, self-reflection, and internal work are the first and most important steps we can take to start the transformation. The goal at this time is to continue to build Dr. King's (1957) "beloved community" so that we can collectively work toward deep, transformational change.

12

Systems Change

Jen Neitzel

For most of us, 2020 was a challenging year with the pandemic and then the murder of George Floyd and the ongoing unrest throughout the summer of 2020. We all looked forward to the new year of 2021. We felt that it was a new beginning that would usher in peace and tranquility. The pandemic would be ending. We would start addressing racial justice in a more meaningful way. However, these idyllic wishes came to a halt almost immediately with the insurrection on January 6, 2020. There was an increasing realization that all was not going to go back to "normal"—whatever that was.

Throughout history, we have been fed false narratives about who we are as a nation and what it means to be American. We have been fed lies about American exceptionalism that serve to uphold the status quo. Believing that we are the greatest country in the world allows us to ignore the hard truths regarding racial injustices in our society that were slowly unearthed throughout 2020. This exceptionalism, in combination with whiteness, pushes a sense of urgency to return to the way things used to be (another false narrative).

Since 2020, events have driven us to realizations that are often ignored because they are uncomfortable. It is and always has been easy for White people to ignore the fact that our nation has always been political. The divide-and-conquer strategy, which is the bread and butter of white supremacy, has pitted us against each other. We are witnessing this strategy at its climax right now, which presents us with two options. We can withdraw because it all seems so overwhelming, or we can choose to face our hard truths. It has always been easy for White people to look away because they have not been directly affected by white supremacy in a way that infringes on their rights and privileges within society. I have ongoing conversations with my two teenage sons (one of whom can now vote) about the importance of voting. Both are disillusioned, like many teens, about what they are witnessing politically within our country. What they, and a lot of other White people, need to understand is that we can choose to be unengaged without any real consequences on our daily lives. However, elections and the subsequent policies detrimentally affect voting rights, women's rights, and the young children and their families that we have dedicated our lives to serve.

Another false narrative is that we have become so divided and that talking about race and racism is divisive. The fact is that we have always been divided. There has not been a time in our history when we have been fully united—even after 9/11. Black people and other people of color have always been pushed to the fringes, on the outskirts of White society. When we talk about our nation being united, we are talking about White people being united. The White worldview allows us to pass over the lived experiences of Black children and families within society. They have never been included in the United States. Our policies and practices prevent them from attaining the fruits of American society.

Our goal now must be to work toward that ideal of being united, which happens when we engage in racial healing. As author Kate Bowler stated in a recent *On Being* podcast episode, "It was always about all of us. We belong to each other" (Bowler & Ali, 2021). We will only belong to each other when we begin to face our false narratives and understand that we can continue to look away; however, the murders of Black people and violence by white nationalists will not end until we force ourselves to confront our nation's extremely complicated and broken past. Kate Bowler goes on to say, "Brokenness is an indictment on all of us" (Bowler & Ali, 2021). Our nation is, and always has been, broken. We all, in some way, have been complicit and/or complacent at some point in our lives. We must all come to the realization that unity will only come through healing. When we heal individually, we can then heal collectively. Only then can we move forward together to change the systems to be more equitable and just.

FIRST-GENERATION EQUITY WORK

Bryan Stevenson says, "Hopelessness is the enemy of justice." For those of us engaged in racial equity work, it is easy to lose hope from time to time. Sometimes, it feels like we are banging our heads against an impenetrable wall. It can feel like no one is listening or that no one cares about making amends for past harms and becoming a country where the ideals set forth in the Constitution and Declaration of Independence are achieved. Too many of us only focus on racial justice when we are presented with events that make it hard for us to ignore or look away. As with the murder of George Floyd and the insurrection on January 6, 2021, many people had to face racism, but were still unwilling to fully do so because of the discomfort and shame that come along with the acknowledgment of the atrocities of slavery, Jim Crow, the Trail of Tears, the American Genocide, and Indian boarding schools. Many organizations began to check the box of "equity" by attending a training or a workshop but were unwilling to commit to deep transformational change.

We live in a society of white shame, not one of white guilt. We are so afraid to bear witness to our brutal past because it counters the narrative that we are the greatest country in the world. It is long past time for White people (read: affluent White women) to pull themselves out of their complicity and complacency. Reading books focused on racial inequities in our book clubs is fine, but what happens after the books are read? What are White women willing to do with the knowledge that they have been given? Will they go back to their lives of privilege and complacency? Or will they stand up in their communities and at the voting booth because their actions or inactions have very real consequences for the lives of children and families of color—particularly Black children and families?

The inability or unwillingness to take measurable actions against racism is not just limited to White people. There is a significant amount of complicity and complacency operating within our systems. Too often, our systems, including our educational system, try to solve incredibly complex problems with bandages. For example, in the school system that my three sons attend, there has been an increase in violence that takes the form of fights and of guns being found in backpacks. This school system has chosen to solve this problem by consulting with law enforcement leaders rather than mental health experts. Even my 18-year-old saw the absurdity in this approach. His response was, "That's not going to solve anything."

Their solution is to require all high schoolers to use clear backpacks while they install metal detectors in schools and do an increased number of security checks. What they do not realize is that they are just putting bandages on gaping wounds. They are failing to recognize what our children, particularly our teenagers, have been through over the last 2 years. Their young brains and bodies have witnessed and experienced a global pandemic, community shutdowns, mask wearing, disruption of daily life, the murder of George Floyd, the subsequent unrest in the summer of 2020, and the insurrection on January 6th. They also are witnessing societal unrest within our nation at this very moment and the role white supremacy is playing in it.

Rather than addressing the mental health of our children, we have thrust them back into schools expecting them to resume business as usual. What we are seeing with the increased violence is that our children are crying out. They have experienced traumas, some more than others because of intergenerational historical and racial traumas, and we have failed them. The current whack-a-mole strategy is not working and has never worked within education. We are too entrenched in the status quo to think more deeply and critically about how to solve centuries-old problems. This superficial approach to addressing racial inequities is what I call *first-generation equity work*.

For generations, we have focused on solving extraordinarily complex problems (e.g., violence, racial inequities) by implementing highly specific educational practices that are focused on promoting isolated skills (e.g., literacy, math, social-emotional) by putting bandages on the problem instead of focusing on the root causes of the very issues we are trying to address. With regard to racism, we promote equality rather than equity. In Chapter 3, we talked about the difference between equality (i.e., everyone gets the same regardless of need) versus equity (i.e., individuals get resources based on what they need). Focusing on equity forces us to move out of a color-blind ideology. The term *color blindness* comes from the book *Racism Without Racists: Color-Blind Racism and the Persistence of Racial Inequality in America* by Eduardo Bonilla-Silva. In his book, Bonilla-Silva (2003) argues that color blindness is the belief that there is no racial hierarchy, which is sustained by a failure to consider the permanence of race's role within our nation's institutions.

Prior to the election of 2016 and the murder of George Floyd, many of us (i.e., White people) thought that we were living in a post-racial society. This is because racism is highly fluid and adapts to the cultural norms and historical events of a particular time. For example, during slavery and Jim Crow, most of our nation found it socially acceptable to discriminate based on skin color and to explicitly believe that Black people were "less than" or "other." However, following the Civil Rights movement, discriminatory policies were banned, and these overt attitudes became increasingly considered racist. Because of this, the grounding ideology that whiteness is the norm and superior went underground where it became a part of our deeper subconscious. During the era of color blindness, there has been an increasing resistance to talk about race and acknowledge the role of racism in perpetuating the ongoing inequities within the educational system and our larger society.

This unwillingness to talk about race and racism persists in education despite the social unrest that took place in the summer of 2020 following the murder of George Floyd. Enough time has now passed that many White people, particularly those in leadership positions, have moved on or tried to get back to the "idyllic" way things were (i.e., not focusing on racial justice). A compounding factor is that COVID-19 shone a light on our highly fragile systems, particularly early childhood, which has been held together by a thin layer of glue for decades. Child care is in crisis. Early intervention is in crisis because of decades of underfunding and the failure to acknowledge the significant role that early childhood providers have in the lives of our young children. We continue to devalue their important work and fail to pay them a living wage.

Because of underfunding and the role that the No Child Left Behind Act of 2001 has played in the deterioration of our early childhood system, we are now facing the ramifications of those decisions. No Child Left Behind created an era of high-stakes accountability that seeped down into early childhood. We pushed down developmentally inappropriate learning expectations at the expense of our children's social-emotional health. We then continue to send these very children off to a K–12 system with teachers who have been educated in preservice programs that place a primary emphasis on pedagogy while ignoring the need to focus on behavior management, classroom management, and social-emotional well-being.

We often hear from early childhood professionals that we cannot address racial equity right now because our system is in crisis. What we need to acknowledge is that racial equity and the restructuring of the early childhood system go hand in hand.

This will require a second-generation approach to equity. It is remarkably easy for White people to say "slow down" or "not now" when they and their families have not been directly affected by the atrocities throughout the history of our country. It is easy for White people to put racial equity on the back burner because they and their children are not affected by the disproportionality in suspensions and the woeful underfunding in education, including early care and learning.

Too many White people, particularly affluent White women, have knowingly or unknowingly swallowed the false notions of success and attainment within our educational system that, at its basis, was designed to dehumanize and control Black children while advancing the educational achievements of White children. Affluent White families too quickly absorb the false narratives of our educational system because they ultimately benefit from the advancement of their children within society and feed into our false notions of success. There is a laser focus on piling on Advance Placement classes (often at the expense of the mental health of our children), promoting elite athletics from an early age (often at the expense of our children), and perpetuating the ideal that the right house, the right neighborhoods, the right car, the right vacations, and the right country clubs are what it means to be successful within our society. All this occurs without the understanding that these falsehoods are grounded in individualism and competition (characteristics of white supremacy culture), which lead to disconnection rather than connection.

As a society, we are hungry for connection; however, this affluent White notion of educational and life success leads to more disconnection. Individualism and competition lead to superficial, materialistic relationships that are lacking in vulnerability. According to Brené Brown (2021), "In a world where perfectionism, pleasing, and proving are used as armor to protect our egos and our feelings, it takes a lot of courage to show up and be all in when we can't control the outcome" (p. 14). She goes on to say, "Vulnerability is not weakness, it's our greatest measure of courage" (p. 15). White supremacy does not nurture vulnerability. Rather, it promotes division, competition, individualism, and power hoarding. If we are to move into a more equitable and just society, we are going to need to let go of all that we know about ourselves and our nation. Racial equity work is shared humanity work—to see ourselves in others. We cannot begin to dismantle the systems until we understand that the numbers and strategies are actually faces and people with stories—stories that must be listened to with humility. When we can do this, we can move into a more empathetic response that is deeply lacking in our nation today. According to Brown (2021), "We need to dispel the myth that empathy is 'walking in someone else's shoes'" (p. 123). True empathy is believing another person even when it does not match our experiences. Racial justice work requires that we move out of our heads and into our hearts. It requires moving past jumping to the solution and trying to understand the issues from a scientific or data-driven standpoint. The basis for empathy is love; not a romantic love but a love of choice. In her work, bell hooks wrote about love extensively. In her book *all about love* (2001), she said, "To truly love, we must learn to mix various ingredients—care, affection, recognition, respect, commitment, and trust, as well as honest and open communication" (p. 5). She goes on to say, "There can be no love without justice" (p. 19).

Current racial equity work is stuck in the head space. We focus on concepts and definitions (all of which are important); however, when we stay in this intellectual space, we fail to recognize the need for shared humanity. Racial equity work must invest in heart work—cultivating vulnerability, empathy, connection, and love. We must move out of racial equity work as an intellectual practice into one that is grounded in the knowing that justice will not be achieved without authentic human connection and relationships.

Current racial equity work is grounded in disconnection. Rather than investing in authentic relationship building and empathy of experience, we make decisions about children and families. We change policies and practices without the input of children and families. This is because we are not grounded in what bell hooks calls "an ethic of love." An ethic of love requires that we believe in our hearts and bodies that "everyone has the right to be free, to live fully and well. To bring a love ethic to every dimension of our lives, our society would need to embrace change" (p. 87).

Currently, those who sit in early childhood leadership positions tend to be White women who knowingly or unknowingly make decisions about Black children and families from a white-centered worldview that presupposes what is needed to reduce ongoing inequities within early childhood. Black women and other women of color are relegated to underpaid jobs within childcare centers and teacher assistant positions in early learning programs. Their voices are not included when making decisions about whether it is time to address racial equity in early childhood education. The families in these underresourced programs are not given a seat at the table when deciding whether it is time to focus on racial equity.

For decades, we have systematically marginalized the very people who kept the childcare system in operation throughout the pandemic. It is long past time that their voices, as well as those of the families who are on the receiving end of the inequities, are included in discussions about funding; what is important to address; and how to meet the needs of young Black children, other children of color, and their families. Presently, within early childhood leadership, there is "a gap between the values they claim to hold and their willingness to do the work of connecting thought and action, theory and practice to realize these values and thus create a more just society" (hooks, 2001, p. 90). This will require a different way of approaching systems change—one that is grounded in a love ethic. We must move out of individualism and competition, not only in our systems but also within the larger society, to have an authentic concern for the "collective good of our nation, city, or neighbor" (hooks, 2001, p. 98) that is more focused on *us* rather than *me*. When we can move collectively into that way of being, we will be able to eradicate the ongoing inequities within our society.

SECOND-GENERATION EQUITY WORK

The cornerstone of this new way of approaching systems change requires a reliance on relationship building, open communication, and the cultivation of authentic empathy and compassion. According to Peck (2010), community is defined as "a group of individuals who have learned how to communicate honestly with each other, whose relationships go deeper than their masks of composure, and who have developed some significant commitment . . . . to make other's conditions our own" (p. 59). Many will say, "What does any of this have to do with systems change?" Here is our answer: our educational system, like every other system, is grounded in white supremacy culture, which includes division, disconnection, individualism, and competition. These underlying principles need to be disrupted to bring about transformational change. Too often, we jump to solutions without doing the foundational work of building authentic relationships and connection that serve as the basis for bringing about justice within the educational system. To achieve change, we must first build community.

The term "second-generation" work is borrowed from an article written by Guralnick (1993). In the 1990s, Guralnick argued that early intervention was in the midst of a period of rapid change that was marked by a movement away from superficial analyses regarding the effectiveness of services and supports for young children with disabilities into a new era in which researchers and policy makers were being pushed to ask more specific questions and develop a more nuanced understanding about how to meet the needs of young children and their families. Much has changed since I first wrote about second-generation work in 2019. First, I think that I was still painfully naïve about the realities of white supremacy. Yes, we can understand white supremacy at an intellectual level, but once in the trenches, you begin to fully realize the many layers that continue to be unpeeled. White supremacy culture and thinking are so deeply embedded within our nation's institutions, including early childhood, that we can no longer see it. However, when you get into the weeds of racial equity work, you begin to see how incredibly difficult it will be to change current policies and practices in a way that will transform the lives of Black children, other children of color, and their families.

Second-generation work requires commitment and determination. There is nothing easy about transformational racial equity work that is focused on disrupting the status quo. Diversity, equity, and inclusion work is rampant, and this will not lead to real, meaningful change. The first and most major step of equity and justice work is generating a paradigm shift. Many people would like to achieve this change within a single training or workshop; however, there needs to be a commitment and investment in cultivating the ethic of love that bell hooks talked about. This work takes time and is foundational to achieving equity and justice in early childhood. Too many system leaders are stuck in first-generation work. As a field, we have yet to emerge from a first-generation approach to equity in which we are in a constant cycle of implementing the latest intervention or relying on what we have always done without thinking critically and examining the underlying issues surrounding equity in education while also generating an ethic of love.

SYSTEMS CHANGE

Systems change work is daunting but necessary work. It is foundational to achieving equity and justice in early childhood education. In the next section, I will lay out the strategies and steps we can use to work toward deep transformational change within early childhood.

Paradigm Shift

As I said previously, many people, particularly those in leadership positions, want to jump straight to solutions. They want to "solve" racism. However, when we push for action without unpacking the many layers of white supremacy and racism, we run the risk of perpetuating the very problems we are trying to solve. In our trainings, we always push people to commit to nonclosure, which is hard for most of us. We have been conditioned to check off tasks, generate solutions, and move into action without making space for what is needed, which is the building of a collective community of early childhood professionals who are committed to equity and justice. Yes, solutions and impatience are important, but we must begin to disrupt *the way things have always been done* with a new way of being. When we fall back into the narrative that business as usual is sufficient, we perpetuate the status quo and fall back into first-generation equity work.

Part of the paradigm shift is not only learning about the accurate history of our country and how our systems were set up to perpetuate racism and white supremacy, but we also must challenge our current ways of being within our organizations and institutions that uphold the status quo. Two characteristics of white supremacy culture that are present within most organizations and institutions are (a) a sense of urgency and (b) quantity over quality.

With a sense of urgency, we often place unrealistic timelines on ourselves and others to complete tasks and get things done, which makes it difficult to be inclusive, encourage democratic and/or thoughtful decision making, think long-term, and consider consequences (Okun, 2021). What this does is sacrifice relationships just so we can check boxes for getting tasks done. With racial equity work, we must create space and time to build relationships and discuss the ways in which white supremacy shows up in our organizations and institutions as well as within early childhood education itself.

A large part of racial equity work is unpeeling the layers so that we can get to the root of the problems we are trying to address. This takes time. It requires authentic relationships grounded in trust and vulnerability. If we say that we are committed to racial equity work, then we must move beyond this sense of urgency. Yes, impatience is good; however, we do not want to get into a mentality where we are just trying to check off the box of racial equity. It took us more than 400 years to get to this point. We are not going to solve racial equity with a single training or even in our lifetimes. It has become increasingly apparent to me that this beast we call white supremacy is so deep and entrenched that we are going to need to commit to small wins. I struggle with this sense of urgency from time to time because the current climate within our nation and the issues feel so immense. This causes us great discomfort, and we seek to find solutions so that this nasty unease will go away. We need to say to ourselves repeatedly, "We will not see the end of this, but we can plant the seeds so that generations after us, Black children and families can enjoy the shade." We must commit to that or else we will become stagnant, which is exactly what white supremacy wants us to do.

With quantity over quality, we are so fixated on achieving measurable goals that we lose sight of the process. For example, we once worked with a large organization. We had just started and it was our first meeting. Many on the video call wanted us to tell them what to do and how to fix the issues. It is essential that all of us who are engaged in racial equity work, including me, sit in a space of humility. The issues are so deep and so complex that none of us have all the answers, not even the so-called experts. That is why relationship building, where we are engaged in listening and learning while also learning to love and accept others and their stories, is so critical to this work. We each bring something to the table when we are trying to figure out how exactly we are going to go about disrupting centuries-old institutions. A collective effort is needed, one that is grounded in love for the other. To accomplish this task, we must move beyond measuring progress through quantifiable goals to achieving a manner where we are engaged in a more democratic process that ensures we have a deep understanding of the issues and everyone feels listened to and heard.

Generating a paradigm shift moves beyond the intellectual into the heart. In our trainings, we say that social justice work is holy work. This is not meant in a mere spiritual sense but in an understanding that the root of *holy* means *to become whole*. Part of changing mind-sets is aligning ourselves with a purpose that goes beyond our own individual intentions. Social justice work requires that we commit to healing from the wounds of racism and white supremacy, both individually and collectively. When we can do that, we will continue to build what Dr. King referred to as the beloved community, and we can truly work together to dismantle and rebuild the early childhood system.

An Appreciative Inquiry Approach to Systems Change

Recently, we have been working with organizations to promote systems change through an appreciative inquiry framework. This approach is counter to what has traditionally been done; however, it is promising because it centers the voices of those most affected by the issues and offers a roadmap for collaboratively working toward deep transformational change. Several key steps are needed to lay the groundwork before this framework can be implemented. For example, a key first step is to establish a "keeper of the vision." Although our overall goal is to promote cross-sector systems change, we fully understand the complexities of engaging in this type of work. Because of this, we recognize that starting with a single organization or institution is the most productive way to move through this work at this time. We can continue cross-sector conversations; however, each sector must be engaged in the paradigm shift work that I discussed previously. This simply is not happening right now. Too many organizations and institutions are still engaged in first-generation equity work, which is surface level, quick-fix work. Each person committed to racial equity and justice must begin to identify how they can apply an appreciative inquiry approach to equity in their spheres of influence.

Establishing a Keeper of the Vision We encourage organizations and institutions that have committed to deep transformational change to become the keeper of the vision in their spheres of influence. For example, this could be a child care resource and referral agency or a local Head Start chapter. When an organization commits to being the keeper of the vision, they become a role model and visionary for others to follow. The light will spread, and more and more organizations will begin to engage in transformational change.

Bringing Together the Strategic Planning Team The keeper of the vision will be responsible for ensuring that the goals of systems change are accomplished, which includes establishing a strategic planning team. This team should include leadership within the organization, leaders of grassroots organizations within the community, community members, and most important, parents and family members who are most deeply affected by the ongoing inequities within early childhood education. When identifying members of the strategic planning team, it is critical that we follow the tenets of diversity, inclusion, and equity/justice.

With diversity, we ensure that the team looks like and represents the community at large. This means that we go beyond race and ethnicity, but we also include socioeconomic status, gender identity, sexual orientation, and ability. A central concept in racial equity work is that none of us are defined by a single identity, which is called *intersectionality* (coined by Kimberlé Crenshaw [1989]). When utilizing an intersectional lens, we understand that a queer Black mother is going to have a completely distinct experience within the early childhood system than a Latino father with a learning challenge. This understanding recognizes that each of us brings our unique experiences to help us develop a more nuanced understanding about the issues and what is needed to address them.

Conducting a Root Cause Analysis   This intersectional framework also will help the strategic planning team engage in a root cause analysis of individual issues. For example, they can work to understand why young Black boys are getting suspended and expelled from early childhood programs at a higher rate than White children. With a root cause analysis, we first define the problem. What is it that we are trying to address? Next, we gather all the information and data we have regarding the problem. With this step, it is essential that we find as much intersectional data as possible so that we can develop a more nuanced understanding of the issue. Listening to the experiences of family and community members is a key component to this information-gathering process. Following this step, we can then work to identify any issues that might be perpetuating the disparities. For suspensions and expulsions, this might be a lack of training and professional development for early childhood providers regarding equity, implicit bias, behavior management, or social-emotional development.

The next, and most important, step is to identify the root causes. Where did the problem originate? What structures, barriers, attitudes, or beliefs created this problem? Most often, the roots of the inequities are grounded in racism, anti-Blackness, and white supremacy. However, other root causes may be specific policies and practices (which are grounded in racism and anti-Blackness) that continue to perpetuate how and where Black children and families are identified for and receive services. Root cause analysis forms the basis for all other work that follows. This is a step where we must fight back against that sense of urgency. It is essential to continue to make space and time for open, authentic discussions where everyone on the strategic planning team feels listened to and heard. The voices of those most affected by the issues are particularly important at this stage in the process. After the root cause analysis, we can then generate recommendations, identify strategies, and begin working toward solutions.

Appreciative Inquiry Framework   All the groundwork that is done with forming a strategic planning team and conducting a root cause analysis creates an atmosphere where the appreciative inquiry framework can flourish. According to Moore (2008), appreciative inquiry is an approach to personal and organizational change that questions and generates dialogue about strengths, successes, values, hope, and dreams, which is transformational in and of itself. This approach is based on the belief that people, individually and collectively, have unique gifts, skills, and contributions that can help organizations shift their attention and action away from problem analysis to identify possibilities for the future. With appreciative inquiry, there is an emphasis on relationship building and equity within the strategic planning team—where there is shared power and all voices, experiences, and opinions are honored.

The appreciative inquiry framework includes the five Ds: define, discover, dream, design, and destiny. With the first D, define, the strategic planning team has already defined the problem through the root cause analysis. They can then move into discovering, which helps organizations identify their strengths and what they are already doing well. Questions the team might answer are (a) What are current equity-related efforts? (b) What are we doing well for children and families? and (c) How do we know that we are doing these things well? This is a crucial step because it serves as a launching pad for building on current strengths to address equity.

The next step is to dream. This is where the team identifies its dreams and aspirations for the organization and how it serves Black children and families. The team discusses its ideal vision for promoting equity in early childhood while also reflecting on opportunities, resources, and supports within the organization and/or funding agencies that could promote equity-related efforts. The design phase allows the strategic planning team to (1) reflect on the organization's strengths, opportunities, and aspirations and (2) discuss what is needed to get to the ideal vision for equity within the early childhood organization and early childhood system at large.

This phase also includes an effort to identify any threats that might hinder the work of equity in the organization. This might come from individuals within the organization who have not bought in to the approach. State legislation also serves as a significant barrier at this time. Identifying threats and barriers is critical because it allows the keeper of the vision to create and control the narrative regarding racial equity work in early childhood. Cultivating relationships is critical when we are trying to turn threats into opportunities. Finding common ground and building on what is important to oppositional individuals can shift their understanding and buy-in to addressing racial equity.

Finally, the strategic planning team can then focus on destiny. That is, they begin the process of writing SMART goals, which is essential if we are to bring about lasting change. Many times, goals are created that are too broad and lack clear definition about what is to be accomplished. The SMART format provides a structure for creating goals that are specific, measurable, achievable, relevant, and time bound. Common types of goals are to (a) increase something, (b) make something, (c) improve something, or (d) reduce something. Highly specific questions are much more successful in supporting implementation work, as opposed to more general goals that offer little insight into what needs to be accomplished. Specific goals should be objective, not subjective. That is, anyone reading the goals should come to the same conclusion about the intention of the goal rather than relying on their own interpretation of what it might look like in practice.

Goals should also be measurable—that is, what metrics are going to be used to determine if the goal is met? For example, a goal might be focused on reducing in- and out-of-school suspensions by 85% or increasing the third-grade reading level from 30% to 60% proficiency for specific populations of children. Measurement methods can be both quantitative (percentage, statistics) or qualitative (anecdotal data); however, it is essential that the goal is specifically written to provide a feasible way to measure its success.

When writing systems change goals, it is especially important that they are achievable. Achievable goals are meant to inspire motivation, not discouragement. As such, the strategic planning team should think about (a) how to accomplish the goal and (b) what resources and skills will be needed to accomplish the goal. Systems change goals also must be relevant to the current situation. This is why looking at the existing data regarding educational disparities is essential when first beginning the work. The group must have an accurate understanding of the current needs to write goals that have relevance within the context of the educational community.

   Ensuring that goals are time bound is an incredibly important part of the goal development process. The strategic planning team should provide a target date for deliverables for each goal. Team members ask specific questions about the goal deadline and what can be accomplished within that time period. If the goal will take 3 months to complete, it is important to break this down into short-, medium-, and long-term goals. Creating time points along the way for goals that take longer to accomplish will ensure that the necessary steps are being taken to meet the deadline. Providing these types of time constraints also creates a sense of urgency for the group to achieve the goal in the time allotted (University of Southern California, 2017).

WHERE TO START

Systems change can feel like an overwhelming and daunting process. It is a huge undertaking but one that is necessary to bring about the deep transformational change that is needed at this time. This leads to the question, "What can you do right now that will help you feel like you are getting those small wins that are so important right now?" The first thing you can do is commit to your own deep transformational change. Educate yourself on the issues by listening to podcasts, reading books, and watching movies and documentaries (see Resource Guide in Appendix B). As you are doing this, you can also work to bring authentic racial equity trainings (not diversity, equity, and inclusion trainings) to your organization. These types of efforts can begin to shift mind-sets within the organization. Finally, create space and time for relationship development and authentic conversations about issues related to race, racism, and white supremacy within yourselves, your organization, and the work that you do with young children and their families. These types of efforts are foundational to the work of systems change. Everything else will naturally unfold if we can all commit to this.

Afterword

Throughout this book, we have tried to paint a broad picture of the issues surrounding racial equity in early childhood education and what is needed right now to bring about deep transformational change. Whenever there is progress toward racial equity within our society, there is always backlash. After the murder of George Floyd, we saw a groundswell of support and a reawakening about the racial inequities within our society. However, following the summer of 2020, we began to feel opposition toward progress creeping in again. There was increased chatter and noise regarding critical race theory and the danger it poses to White children within education. The noise became louder during gubernatorial elections, and an alarming number of states began instituting legislation that prohibits the teaching of the true history of our country. This opposition has made it increasingly difficult to speak and learn about the root causes of the inequities within our society.

What is needed right now is the building of a movement in education to drown out the falsehoods that permeate our society at the current moment. We need early childhood educators who are committed not only to justice but also to the deep internal work of examining our beliefs, actions, insecurities, and discomfort with being a part of the change. A commitment to this work requires vulnerability, a willingness to discuss once-taboo subjects with others, humility, and a willingness to make and own our mistakes. Hard ongoing conversations are necessary—about race, racism, and white supremacy, including how it shows up in ourselves, our organizations, and the work that we do with young children and their families. What can you do right now?

1. *Educate yourself.* Read books and articles; listen to podcasts focused on race, racism, and racial healing; watch historical and current-day movies and documentaries. These activities are crucial because they facilitate that deep internal work that is needed to undo racism within ourselves and our society.

2. *Reflect.* Take time to reflect on what you are learning. You can journal or just take time to better understand our history and how you have been complicit in some way in upholding the status quo.

3. *Notice.* In your daily life, observe situations, news stories, and television shows and take note of discrimination and bias. Racism is insidious and shows up in many ways and takes many forms within our lives.

4. *Have grace.* As you embark on this journey, have grace for yourselves and others. We have all been socialized in a society where White is the norm. You may feel guilt or even shame. Whereas guilt is healthy because it allows us to atone, apologize, and do better, shame is stagnating. Guilt is "I did something bad." Shame is "I am bad." Healthy guilt is expected; however, you need to move through that guilt. Allow yourself to feel the pain, but do not let it define you.

Again, welcome to your anti-racism journey. This is not a sprint or a destination. Anti-racism work requires commitment and determination. With each commitment, we get closer to creating what Dr. King called the "beloved community."

Appendix A

Positive Racial
Identity Development

First Person Voices
Aisha White

In a series of conversations with African American scholars, educators, students, and a parent, interviewees shared their experiences, opinions, and hopes and dreams for a world where support for the positive racial identity development of Black children is the norm. Participants responded to questions about their own racial journeys, their research, practice, challenges facing educators, and passion for this topic. All interviews were conducted by Aisha White, PhD, of the P.R.I.D.E. Program at the University of Pittsburgh.

Marc Peters, Self-Employed Father and Grandfather

Aisha White (AW): A while back you told me a story about being teased in school because of your skin color. Can you tell me a little about that again if you don't mind?

Marc Peters (MP): Yeah, when I would go to school, kids would call me "blacky" and "darky" and as a result of that I thought it was bad to be darker than some of the other students. Kids would say things like that, and I began to develop a complex about it and wanted to change how I looked. I even went to the drugstore to see if they had anything to lighten my skin tone. I didn't have enough money because I was little so then I thought okay, maybe if I put some bleach in the bathtub, I can use that to make my skin lighter. And although over time I was able to ignore it, I was still getting into fights with people—telling them things like "Call me black again and see what happens." I even sometimes wanted to fight. None of it worked, though, and when I took that bath with bleach, I didn't get lighter.

AW: How old were you at the time?

MP: At the time, I was in fourth or fifth grade. I remember that I was still going to elementary school. And as I think about it, some of the other kids who seemed to me to be the same complexion as me, you know, who were also kinda dark, they even teased me. It didn't seem to me that they were lighter than me, but I still felt like an outcast. I even wanted to start being around some of the guys who were lighter than me because of that.

AW: Did you ever have conversations with your parents about this?

MP: No, no, I didn't because it seemed like they never talked about how dark they were or how dark I was. It seemed to me that they didn't want me to know, it just wasn't a thing they acknowledged. But my parents hid a lot from me, things about how they felt or if they had any sickness or other things. They never told me about them because I think they felt that if I found out about it, I'd be so upset. As I think about it, even those kids that used to tease me, evidently, they weren't taught anything either, so they needed to have conversations with their parents too.

AW: What do you know about positive racial identity?

MP: I know that it has to do with the culture you are and how you name yourself—are you Afro-American, Black, or how do you describe yourself, your identity? I think it also is related to where those names or labels for our people came from and how we determine how we define ourselves. Some of the names we've been given are labels from someone else.

AW: Did you do things to help your children appreciate their race, culture, and ethnicity as a parent?

MP: Pretty much, yes. I taught them that they were Black, and I used that word. I also exposed them to clothes, different African garments, and I shared different books they would read about honesty and Black culture. I wanted them to experience that because I felt schools lots of times left those things out.

AW: Is it something you do as a grandparent? Is it something you would like to be able to do?

MP: Yes, I do; I try to. I try to get them on board as far as them knowing that they are Black, how to respond if someone says the wrong things to you about being Black, like the things I experienced growing up in school. I started telling them about education about different types of schools—elementary, middle, high school, college, trade schools, all the way up.

AW: Do you think most parents know how to help children develop a positive racial identity?

MP: No, I don't, because I didn't learn too much about that from my parents and I know my parents didn't learn about it from their parents, so it just keeps passing down in the same direction, the same way—not sharing information. And sometimes, in families, even if there's a man and a woman in the same household, sometimes the two of them don't have the same experiences and they might not agree about how to socialize the child. I strongly believe there should be more conversations about our identities and who we are, who we really are.

AW: What kinds of things do you think parents need to be able to support their kids in feeling good about how they look and their race in general?

MP: I think sometimes the kids need to ask them questions but then sometimes children don't know what questions to ask. With that in mind, I feel parents need to be reeled in and given information about how to talk to their kids about these things.

AW: Do you think teachers have a role to play in helping children feel good about their race or ethnicity? Why or why not?

MP: Yeah, they have a lot to do with it I think because they're with the children sometimes more than you are as a parent who might only see them for a few hours of the day after they get home. Teachers have a lot of time to spend with the kids to share with them what they need to know.

AW: Do you think teachers know how to do that?

MP: No. In all honesty, I think some of them only want to get a degree to be a teacher. And still others, I hate to say it, but some are racist, which creates all kinds of problems for children and parents. However, there are others that just don't know what to do. Those teachers need to be taught the honest truth.

Dr. Sherlyn Harrison, EdD, Early Head Start Coordinator, Pittsburgh Public Schools

Aisha White (AW): Tell me about a time you recall being treated differently because of your race.

Sherlyn Harrison (SH): My earliest memory of a racialized experience is me bundled up in a little red coat that was a favorite of mine and my parents. At 3 years old, I went to a private nursery school in Pittsburgh where most of my classmates were White children from affluent families. We were fortunate enough to have gym and swimming classes, and one day, after gym class, when I went to get my coat, it wasn't there. When it was time for me to be picked up, I remember standing outside in the cold in the dead of winter with no coat on worried that I would be in BIG trouble. What I do remember most about that experience was my dad and how upset he would get every time he recalled the story saying: "They had my baby standing out in the cold with no coat on!" He could never understand why an adult would not take off their coat (a White female teacher was standing right beside me wearing her winter coat) and wrap it around a young child. The school administration also insinuated to my mom that I had hidden my coat somewhere.

AW: Tell me a little about your interest in positive racial identity.

SH: I was so excited to see the P.R.I.D.E. scan in 2016. Reading it opened the door to all the research questions and all the passions I've had over the years about young African American children and academic achievement.

AW: Why is having a positive racial identity important?

SH: Because racism is so prevalent in society, all over the world, having a positive racial identity is necessary in order to be successful. It's a belief that an individual has in themselves that they are able and worthy and capable of doing whatever they want to do. Everyone should have a positive identity but, in this country, and around the world, because racism is such a widespread thing and because it's embedded in everything you do, it's really needed in Black children and children of color. One of the things I realized as I started my doctoral work is that parents are racial socialization agents, but children spend half their waking hours in school. I saw a disconnect between messages kids get at home and school, but just as parents want the best for their children, teachers want their students to succeed. Once they (teachers) become aware that positive racial identity helps their students become successful, how can they not want to do things to support it?

AW: Tell me about your research.

SH: In my dissertation work, I was trying to uncover the ways parents can inform teachers about all the wonderful things they do at home to build up children's racial identity and what might be a way parents could transfer that knowledge to teachers. I wanted to understand what the platform for parents might be to communicate that to teachers, so one of the questions I wanted to answer was what parents and teachers needed. I found that all of the parents felt supporting children's positive racial identity in the classroom is not only possible but should be happening on a regular basis.

AW: What challenges do teachers face?

SH: Systems are a big obstacle to this work. Our educational systems have to decide that educating all children is the purpose of what they're doing because our systems are so driven by our discriminatory culture that they are just replaying and manifesting the flaws of the wider society. Once systems decide to be anti-racist, then we will have overcome the biggest obstacle. Another challenge might be parents, but if parents object to teachers talking about race, I think addressing this is connected to relationship building. Early childhood education teachers have a great opportunity to build strong relationships with parents, relationships that start with trust. Teachers have other hard conversations, and like those conversations, dialogue about race can be had more easily when teachers have a relationship with parents.

AW: What advice do you have for educators?

SH: Educators should know that following the murder of George Floyd, there was an explosion of resources that were made available to parents and educators about talking to children about race, from *Sesame Street* to *EmbraceRace,* the NAEYC (National Association for the Education of Young Children), Trying Together (a local early childhood organization), and Zero to Three. I would also say to teachers, we should be careful not to think of the Black experience as being one way—one sided. All African American teachers are not of the same mind-set about positive racial identity, so we shouldn't assume they buy into this notion. Sometimes, they might need just as much support as a White teacher.

AW: Looking to the future.

SH: I want to see interest grow, for this message to reach everyone in the Pittsburgh Public Schools early education program. I'm already seeing the impact program-wide, but I would love to see P.R.I.D.E. in all classrooms. Imagine if 20 teachers would go back and create a P.R.I.D.E. classroom. Think about what that would look like! A classroom that would be totally immersed in what it means to build positive racial identity in young people for the whole school year or for whatever time period. I also would like to see P.R.I.D.E. implemented from pre-K to 12th grade. One other thing I think would be great is to have a collaborative of programs that are doing similar work, doing similar things. Lastly, I think we really need more outcome data related to positive racial identity that answers the question of how this work is impacting our kids.

Chelsea Jimenez, PhD Student, Urban Education, Predoctoral Fellow, Remake Learning, and Former Elementary School Teacher

Aisha White (AW): Tell me about your personal experiences and interest in positive racial identity.

Chelsea Jimenez (CJ): I can remember that on the first day of school, the teacher kept asking me to repeat myself. By the third day of school, not only was I repeating myself, but I realized that the teacher was actually looking over me. There was no conversation with my parents before they pulled me into a class for students whose home language was not English even though English was my first language. I wasn't able to test out of that class until I reached high school. While I could listen and understand something in English and point to something that was described in English, and write about it, when it came to speaking, it was the dialect that prevented me from moving out of that class. They said the way I spoke "didn't sound right." Although my first language was English, that wasn't the case for either of my parents. When I failed the tests, they never told me why I wasn't testing out.

AW: What is positive racial identity to you?

CJ: For me it's how a person associates themselves with their identity in relation to their race and their culture. It's not just how one perceives Blackness as an identity but how I see myself in relation to it. Do I see myself positively as a reflection of how I see Blackness? They both need to happen—as culture and identity. We popularize Black identity a lot, but we don't always see ourselves in the best light. While "Black" might be cool, knowing how your White teacher sees you as a Black person is something different. The White students may be perceived as more civilized, as prettier, things of that nature.

AW: What challenges do teachers face?

CJ: I believe educators are hesitant to practice teaching that supports children's positive racial identity because, first, there's no extra time. They already have to teach 20 things and now you're saying I have to teach about culture, which isn't in the standards, so now I have to teach 25 things. I don't know where I would begin doing that, and on top of that, these kids aren't even at grade level. Second, sometimes it's how it's perceived. Will I get pushback from leadership? In K–12, you don't have tenure, so if you push the boundaries, you might not have a job anymore.

AW: Why is helping children develop a positive racial identity important?

CJ: Because schools are the first and main place children get socialized outside their households. The school is the primary place where they learn about who they are and how they're viewed, so it's dangerous to not teach a student about their own race or culture in positive ways. Also, it's important because society often teaches them deficit views that they internalize. That can turn into self-hate and cause them to hide who they are. On top of that, students of other cultures might begin to view them the same way—negatively.

AW: When you were teaching, what practices did you use to support children's positive racial identity as it relates to their language?

CJ: I had a lot of students who were speakers of African American language (African American Vernacular English [AAVE]), and I would see them talk to friends or me and would hear them speak one way using AAVE. But in their writing, in most cases, they would use standardized English. I decided to talk to my students about language and history and how we got here and how language has shifted. We talked about Black people being scientists and kings and queens before slavery and how there was language banning during the slavery era in order to minimize rebellion. We also talked about the rules in AAVE and focused on the "habitual be." They told me that they really enjoyed listening to music during lessons and I asked if they thought music artists spoke a different language—Cardi B, for example, has a refrain that goes, "You know where I'm at, you know where I be," and the kids talked about how they talk that way too. So, we listened to a song and read the book *Flossie and the Fox*. I asked them to write two sentences using AAVE and then draw a picture, and one of my students wrote 12 sentences. The kids were so excited to discover that they were bilingual!

AW: What should educators do if parents object to them talking about race or supporting children's positive racial identity?

CJ: I can speak to that from personal experience because I've been in spaces where parents pushed back and, in many ways, education is like retail—the customer is always right, and in education the parent is the customer. If it's possible, teachers can fall back on standards, but it's even better if they have the support of the principal—then they're good to go. Sometimes, we tell parents that their children are going to learn about these things anyway—and in elementary school, not high school. We tell them that children will learn these things through implicit ways so they should be aware that it's easier to get ahead of this before their children are socialized by outside actors. And, in many cases, they are going to learn these things from a deficit perspective, which we don't want to see. If, after all that, parents still say they don't want their child to participate, I would have the principal call them and, in some cases, they ended up pulling their students out of class. The thing is, none of this is mandated.

AW: What advice do you have for Black educators and educators of color?

CJ: I would say that for all teachers, when you're dealing with nonstandard languages or cultures, you have to check your biases at the door and acknowledge biases in society and how it's reflected in your own work. You may say "I'm not racist" on the one hand, but on the other you're constantly correcting your students' language. Educators have to learn about who their students are and what the languages are in their household— develop cultural consciousness. Specifically for Black teachers, I would say that it's important that we fully understand what AAVE is. We all need to do some research of our own. Even if you mean well, there's still the potential for approaching this in an unsafe way. I've made mistakes myself, so even if you're a Black teacher, you can still do harm.

AW: Moving forward.

CJ: I hope that we can begin to include aspects of students' home language into the curriculum because it makes a difference in who these students become. If this work was mandated, then it could go so much further. More and more people are learning about it, so there's room for growth, but because it's not required then it just becomes an extra lesson that may or may not be integrated. Also, a lot of educators have not been educated themselves to teach about these things. Positive racial identity could really be integrated into everything if it's mandated, so one of my hopes is that requiring it would happen.

Jessica Cochran—Graduate Student, Second- and Third-Grade Teacher, and Member of the P.R.I.D.E. Teacher Cohort Group

Aisha White (AW): What got you interested in the teacher cohort group?

Jessica Cochran (JC): It was during my third year here in Pittsburgh that I came across information about the P.R.I.D.E. teacher cohort while I was searching online and thought it would be amazing. I had wanted to study similar concepts in graduate school, and I thought it would be cool to be with a group of educators in order to think of new ideas to incorporate positive racial identity in Black and brown children in the classroom. And this sense of community that would come from working with a group of educators was very inspiring and appealing to me.

AW: What racial identity issues have you seen in the classroom?

JC: The school I work at has a student body that is 30% Black and 70% White, and a good number of the African American students are involved in interracial family adoption. Because of that, I've seen a lot of big questions with students of color specifically who have White parents. For example, one student who is Black has a White mom and dad, and he didn't know how to fill out a test form that was asking him to choose his race. He was clearly Black presenting, but he said: "I'm Black but I don't know what to do because my mom and dad are White." I believe that we see these kinds of things when students aren't talking about it in the earlier grades. In that situation, I wasn't sure what to say so I just told him to fill in the bubbles with however he felt they apply to him. But when I did introduce the topic in the classroom, it was like everyone was sort of holding their breath, but once we started talking about it, students were really engaged.

AW: What is positive racial identity?

JC: I would describe it as having a sense of honor and pride and clarity as to your racial identity and being able to celebrate it and identify, for example, with aspects of my identity I connect with my race. Things like music, or skin tone, or family traditions, or all sorts of things that can be connected and celebrated in that way.

AW: How do you celebrate positive racial identity in your teaching?

JC: One of the biggest ways is by using literature and books. I like having a lot of books around the room so children can see people who look like them in different roles and different professions. I think that's something that is powerful for all students. To see all different people, different shades and races doing amazing things is so important. I try to keep those books out and try to keep pictures around the room as well. Another way is by incorporating topics into our curriculum. In my classroom, we integrate a lot of Black voices into our units, including Black artists and scientists, or geographers. By including the whole history into what we learn or do, in the process we're incorporating all kinds of people who have done really cool things.

AW: What about challenges—why do educators hesitate to talk about these issues?

JC: I think they hesitate because when you start talking about race and open this topic up, kids have questions and I think the questions freak people out. For Martin Luther King Day, a co-teacher introduced Dr. King to the classroom, and in the process answered a student's question about Blackness that she felt she completely dropped the ball on. It caused her a lot of stress. Later she came to me and said, "I made a mistake" and described the situation to me. I think that's just one example of how the conversation can get really tricky, and it's tough for adults to embrace the idea that they don't really have answers.

AW: Why is it important to support young children's positive racial identity development?

JC: I think one reason that comes to mind is children will be coming to conclusions in their heads regardless of whether it's talked about in a positive or guided or safe way or not, and that's something we've talked about a lot in our P.R.I.D.E. cohort sessions.

Children take whatever is around them and then form their own conclusions. If they are seeing things that don't reflect them, or if people who look like them or even they themselves are presented or represented in a negative way, then that snowballs through their life. I think it's one of the most important things we can do to help make them a whole person.

AW: What do you think are the greatest obstacles for educators?

JC: Fear. And also not being able to discern what is a quality resource or book and what is harmful, and I've seen attempts in classrooms that are actually harmful and should not even be done. For example, things like the egg activity where teachers take a white egg and a brown egg, talk about the outside of the egg, crack it open and then say, "See, both look the same inside." After that, one teacher went from child to child actually telling them what their race was, saying, "You're Black and you're White." It was mortifying. Choosing resources and being able to decipher what is good and what you shouldn't do I think are key.

AW: What should educators do if parents object to them talking about race or engaging in positive racial identity activities?

JC: Sometimes, I think things I've done have surprised parents, but that hasn't happened to me (parents objecting) in the classroom. However, if it did happen, I would hope that I would get support from the school in giving pushback to parents in respectful ways.

AW: What resources would you recommend for educators?

JC: I actually started the year out talking about race through discovery art activities that looked at skin tone and using language to describe the color brown, like *honey* or *caramel*. I gave students opportunities to discover or explore self-portraiture by using a range of tones of brown that they can mix to create something that reflects their own image. I think that's a simple way for any educator to begin. But honestly, whenever anyone asks me for resources, I send them links to P.R.I.D.E.—the "In My Skin" podcast—and other resources on the site.

AW: What advice do you have for educators of color and Black educators?

JC: First, DO IT! Second, find each other for support and ideas—pushback is real, and not everyone likes what we're doing.

AW: Moving forward, what are your hopes and concerns?

JC: I'm worried about the banning of books. I hope that as there are more Black educators and Black policy advocators, this work is incorporated into the curriculum—into Common Core—and that there are standards put in place just like there are other standards for other subjects in order to offer clarity and accountability for teachers.

Ebonyse Mead, Family Scientist, Racial Justice Consultant and President, Educational Equity Institute

Aisha White (AW): Could you tell me a little about when you were younger and the positive racial identity messages you received from your father?

Ebonyse Mead (EM): My father was and is what people would refer to as "pro-Black," and when I was younger, I didn't really know what that was. On this particular day, he was watching a program on PBS (the Public Broadcasting System), and I had this habit of sitting under my dad and watching with him. The program was about the Egyptians, so I asked him what he was watching, and he told me, "Never let anyone tell you that the Egyptians were not Black." I was around 9 years old, so my 9-year-old brain didn't know how to conceptualize that, but I do remember that because of his tone, he meant business. He often talked about who they were, and I remember him saying something about the hieroglyphics, explaining that they were written by the Egyptians (who were African), despite other narratives swirling around about them being written by other people. As I grew up, those were the kinds of messages I received. In my family, we talked about Angela Davis and Malcolm X and Marcus Garvey and Denmark Vesey. My father was very much in support of Black liberation in all aspects. We didn't necessarily always celebrate Kwanzaa, but it was something we did in our house along with celebrating holidays like Juneteenth. When I was 19, my father bought a book for me called *The Politics of Color* and it was my introduction to colorism. After reading that book, I became very aware of colorism and my own experiences. My dad always instilled in me the message to be proud of who I am and the way that I look and even to this day he still sends me birthday cards and Mother's Day cards saying "proud Black woman," so his job of instilling racial pride in me didn't stop just because I became an adult.

AW: What is positive racial identity?

EM: It's a combination of things. First, helping Black children in particular to be able to navigate this racist society. It gives them the tools they need to try to survive and thrive. It's sobering when you think about it, because it's kinda sad that we have to have these conversations with our children. On the other hand, I really feel it's giving them the tools to navigate this racist society in the best fashion as possible. Second, the other thing it does is help children keep their mental health intact, which is where positive racial identity comes in. It's doing those two things at the same time. It involves having a two-part conversation with your child; first, helping them to understand that some people will see you as a threat, you won't be trusted, or you'll be viewed as a criminal. But second, it also involves telling them that because of your Blackness you are dynamic, you're great, and you come from excellence, so it's this dual message. When I talk about this, it breaks my heart because how confusing is that? You're telling me because I'm Black these things will happen to me, but you're also telling me that because I'm Black these things are phenomenal about me. So, to me that's what positive racial identity does. It helps children at a young age be able to hold both of those things in their hands and their minds at the same time.

AW: How does positive racial identity development come into play in your work as a professor and professional trainer?

EM: When you have faculty of color who are conscious like me, I feel that it's my responsibility to bring issues into the classroom that might not necessarily be addressed in the book. For example, while a chapter I'm currently teaching is talking about adoptive families, I go a little deeper to talk about transracial adoptive families. The students that I'm preparing to go work in communities with families probably won't look like those families; they probably will have a different racial, socioeconomic, and religious background. So, as a trainer, as a professor, I have a responsibility to bring awareness to that and to help students be not just culturally responsive but to be anti-racist practitioners as well. With young Black children, my fear is that there will be teachers who will go into the classroom and unintentionally cause harm to them because of their unwillingness to talk about race. There's this willful ignorance that talking about race is divisive, but when you're teaching Black children and other children of color, how can you possibly do that—teach them in the absence of race? You can't, and that's another reason it comes into play. In too many of our teacher prep programs, we focus on the children but we don't really help teachers learn how to connect with families and partner with them. Children exist in the context of their families and communities. So, I strongly believe you can't talk about child development without addressing race and racism because it plays a part in children's outcomes particularly when you have teachers in the classroom who don't look like them but who are also unwilling to address these difficult issues.

AW: Are educators aware of positive racial identity?

EM: I think so—but not a lot. Some are aware and understand its importance but don't know what to do. That's one of the themes that emerged from my dissertation work. Teachers wanting to promote positive racial identity but just not knowing what to do. And because a lot of the teachers were White, they were also afraid of coming off as racist and I think that's a huge barrier in this work. It goes along with the unwillingness to confront race because they don't want to be perceived as racist.

AW: Why is it important for educators to support children's positive racial identity?

EM: I'll start with two things—colorism and anti-Blackness. I think both are prevalent in education, so prevalent that educators don't even know that it's happening. Let's begin with colorism (prejudice or discrimination against individuals with a dark skin tone, typically among people of the same ethnic or racial group). We know that children with darker skin tones are punished more severely and more frequently than children with lighter skin tones, and that has been such a part of the practice in the education setting that I don't even think teachers know that those things are happening.

That's one reason we need to help teachers increase their capacity to support positive racial identity. But it's also connected to what we know about the importance of social-emotional well-being in children. When children receive negative messages, for example anti-Black messages, about who they are, children internalize those messages whenever or wherever they receive them. They reinforce how children feel about themselves, so it's important to help children build their positive racial identity in a world that doesn't view them positively to begin with. Also, as children get older, they can internalize racial oppression and one of the ways that can manifest is as "stereotype threat" (the fear or anxiety of confirming a negative stereotype about one's social group). And while it's something we may not see in pre-K or kindergarten, we do see it in later grades so we can help them build that positive racial identity to combat those kinds of things early on.

AW: What obstacles or challenges do educators face?

EM: One is perhaps parents, particularly White parents who may not be comfortable and who may think it's controversial. We can see that right now with this anti–critical race theory backlash we're going through. But I also think it's laws that have been put in place as a result of the banning of critical race theory. I think districts are afraid to step into these conversations because of parents and/or political affiliations.

Also, when teachers don't have buy-in from their leadership, that can be a problem as well. In my nonprofit training work, we had a contract terminated because the school district we worked with didn't want us to talk about the education system being rooted in white supremacy culture. I even see pushback at the university level in the form of a university not wanting us to use certain terms in describing white supremacy in American society. All these things serve as barriers to having these necessary authentic conversations. We've even begun to recommend that states look at their curriculum laws to see where the restrictions apply from pre-K to K–12.

One other thing I've learned in doing this work is White shame in this country is a huge barrier. Shame and guilt are not the same thing and to do this work as White people, individuals really have to engage in some critical self-evaluation about who they are at their core and confront the fact that the things they have accumulated in this country maybe they didn't fully earn. Another thing I've learned is that we're so conditioned when we think about diversity and inclusion that now we look at is as a check the box kind of thing: "Check, we're all diverse so now we can move on." We have an incredible amount of work to do, and although it won't happen in our lifetime, I still have hope.

AW: What should teachers do if parents object to them talking about race?

EM: Well, while the rebel in me says do it anyway, I do think there are ways that you can enter into conversations with children in developmentally appropriate ways that get around those parent objections. Think about the way that multicultural education has shifted in our country. It now allows for us to talk to children about things like difference and sameness. There are lots of activities teachers can use to do that. I think reading picture books about being different and the same at circle time with kids and having discussions with them is really good, doable, and something most parents would not object to. They can engage in activities such as using a Venn diagram on a whiteboard and talk about the differences and similarities in the classroom. So again, I think there are ways to talk with children without explicitly discussing race but instead talking about skin tone. There are ways teachers can interject that content into daily classroom conversations because we're not talking about abstract concepts like race with very young children anyway. If you couch it in diversity, parents are okay with that because we've been conditioned to think about diversity as "okay."

AW: What resources and advice would you offer to educators?

EM: I always reference the P.R.I.D.E. program any time I'm talking to someone about this topic. There are also lots of good videos from PBS—I even use them in my class in a module about children and race. The videos show how children are having these conversations with parents (e.g., *PBS Kids Talk About: Race & Racism*). Also, there are so many books now that talk about hair and skin and all those types of things, and many of them are by Black authors. Basically, I would recommend (1) organizations that are doing this type of work, (2) videos of parents talking with children, and (3) books. I think those are three concrete, easy things that parents or educators can use.

AW: What advice do you have specifically for educators of color and in particular Black educators?

EM: First, I would like to make it clear that the fact that you're an educator of color doesn't mean you're conscious of the issues or even that you're brave enough to talk about them. When we're talking about what's needed, we have to say educators of color who are conscious of the issues and who have the language necessary to have rich, authentic conversations. Having the language to name it is really important too, because with the language you know what you're fighting against and you're able to think about how you can embed this into the content in a developmentally appropriate way. Second, I would say that if you don't know, ask! And that goes for all educators. Don't shy away from the shocking kinds of questions that young children will ask you. And yes, you probably will be shocked by some of the questions as well as some of the things children may do.

During one of our recent trainings, a Black participant (woman) told a story about a White girl who licked her arm because she thought she would taste like chocolate. When those things happen, it takes us aback, but we have to look at it from a child's perspective and view it as a teachable moment. Children are coming from a place of curiosity, they really want answers to their questions, and they want us to answer with honesty, with bravery. If we (Black educators and educators of color) don't do it, it's less likely that White educators will. It's important that these things are brought up in an authentic way, not a watered-down way. And I would say be brave enough to bring it.

AW: Where would you like to see this growing interest in race, young children, and positive racial identity go?

EM: I would really hope that more people will begin to be more proactive than reactive. I think that when something horrible happens to a Black person, people are more reactive, but we need to begin to sort out how to do things when something bad doesn't happen. I also would like to see that when there is a reaction, the momentum lasts long enough for real change and not just organizations and companies putting something about equity on their web page—we saw a whole lot of that recently. Related to that, I would like to see people care about Black people not just when a Black person is murdered. I want to see them doing more long-term transformational work—and in the process, make sure that the voices of Black parents and other parents and people of color are centered in the work. I'll close by saying we really need to have a paradigm shift in how we do all of this work. Equity work cannot just be sprinkled around here or there—it should become the way we do everything. We should be viewing everything from an anti-racist lens so that it becomes who we are and how we operate. It needs to be embedded in the culture. That's what I would like to see—transformational change.

Appendix B

Anti-Racist Resources

EDUCATION READING LIST

Azzi-Lessing, L. (2017). *Behind from the start: How America's war on the poor is harming our most vulnerable children.* Oxford University Press.

Chaudry, A., Morrissey, T., Weiland, C., & Yoshikawa, H. (2017). *Cradle to kindergarten: A new plan to combat inequality.* Russell Sage Foundation.

Chen, W. D., Nimmo, J., & Fraser, H. (2009). Becoming a culturally responsive early childhood educator: A tool for support reflection by teachers embarking on the anti-bias journey. *Multicultural Perspectives, 11*(2), 101–106.

Davis, M. B. (2007). *How to teach students who don't look like you: Culturally relevant teaching strategies.* Corwin Press.

Derman-Sparks, L., & Edwards, O. J. (2010). *Anti-bias education for young children and ourselves.* NAEYC.

Gay, G. (2000). *Culturally responsive teaching: Theory, research, & practice.* Teachers College Press.

Iruka, I., Cureton, S., & Durden, T. (2020). *Don't look away: Embracing anti-bias classrooms.* Gryphon House.

Kea, C., Campbell-Whatley, D. G., & Richard, V. H. (2006). *Becoming culturally responsive educators: Rethinking teacher education pedagogy.* Research to practice brief (pp. 1–15). National Center for Culturally Responsive Educational Systems.

Ladson-Billings, G. (2009). *The dreamkeepers: Successful teachers of African American students.* Jossey-Bass.

Love, B. (2019). *We want to do more than survive: Abolitionist teaching and the pursuit of educational freedom.* Beacon Press.

Singleton, G. E. (2015). *Courageous conversations about race: A field guide for achieving equity in schools* (2nd ed.). Corwin.

Watson, D., Hagopian, W., & Au, W. (2018). *Teaching for black lives.* Rethinking Schools.

York, S. (2016). *Roots and wings: Affirming culture and preventing bias in early childhood.* Redleaf Press.

RACE AND RACISM READING LIST

Alexander, M. (2012). *The new Jim Crow: Mass incarceration in the age of colorblindness.* The New Press.

Anderson, C. (2017). *White rage: The unspoken truth of our racial divide.* Bloomsbury.

Coates, T. (2015). *Between the world and me.* Spiegel and Grau.

Desmond, M. (2016). *Evicted: Poverty and profit in the American city.* Penguin Random House.

DiAngelo, R. (2018). *White fragility: Why it's so hard for white people to talk about racism.* Beacon Press.

Harvey, J. (2017). *Raising white kids: Bringing up children in a racially unjust America.* United Methodist Publishing House.

Hooks, B. (2011). *All about love.* William Morrow.

Kendi, I. X. (2017). *Stamped from the beginning: The definitive history for racist ideas in America.* Nation Books.

Kendi, I. X. (2019). *How to be an anti-racist.* One World.

Kendi, I. X. (2021). *Four hundred souls: A community history of African America from 1619–2019.* Random House.

Menakam, R. (2017). *My grandmother's hands: Racialized trauma and the pathway to mending our hearts and bodies.* Central Recovery Press.

McGuire, D. L. (2011). *At the dark end of the street: Black women, rape, and resistance. A new history of the civil rights movement from Rosa Parks to the rise of black power.* Vintage Books.

Oluo, I. (2018). *So you want to talk about race?* Seal Press.

Sensoy, O., DiAngelo, R., & Banks, J. A. (2011). *Is everyone really equal? An introduction to key concepts in social justice.* Teachers College Press.

Smith, C. (2021). *How the word is passed: A reckoning with the history of slavery across America.* Little, Brown.

Stevenson, B. (2014). *Just mercy: A story of justice and redemption.* Spiegel & Grau.

Waziyatawin. (2008). *What does justice look like?* Living Justice Press.

Wilkerson, I. (2020). *Caste: The origins of our discontent.* Random House.

Wilkerson, I. (2020). *The warmth of other suns: The epic story of America's great migration.* Random House.

WEBSITES

10 Things Every White Teacher Should Know When Talking About Race
https://thecornerstoneforteachers.com/truth-for-teachers-podcast/10-things-every-white-teacher-know-talking-race/

Learning for Justice
https://www.learningforjustice.org/topics/race-ethnicity

Top Education Equity Reads of 2015
   https://medium.com/@NYCLeadership/top-education-equity-reads-of-2015
   -4abd8e37a03c

The Characteristics of White Supremacy Culture
   https://surj.org/resources/white-supremacy-culture-characteristics/

TED TALKS

Bryan Stevenson: *We Need to Talk About an Injustice*
https://www.ted.com/talks/bryan_stevenson_we_need_to_talk_about_an_injustice

Mellody Hobson: *Color Blind or Color Brave?*
https://www.youtube.com/watch?v=oKtALHe3Y9Q

Rosemarie Allen: *School Suspensions Are an Adult Behavior*
https://www.youtube.com/watch?v=f8nkcRMZKV4&vl=en

Megan Ming Francis: *Let's Get to the Root of Racial Injustice*
https://www.youtube.com/watch?v=-aCn72iXO9s&feature=youtu.be

PODCASTS

On Being
https://onbeing.org/series/podcast/ (also on Apple)
   Bryan Stevenson
   John Lewis
   Robin DiAngelo and Resmaa Menakem
   Resmaa Menakem
   Isabel Wilkerson

Armchair Expert with Dax Shepard: Michael Eric Dyson
https://armchairexpertpod.com/ (also on Apple)

Pod Save the People
https://podcasts.apple.com/us/podcast/pod-save-the-people/id1230148653 (also on Apple)

1619 Project Podcasts
https://podcasts.apple.com/us/podcast/1619/id1476928106 (also on Apple)

Unlocking Us with Brené Brown
   Austin Channing Brown (https://brenebrown.com/podcasts/; also on Spotify)
   Clint Smith Jr.

Undistracted with Brittany Packnett Cunningham (on Apple)

Into America (on Apple Podcasts)

DOCUMENTARIES

I Am Not Your Negro (Netflix or Amazon) (Trailer: https://www.youtube.com/watch?v=
   rNUYdgIyaPM)

13th (Netflix) (Trailer: https://www.youtube.com/watch?v=K6IXQbXPO3I)

The African Americans: Many Rivers to Cross
https://www.pbs.org/show/african-americans-many-rivers-cross/

John Lewis: Good Trouble
https://www.amazon.com/John-Lewis-Good-Trouble/dp/B087QQ4X73

Freedom Riders
https://www.amazon.com/Freedom-Riders-Stanley-Nelson/dp/B084F1DDZ6

Amend (Netflix)

High on the Hog (Netflix)

The Rape of Recy Taylor (Hulu and Amazon)

Black Boys (Amazon)

FILMS

American Skin (Amazon)

Judas and the Black Messiah (HBO Max)

Ma Rainey's Black Bottom (Netflix)

Malcom X (Amazon)

Moonlight (Netflix)

Mudbound (Netflix)

One Night in Miami (Amazon)

Selma (Amazon)

When They See Us (Netflix)

Concrete Cowboy (Netflix)

Monster (Netflix)

In Our Mother's Garden (Netflix)

Bibliography

Administration for Children and Families. (2016). *Head Start Program Performance Standards. 45 CFR Chapter XIII.* Office of Head Start, Administration for Children and Families, U.S. Department of Health and Human Services. https://eclkc.ohs.acf.hhs.gov /sites/default/files/pdf/hspps-appendix.pdf

Akua, C. (2020). Standards of Afrocentric education for school leaders and teachers. *Journal of Black Studies, 51*(2), 107.

Allen, R. (2016, August 6). *TED×MileHigh: School suspensions are an adult behavior* [Video]. YouTube. https://www.youtube.com /watch?v=f8nkcRMZKV4&t=152s

Allen, R. (2022a). Preschool suspensions: A civil rights issue. In D. Jackson (Ed.), *A community in transition: Key issues confronting the Black community in Denver, CO* (pp. 63–100). Cambridge Scholars Publishing.

Allen, R. (2022b, January 11). *TED×Cherry-Creek Women: What if schools are the source of trauma?* [Video]. YouTube. https://www .youtube.com/watch?v=p2lXtMoIQx8

Allen, R., Shapland, D., Neitzel, J., & Iruka, I. (2021). Creating anti-racist early childhood spaces. In I. Alanís & I. U. Iruka (Eds.), *Advancing equity and embracing diversity in early childhood education: Elevating voices and actions* (pp. 114–119). National Association for the Education of Young Children.

American Psychological Association. (2008). *Zero Tolerance Task Force report: An evidentiary review and recommendations.*

Anderson, J. D. (1988). *The education of Blacks in the South, 1860–1935.* University of North Carolina Press.

Andrews, K., Parekh, J., & Peckoo, S. (2019). *A guide to incorporating a racial and ethnic equity perspective throughout the research process.* Child Trends. https://www.childtrends .org/publications/a-guide-to-incorporating -a-racial-and-ethnic-equity-perspective -throughout-the-research-process

Annie E. Casey Foundation. (2021). *Equity vs. equality and other racial justice definitions.* https://www.aecf.org/blog/racial-justice -definitions

Ardrey, T. A. (2020). Bridging the gap: An early childhood framework for implementing culturally engaging practices for African American preschoolers. *Nurture.*

Avalos, N. (2021). What does it mean to heal from historical trauma? *AMA Journal of Ethics, 23*(6), 494–498.

Bailey, Z. D., Feldman, J. M., & Bassett, M. T. (2021). How structural racism works: Racist policies as a root cause of U.S. racial health inequities. *New England Journal of Medicine, 384*(8), 768–773.

Baker, C. N. (2005). Images of women's sexuality in advertisements: A content analysis of black- and white-oriented women's and men's magazines. *Sex Roles: A Journal of Research, 52*(1–2), 13–27.

Baker, J. T. (2021). Higher-class whites. In Z. A. Casey (Ed.), *Encyclopedia of critical whiteness studies in education* (pp. 250–257). Koninklijke Brill NV.

Banaji, M. R., & Greenwald, A. G. (2013). *Blind spot: Hidden biases of good people.* Delacorte.

Banks, J. (2008). *Teaching strategies for ethnic studies.* Allyn & Bacon.

Banks, J. A., & Banks, C. A. M. (Eds.). (2001). *Multicultural education: Issues and perspectives* (4th ed.). Allyn & Bacon.

Barbarin, O., & Crawford, G. M. (2006). Acknowledging and reducing the stigmatization of African American boys. *Young Children, 61*(6), 79–86.

Barnett, S., Carolan, M., & Johns, D. (2013). *Equity and excellence: African-American children's access to quality preschool.* National Institute of Early Care and Education. https://nieer.org/2013/11/18/equity-and -excellence-african-american-childrens -access-to-quality-preschool

Barnett, S., & Nores, M. (2013). *Equitable access to quality preschool* [Webinar]. Center for Early Learning Outcomes, National Institute for Early Education Research. http://ceelo .org/wp-content/uploads/2013/10/SLIDES _EquitableAccesstoQualityPrek.pdf

Barnett, W. S. (1998). Long-term cognitive and academic effects of early childhood education on children in poverty. *Preventive Medicine, 27,* 204–207.

Bartlett, J., Smith, S., & Bringewatt, E. (2017). *Helping young children who have experienced trauma: Policies and strategies for early care and education.* Child Trends. https://www .childtrends.org/publications/ecetrauma

Barton, E., & Smith, B. J. (2015). Advancing high-quality preschool inclusion: A discussion and recommendations for the field. *Topics in Early Childhood Special Education, 35*(2), 69–78.

Baugh, J. E., & Rajaei, A. (2022). Family life education with Black families. In S. M. Ballard & A. C. Taylor (Eds.), *Family life education with diverse populations* (pp. 239–262). SAGE.

Becker, M. (1999). Patriarchy and inequality: Towards a substantive feminism. *University of Chicago Legal Forum, 1999,* Article 3. http://chicagounbound.uchicago.edu/uclf /vol1999/iss1/3

Belfield, C. R., Nores, M., Barnett, W. S., & Schweinhart, L. J. (2006). The High/Scope Perry Preschool Program: Cost-benefit analysis using data from the age-40 follow-up. *Journal of Human Resources, 41*(1), 162–190.

Bell, E. L. (2004). Myths, stereotypes, and realities of Black women: A personal reflection. *Journal of Applied Behavioral Science, 40,* 146–159.

Beneke, M. R., Park, C. C., & Taitingfong, J. (2018). An inclusive, anti-bias framework for teaching and learning about race with young children. *Young Exceptional Children, 22*(2). https://doi.org/10.1177/1096250618811842

Bierdz, B. (2021). Whiteness as property. In Z. Casey (Ed.), *Encyclopedia of critical whiteness studies in education* (pp. 708–713). Brill Sense.

Black girls viewed as less innocent than white girls. *The Georgetown Law Center on Poverty and Inequality.* (2017, June 27). Retrieved November 21, 2021. https://www .law.georgetown.edu/news/black-girls -viewed-as-less-innocent-than-white-girls -georgetown-law-research-finds-2/

Blair, C., Granger, G., Willoughby, M., Mills-Koonce, R., Cox, M., Greenberg, M., Kivlighan, K., Fortunato, C., & FLP Investigators. (2011). Salivary cortisol mediates effects of poverty and parenting on executive functions in early childhood. *Child Development, 82*(6), 1970–1984.

Blair, I., Ma, J., & Lenton, A. (2001). Imagining stereotypes away: The moderation of implicit stereotypes through mental imagery. *Journal of Personality and Social Psychology, 81*(5), 828–841.

Blaise, M. (2005). A feminist post structural study of children "doing" gender in an urban kindergarten classroom. *Early Childhood Research Quarterly, 20*(1), 85–108.

Bodovski, K., & Farkas, G. (2007). Do instructional practices contribute to inequality in achievement? *Journal of Early Childhood Research, 5,* 301–322.

Boehm-Turner, A., & Toedt, E. (2021). Social class and whiteness. In Z. A. Casey (Ed.), *Encyclopedia of critical whiteness studies in education* (pp. 638–645). Koninklijke Brill NV.

Bonilla-Silva, E. (2018). *Racism without racists: Color-blind racism and the persistence of racial inequality in the United States* (5th ed.). Rowman & Littlefield.

Boscardin, C. K. (2015). Reducing implicit bias through curricular interventions. *Journal of General Internal Medicine, 30*(12), 1726–1728. https://www.ncbi.nlm.nih.gov /pmc/articles/PMC4636582/

Boutte, G. S. (2012). Urban schools: Challenges and possibilities of early childhood and elementary education. *Urban Education, 47*(2), 515–550.

Boutte, G., Lopez-Robertson, J., & Powers-Costello, E. (2011). Moving beyond colorblindness in early childhood classrooms. *Early Childhood Education Journal, 39*(5), 339–342.

Bowden, J. (2021). Arkansas governor allows bill targeting critical race theory in state agencies to become law. Retrieved from: https://thehill.com/homenews/state -watch/551609-arkansas-governor-allows -bill-targeting-critical-race-theory-in-state/

Bowler, K., & Ali, W. (Hosts). (2021, September 16). *Kate Bowler and Wajahat Ali: The future of hope* [Audio podcast episode]. On Being With Krista Tippett. https://onbeing .org/programs/kate-bowler-and-wajahat-ali -the-future-of-hope/

Bowman, P. J., & Howard, C. (1985). Race-related socialization, motivation, and academic achievement: A study of black youths in three-generation families. *Journal of the American Academy of Child Psychiatry, 24*(2), 134–141.

Boykin, A. W., & Toms, F. D. (1985). Black child socialization: A conceptual framework.

In H. P. McAdoo & J. L. McAdoo (Eds.), *Black children: Social, educational, and parental environments* (pp. 159–173). SAGE.

Brave Heart, M. Y., Chase, J., Elkins, J., & Altschul, D. B. (2011). Historical trauma among Indigenous Peoples of the Americas: Concepts, research, and clinical considerations. *Journal of Psychoactive Drugs, 43*(4), 282–290.

Bredekamp, S. (1997). NAEYC issues revised position statement on developmentally appropriate practice in early childhood programs. *Young Children, 52*(2), 34–40.

Brooks-Gunn, J., & Duncan, G. (1997). The effects of poverty on children. *The Future of Children, 7*(2), 55–71.

Brown, A. (2011). Same old stories: The Black male in social science and educational literature, 1930s to present. *Teachers College Record, 113*(9), 2047–2079.

Brown, B. (2010). *The gifts of imperfection: Let go of who you think you're supposed to be and embrace who you are.* Hazeldon.

Brown, B. (2017). *Braving the wilderness: The quest for true belonging and the courage to stand alone.* Penguin.

Brown, B. (2018). *Dare to lead.* Random House.

Brown, B. (2021). *Atlas of the heart: Mapping meaningful connection and the language of human experience.* Random House.

Brown v. Board of Education, 347 U.S. 483 (1954). https://www.oyez.org/cases/1940-1955 /347us48

Brown-Jeffy, S. L., & Cooper, J. E. (2011). Toward a conceptual framework of culturally relevant pedagogy: An overview of the conceptual and theoretical literature. *Teacher Education Quarterly, 38*(1), 65–84.

Bryk, A. S., & Schneider, B. (2003). Trust in schools: A core resource for school reform. *Educational Leadership, 60,* 40–44.

Burch, P. (2007). Educational policy and practice from the perspective of institutional theory: Crafting a wider lens. *Educational Researcher, 36*(2), 84–95.

Burton, M. L., Greenberger, E., & Hayward, C. (2005). Mapping the ethnic landscape: Personal beliefs about own group's and other groups' traits. *Cross-Cultural Research, 39*(4), 351–379.

Bussey, K., & Bandura, A. (1999). Social cognitive theory of gender development and differentiation. *Psychological Review, 106*(4), 676–713.

Butchart, R. (2010). Black hope, white power: Emancipation, reconstruction and the legacy of unequal schooling in the US South, 1861–1880. *Paedagogica Historica, 46*(1), 33–50. https:// doi.org/10.1080/00309230903528447

Buysse, V., & Peisner-Feinberg, E. (Eds.). (2013). *Handbook of response to intervention in early childhood.* Paul H. Brookes Publishing Co.

Callie Silver, H., & Zinsser, K. M. (2020). The interplay among early childhood teachers' social and emotional well-being, mental health consultation, and preschool expulsion. *Early Education and Development, 31*(7), 1133–1150.

Calzada, J. E., Huang, Y. K., Hernandez, M., Soriano, E., Arca, F. C., Dawson-McClure, S., Kamboukos, D., & Brotman, L. (2015). Family and teacher characteristics as predictors of parent involvement in education during early childhood among Afro-Caribbean and Latina immigrant families. *Urban Education, 50*(7), 870–896.

Cannella, G. S. (1997). *Deconstructing early childhood education: Social justice and revolution. Rethinking childhood* (Vol. 2). Peter Lang.

Caporino, N., Murray, J., & Jensen, P. (2003). The impact of different traumatic experiences in childhood and adolescence. *Emotional and Behavioral Disorder in Youth, 4*(3), 63–69.

Carter, P., Skiba, R., Arredondo, M., & Pollock, M. (2017). You can't fix what you don't look at: Acknowledging race in addressing racial discipline disparities. *Urban Education, 52*(2), 207–235.

Carter, T. R. (2007). Racism and psychological and emotional injury: Recognizing and assessing race-based traumatic stress. *Counseling Psychologist, 35*(1), 13–105.

Casey, Z. (Ed.). (2021). American Indians and whiteness. In *Encyclopedia of critical whiteness studies in education* (pp. 33–38). Brill Sense.

Castellanos, G. A., Gomez Izquierdo, J., & Pineda, F. (2009). Racist discourse in Mexico. In T.A. Van Dijk (Ed.), *Racism and discourse in Latin America* (pp. 217–258). Lexington Books.

Caughy, M. O., O'Campo, P. J., Randolph, S. M., & Nickerson, K. (2003). The influence of racial socialization practices on the cognitive and behavioral competence of African American preschoolers. *Child Development, 73*(5), 1611–1625.

Cavafy, C. P. (1975). *Collected poems.* Princeton University Press.

Ceglowski, D. A., Logue, M. E., Ullrich, A., & Gilbert, J. (2009). Parents' perceptions of child care for children with disabilities. *Early Childhood Education Journal, 36*(6), 497–504. https://doi.org/10.1007/s10643-009 -0309-0

Centers for Disease Control and Prevention (CDC). (n.d.). *CDC/ATSDR SVI fact sheet.* https://www.atsdr.cdc.gov/placeandhealth/svi/fact_sheet/fact_sheet.html

Chaddock, N. (2021). Caucasian. In Z. A. Casey (Ed.), *Encyclopedia of critical whiteness studies in education* (pp. 95–97). Koninklijke Brill NV.

Chavez-Duenas, N. Y., Adames, H. Y., & Organista, K. C. (2014). Skin-color prejudice and within-group racial discrimination: Historical and current impact on Latino/a populations. *Hispanic Journal of Behavioral Sciences, 36*(1), 3–26.

Chen, D., Nimmo, J., & Fraser, H. (2009). Becoming a culturally responsive early childhood educator: A tool to support reflection by teachers embarking on the anti-bias journey. *Multicultural Perspectives, 11*(2), 101–106.

Cherng, H. (2016). Is all classroom conduct equal? Teacher contact with parents of racial and ethnic minority and immigrant adolescents. *Teachers College Record, 118*(11), 1–32.

Child Care Aware of America. (2018). *The US and the high cost of child care: A review of prices and proposed solutions for a broken system.* https://cdn2.hubspot.net/hubfs/3957809/COCreport2018_1.pdf

Child Care Aware of America. (2020). *Demanding change: Repairing our child care system.* https://www.childcareaware.org/demanding-change-repairing-our-child-care-system/

Children's Defense Fund. (1975). *School suspensions: Are they helping children?* Washington Research Project.

Children's Defense Fund. (2021). *The state of America's children 2021.* https://www.childrensdefense.org/state-of-americas-children/

Children's Equity Project. (2020). *Start with equity: From the early years to the early grades—Data, research, and an actionable child equity policy agenda.* https://childandfamilysuccess.asu.edu/sites/default/files/2020-10/CEP-report-101320-FINAL_0.pdf

Chopra, D. (1994). *The seven spiritual laws of success: A practical guide to the fulfilment of your dreams.* Amber-Allen.

Chow, K. A., Gaylor, E., Grindal, T., Tunzi, D., Wei, X., & Tiruke, T. (2021). Associations of teacher characteristics with preschool suspensions and expulsions: Implications for supports. *Children and Youth Services Review, 129,* 106162.

Christopher, G. C., Zimmerman, E. B., Chandra, A., & Martin, L. A. (2021). *Charting a course for an equity-centered data system: Recommendations from the National Commission to Transform Public Health Data Systems.* Robert Wood Johnson Foundation. https://www.rwjf.org/en/library/research/2021/10/charting-a-course-for-an-equity-centered-data-system.html

Clark, K. B., & Clark, M. K. (1947). Racial identification and preferences in Negro children. In T. M. Newcomb & E. L. Hartley (Eds.), *Readings in social psychology* (pp. 169–178). Henry Holt.

Clark, P., & Zygmunt, E. (2014). A close encounter with personal bias: Pedagogical implications for teacher education. *The Journal of Negro Education, 83,* 147–161.

Clayback, K. A., & Hemmeter, M. L. (2021). Exclusionary discipline practices in early childhood settings: A survey of child care directors. *Early Childhood Research Quarterly, 55,* 129–136.

Coles, L. R. (2006). *Race and family: A structural approach.* Sage.

Conger, R., Ge, X., Elder, G., Lorenz, F., & Simons, R. (1994). Economic stress, coercive family process, and developmental problems of adolescents. *Child Development, 65*(2), 541–561.

Connor, C., Son, S., Hindman, A., & Morrison, F. (2005). Teacher qualifications, classroom practices, family characteristics, and preschool experience: Complex effects on first graders' vocabulary and early reading outcomes. *Journal of School Psychology, 43*(4), 343–375.

Council on School Health. (2013). Out-of-school suspension and expulsion. *Pediatrics, 131*(3), e1000–e1007.

Counts, J., Katsiyannis, A., & Whitford, K. D. (2018). Culturally and linguistically diverse learners in special education: English learners. *NASSP Bulletin, 102*(1), 5–21.

Crenshaw, K. (1989). Demarginalizing the intersection of race and sex: A black feminist critique of antidiscrimination doctrine, feminist theory and antiracist politics. *University of Chicago Legal Forum, 1989,* Article 8. http://chicagounbound.uchicago.edu/uclf/vol1989/iss1/8

Crosnoe, R., Purtell, K. M., Davis-Kean, P., Ansari, A., & Benner, A. D. (2016). The selection of children from low-income families into preschool. *Developmental Psychology, 52*(4), 599–612. https://doi.org/10.1037/dev0000101

Crowley, R. M., & Smith, W. (2015). Whiteness and social studies teacher education: Tensions in the pedagogical task. *Teaching Education, 26,* 160–178.

Crumbley, J. (1999). *Seven tasks for parents: Developing positive racial identity*. North American Council on Adoptable Children. https://nacac.org/resource/seven-tasks-for-parents/

Cunningham, W., Nezlek, J., & Banji, M. (2004). Implicit and explicit ethnocentrism: Revisiting the ideologies of prejudice. *Personality and Social Psychology Bulletin, 30*(10), 1322–1346.

Dale, M. (2020). *For California child care workers, inequality is baked into the system.* LAist. https://laist.com/news/for-california-child-care-workers-inequality-is-baked-into-the-system

Darity, W., Dietrich, J., & Hamilton, D. (2008). Bleach in the rainbow: Latin ethnicity and preference for whiteness. *Transforming Anthropology, 13*(2), 103–109.

Darling-Hammond, L. (2005). New standards and old inequalities: School reform and the education of African American students. In J. E. King (Ed.), *Black education: A transformative research and action agenda for the new century* (pp. 197–224). Routledge.

Dasgupta, N., & Greenwald, A. G. (2001). On the malleability of automatic attitudes: Combating automatic prejudice with images of admired and disliked individuals. *Journal of Personality and Social Psychology, 81*(5), 800–814.

Davis, F. J. (1991). *Who is black? One nation's definition*. Pennsylvania State University Press.

DeGruy, J. (2005). *Post traumatic slave syndrome*. Joy DeGruy Publications.

DeGruy, J. (2009). *Post traumatic slave syndrome: Study guide*. Joy DeGruy Publications.

Dei, G. J. S. (2011, Spring). Defense of official multiculturalism and recognition of the necessity of critical anti-racism. *Canadian Issues, 55*, 15–19.

Dei, G. J. S. (2017). *Reframing Blackness and black solidarities through anti-colonial and decolonial prisms*. Springer.

D'Elio, M. A., O'Brien, R. W., Grayton, C. M., Keane, M. J., Connell, D. C., Hailey, L., & Foster, E. M. (2001). *Reaching out to families: Head Start recruitment and enrollment practices*. U.S. Department of Health and Human Services. https://www.acf.hhs.gov/sites/default/files/documents/opre/complete.pdf

Delpit, L. D. (2012). *"Multiplication is for white people": Raising expectations for other people's children*. The New Press.

Derman-Sparks, L. (1989). *Anti-bias curriculum: Tools for empowering young children* (NAEYC No. 242). National Association for the Education of Young Children.

Derman-Sparks, L. (2016). What I learned from the Ypsilanti Perry Preschool Project: A teacher's reflection. *Journal of Pedagogy, 7*(1), 93–106. https://doi.org/10.1515/jped-2016-0006

Derman-Sparks, L., & Edwards, J. O. (2010). *Anti-bias education for young children and ourselves* (2nd ed.). National Association for the Education of Young Children.

Derman-Sparks, L., & Phillips, C. B. (1997). *Teaching/learning anti-racism: A developmental approach*. Teachers College Press.

Desimone, L. M., & Long, D. (2010). Teacher effects and the achievement gap: Do teacher and teaching quality influence the achievement gap between black and white and high- and low-SES students in the early grades? *Teachers College Record, 112*, 3024–3073.

Devine, P. G., Forscher, P. S., Austin, A. J., & Cox, W. T. L. (2012). Long-term reduction in implicit race bias: A prejudice habit-breaking intervention. *Journal of Experimental Social Psychology, 48*(6), 1267–1278.

DiAngelo, R. (2018). *White fragility: Why it's so hard for white people to talk about racism*. Beacon Press.

DiAngelo, R. (2021). *Nice racism: How progressive white people perpetuate racial harm*. Beacon Press.

Dobbins, D., McCready, M., & Rackas, L. (2016). *Unequal access: Barriers to early childhood education for boys of color*. Robert Wood Johnson Foundation.

Du Bois, W. E. B. (1903). *The souls of black folk*. A. C. McClurg & Co.

Dunbar-Ortiz, R. (2014). *An indigenous peoples' history of the United States*. Beacon Press.

Early, D., Iruka, I., Ritchie, S., Barbarin, O. A., Winn, D. C., Crawford, G. C., Frome, P. M., Clifford, R. M., Burchinal, M., Howes, C., Bryant, D. M., & Pianta, R. C., (2010). How do pre-kindergartners spend their time? Gender, ethnicity, and income as predictors of experiences in pre-kindergarten classrooms. *Early Childhood Research Quarterly, 25*, 177–193.

Early, D. M., & Winton, P. J. (2001). Preparing the workforce: Early childhood teacher preparation at 2- and 4-year institutions of higher education. *Early Childhood Research Quarterly, 16*(3), 285–306.

Eberhardt, J. L. (2019). *Biased: Uncovering the hidden prejudice that shapes what we see, think, and do*. Viking.

Epstein, R., Blake, J. J., & González, T. (2015). *Girlhood interrupted: The erasure of black girls' childhood*. Georgetown Law Center on Poverty and Inequality.

Erickson, R. (1997). The laws of ignorance designed to keep slaves (Blacks) illiterate and powerless. *Education, 118*(2), 206.

Escayg, K. (2018). The missing links: Enhancing anti-bias education with anti-racist education. *Journal of Curriculum, Teaching, Learning and Leadership in Education, 3*(1), Article 4. https://digitalcommons.unomaha.edu/ctlle/vol3/iss1/4

Evans-Winters, V. E. (2005). *Teaching black girls: Resiliency in urban classrooms.* Peter Lang.

Fabelo, T., Thompson, M. D., Plotkin, M., Carmichael, D., Marchbanks, M., & Booth, E. A. (2011). *Breaking schools' rules: A statewide study of how school discipline relates to students' success and juvenile justice involvement.* The Council of States Governments Justice Center and the Public Policy Research Institute.

Falk, T. M. (2021). Wage slaves. In Z. A. Casey (Ed.), *Encyclopedia of critical whiteness studies in education* (pp. 686–693). Brill Sense.

Fantuzzo, J., McWayne, C. M., Perry, M. A., & Childs, S. (2004). Multiple dimensions of family involvement and their relations to behavioral and learning competencies for urban, low-income children. *School Psychology Review, 33*(4), 467–480.

Fast, E., & Collin-Vezina, D. (2010). Historical trauma, race-based trauma and resilience of indigenous peoples: A literature review. *First Peoples Child & Family Review, 5*(1), 126–136.

Feinberg, E., Silverstein, M., Donahue, S., & Bliss, R. (2011). The impact of race on participation in Part C early intervention services. *Journal of Developmental & Behavioral Pediatrics, 32*(4), 284–291. https://doi.org/10.1097/DBP.0b013e3182142fbd

Fergus, E. (2017). Confronting colorblindness. *Phi Delta Kappan.* DOI: 10.1177/0031721717690362

Fernandes, C. A. (2017). *Unpacking "la mochila" of Latino white privilege: Relationships among white privilege, color blind attitudes, and internalized racism among Latinos.* Boston, MA: Northeastern University. Retrieved from: https://repository.library.northeastern.edu/files/neu:cj82r600m/fulltext.pdf

Finn, J. D., & Servoss, T. J. (2014). Misbehaviors, suspensions, and security measures in high school: Racial/ethnic and gender differences. *Journal of Applied Research on Children, 5*(2), 52.

Flores, B. B., Casebeer, C. M., & Riojas-Cortez, M. (2011). Validation of the early childhood ecology scale-revised: A reflective tool for teacher candidates. *Journal of Early Childhood Teacher Education, 32*(3), 266–286.

Fox, L., Dunlap, G., Hemmeter, M. L., Joseph, G. E., & Strain, P. S. (2003). The teaching pyramid: A model for supporting social competence and preventing challenging behavior in young children. *Young Children, 58*(4), 48–52.

Fox, L., & Hemmeter, M. L. (2009). A program-wide model for supporting social emotional development and addressing challenging behavior in early childhood settings. In W. Sailor, G. Dunlap, G. Sugai, & R. Horner (Eds.), *Handbook of positive behavior support* (pp. 177–202). Springer. https://doi.org/10.1007/978-0-387-09632-2_8

Fox, L., Strain, P. S., & Dunlap, G. (2021). Preventing the use of preschool suspension and expulsion: Implementing the pyramid model. *Preventing School Failure: Alternative Education for Children and Youth, 65*(4), 312–322.

Francis, B. (2000). *Boys, girls and achievement: Addressing the classroom issues.* Routledge.

Franco, X., Yazejian, N., LaForett, D., Peisner-Feinberg, E., Kasprzak, C. M., Bryant, D. M., Williams, S. B., Loza, S., De Marco, A., Hong, S. S., Bratsch-Hines, M., Harradine, C., Reid, K., & Zgourou, E. (2020). *North Carolina statewide birth-5 needs assessment: Final report.* Frank Porter Graham Child Development Institute. https://ncchildcare.ncdhhs.gov/Portals/0/documents/pdf/N/NC_Statewide_Birth-5_Needs_Assessment_Report_Final_31120.pdf?ver=2020-04-03-151528-233

Frey, S. (2015). *Art appreciation helps young children learn to think and express ideas.* EdSource. https://edsource.org/2015/art-appreciation-helps-young-children-learn-to-think-and-express-ideas/77734

Fuller, B., Kagan, S. L., Caspary, G. L., & Gauthier, C. A. (2002). Welfare reform and child care options for low-income families. *Future Child, 12*(1), 96–119.

García Coll, C., Lamberty, G., Jenkins, R., McAdoo, H., Crnic, K., Wasik, B. H., & Vázquez García, H. (1996). An integrative model for the study of developmental competencies in minority children. *Child Development, 67*(5), 1891–1914.

Gay, G. (2002). Preparing for culturally responsive teaching. *Journal of Teacher Education, 53*(2), 106–116.

Gay, G., & Howard, T. C. (2000). Multicultural teacher education for the 21st century. *The Teacher Educator, 36*(1), 1–16.

George, J. (2021). *A lesson on critical race theory.* ABA. https://www.americanbar.org/groups/crsj/publications/human_rights_magazine_home/civil-rights-reimagining-policing/a-lesson-on-critical-race-theory/

Georgetown Law. (2017, June 27). *Black girls viewed as less innocent than white girls.* https://www.law.georgetown.edu/news/black-girls-viewed-as-less-innocent-than-white-girls-georgetown-law-research-finds-2/

Gillanders, C., McKinney, M., & Ritchie, S. (2012). What kind of school would you like for your children? Exploring minority mothers' beliefs to promote home-school partnerships. *Early Childhood Education Journal, 40*(5), 285–294. https://doi.org/10.1007/s10643-012-0514-0

Gilliam, W. S. (2005a). *Prekindergartners left behind: Expulsion rates in state prekindergarten systems.* Foundation for Child Development. https://www.fcd-us.org/prekindergartners-left-behind-expulsion-rates-in-state-prekindergarten-programs/

Gilliam, W. S. (2005b). *Prekindergarteners left behind: Expulsion rates in state prekindergarten systems.* Yale University Child Study Center. https://www.researchgate.net/publication/228701481_Prekindergarteners_Left_Behind_Expulsion_Rates_in_State_Prekindergarten_Systems

Gilliam, W. S. (2009). Preschool promises: An introduction, commentary, and charge. *Psychological Science in the Public Interest, 10*(2), i–v. http://www.jstor.org/stable/41038722

Gilliam, W. S. (2015, April 14). Invited testimony, U.S. House of Representatives Committee on Appropriations, Subcommittee on Labor, Health and Human Services, Education, and Related Services, Budget Hearing—Early Education Panel, The Capitol, Washington, DC.

Gilliam, W. S. (2016). *Early childhood expulsions and suspensions undermine our nation's most promising agent of opportunity and social justice.* Robert Wood Johnson Foundation. https://forwardpromise.org/research-resources/early-childhood-expulsions-and-suspensions-undermine-our-nations-most-promising-agent-of-opportunity-and-social-justice/

Gilliam, W. S., Maupin, A. N., Reyes, C. R., Accavitti, M., & Shic, F. (2016a). *Do early educators' implicit biases regarding sex and race relate to behavior expectations and recommendations of preschool expulsions and suspensions? Research study brief.* Yale University Child Study Center, Yale University.

Gilliam, W. S., Maupin, A. N., & Reyes, C. R. (2016b). Early childhood mental health consultation: Results of a statewide random-controlled evaluation. *Journal of the American Academy of Child and Adolescent Psychiatry, 55*(9), 754–761.

Gilliam, W. S., & Reyes, C. R. (2018). Teacher decision factors that lead to preschool expulsion scale development and preliminary validation of the Preschool Expulsion Risk Measure. *Infants & Young Children, 31*(2), 93–108. https://doi.org/10.1097/IYC.0000000000000113

Gilliam, W. S., & Shahar, G. (2006). Preschool and child care expulsion and suspension: Rates and predictors in one state. *Infants & Young Children, 19*(3), 228–245.

Glenn-Applegate, K., Pentimonti, J., & Justice, L. M. (2011). Parents' selection factors when choosing preschool programs for their children with disabilities. *Child & Youth Care Forum, 40*(3), 211–231.

Goff, A. P., Jackson, C. M., Di Leone, B., Culotta, M. C., & DiTomasso, A. N. (2014). The essence of innocence: Consequences of dehumanizing Black children. *Journal of Personality and Social Psychology, 106*(4), 526–545.

Golden, T. (1994). *Black male: Representations of masculinity in contemporary American art.* Whitney Museum of American Art.

Grabb, E., Baer, D., & Curtis, J. (1999). The origins of American individualism: Reconsidering the historical evidence. *Canadian Journal of Sociology, 24*(4), 511–533.

Grant, K. B., & Ray, J. (2013). *Home, school, and community collaboration: Culturally responsive family engagement* (2nd ed.). SAGE.

Greenwald, A. D., McGhee, D. E., & Schwartz, J. L. (1998). Measuring individual differences in implicit cognition: The Implicit Association Test. *Journal of Personality and Social Psychology, 74*(6), 1464–1480.

Gregory, A., Skiba, R. J., & Noguera, P. A. (2010). The achievement gap and the discipline gap: Two sides of the same coin? *Educational Researcher, 39*(1), 59–68.

Grier, W. H., & Cobb, P. M. (1992). *Black rage: Two black psychiatrists reveal the full dimensions of the inner conflicts and the desperation of black life in the United States.* Basic Books.

Guralnick, M. J. (1993). Second generation research on the effectiveness of early intervention. *Early Education and Development, 4*(4), 366–378.

Hamilton, D., & Darity, W. A., Jr. (2017). The political economy of education, financial literacy, and the racial wealth gap. *Review, 99*(1), 59–76.

Hamre, B. K., & Pianta, R. C. (2001). Early teacher–child relationships and the trajectory of children's school outcomes through eighth grade. *Child Development, 72*(2), 625–638.

Han, H. S., & Thomas, M. S. (2010). No child misunderstood: Enhancing early childhood teachers' multicultural responsiveness to the social competence of diverse children. *Early Childhood Education Journal, 37*(6), 469–476.

Hannon, L., DeFina, R., & Brunch, S. (2013). The relationship between skin tone and school suspensions for African Americans. *Race and Social Problems, 5*(4), 281–295.

Hardy, K. V. (2013). Healing the hidden wounds of racial trauma. *Reclaiming Children and Youth, 22*(1), 24–28.

Hawn Nelson, A., Jenkins, D., Zanti, S., Katz, M., Berkowitz, E., Burnett, T., & Culhane, D. (2020). *A toolkit for centering racial equity throughout data integration.* Actionable Intelligence for Social Policy, University of Pennsylvania.

H.B. 377, 2021 Reg. Sess. (ID 2021). https://legislature.idaho.gov/wp-content/uploads/sessioninfo/2021/legislation/H0377.pdf

H.B. 1775, 2021 Reg. Sess. (OK 2021). https://sde.ok.gov/sites/default/files/documents/files/HB%201775%20Emergency%20Rules.pdf

Head Start National Center on Program Management and Fiscal Operations. (n.d.)

Hess, R. S., Molina, A., & Kozleski, E. B. (2006). Until somebody hears me: Parent voice and advocacy in special educational decision-making. *British Journal of Special Education, 33*(3), 148–157.

Hinojosa, M. S., & Moras, A. (2009). Challenging colorblind education: A descriptive analysis of teacher racial attitudes. *Research and Practice in Social Sciences, 4*(2), 27–45. http://digitalcommons.sacredheart.edu/sociol_fac/6

Hinton, P. R. (2000). *Stereotypes, cognition and culture.* Psychology Press.

Hobson, M. (2014). *Color blind or color brave?* [Video]. TED. https://www.ted.com/talks/mellody_hobson_color_blind_or_color_brave?language=en

Hollins, E. R., & Guzman, M. T. (2005). Research on preparing teachers for diverse populations. In M. Cochran-Smith & K. M. Zeichner (Eds.), *Studying teacher education: The report of the AERA panel on research and teacher education* (pp. 477–548). Lawrence Erlbaum Associates.

hooks, b. (2001). *all about love: new visions.* HarperCollins.

Howes, C., & Shivers, E. M. (2006). New child-caregiver attachment relationships: Entering childcare when the caregiver is and is not an ethnic match. *Social Development, 15*(4), 574–590.

Hughes, D., Rodriguez, J., Smith, E. P., Johnson, D. J., Stevenson, H. C., & Spicer, P. (2006). Parents' ethnic–racial socialization practices: A review of research and directions for future study. *Developmental Psychology, 42*(5), 747–770.

Hughes, J. N., Gleason, K. A., & Zhang, D. (2005). Relationship influences on teachers' perceptions of academic competence in academically at-risk minority and majority first grade students. *Journal of School Psychology, 43*(4), 303–320.

Hughes, J., & Kwok, O.-M. (2007). Influence of student–teacher and parent–teacher relationships on lower achieving readers' engagement and achievement in the primary grades. *Journal of Educational Psychology, 99*(1), 39–51.

Hunter, M. L. (2005). *Race, gender, and the politics of skin tone.* Routledge.

Hunter, M. (2016). Colorism in the classroom: How skin tone stratifies African American and Latina/o students. *Theory Into Practice, 55*(1), 54–61.

Hunt Institute. (2016). *How are the children?* https://huntinstitute.org/resources/2016/03/how-are-the-children/

Hyun, E., Marshall, J. D., & Dana, N. F. (1995). *New directions in early childhood teacher preparation: Developmentally and culturally appropriate practice (DCAP).* Paper presented at the National Association of Early Childhood Teacher Educators (NAECTE), Washington, DC.

Indian Health Service (2019). *Indian health disparities.* https://www.ihs.gov/newsroom/factsheets/disparities/

Individuals with Disabilities Education Act of 2004, Pub. L. 108–466, § 1414(b) (A) (2004). https://ies.ed.gov/ncser/pdf/pl108-446.pdf

Irving Harris Foundation. (n.d.). *Diversity-informed tenets.* https://www.irvingharrisfdn.org/how-we-work/special-initiatives/diversity-informed-tenets/

Isaacs, J. (2012). *Starting school at a disadvantage: The school readiness of poor children.* Brookings.

Ishimaru, A. M. (2017). From family engagement to equitable collaboration. *Educational Policy, 33*(2), 350–385.

Jansen, J. D. (2009). *Knowledge in the blood: Confronting race and the apartheid past.* Stanford University Press.

Jarrett, O. (2016). Doll studies as racial assessments: A historical look at racial attitudes and school desegregation. In M. M. Patte & J. A. Sutterby (Eds.), *Celebrating 40 years of play research: Connecting our past, present, and future* (pp. 19–37). Hamilton Books.

Jarrett, R. L., & Coba-Rodriguez, S. (2015). "My mother didn't play about education": Low income, African American mothers' early school experiences and their impact on school involvement for preschoolers transitioning to kindergarten. *Journal of Negro Education, 84*(3), 457–472.

Johnson, C. S., & Hinton, H. III. (2018). A morality of inclusion: A theoretical argument for culturally consonant character education. *Curriculum and Teaching Dialogue, 20*(1–2), 73–87. https://www.infoagepub.com/series/Curriculum-and-Teaching-Dialogue

Johnson-Staub, C. (2017). *Equity starts early: Addressing racial inequities in child care and early education policy.* CLASP. https://www.clasp.org/sites/default/files/publications/2017/12/2017_EquityStartsEarly_0.pdf

Katz, P. A., & Kofkin, J. A. (1997). Race, gender, and young children. In S. S. Luthar, J. A. Burack, D. Cicchetti, & J. R. Weisz (Eds.), *Developmental psychopathology: Perspectives on adjustment, risk, and disorder* (pp. 51–74). Cambridge University Press.

Keels, M., Durkee, M., & Hope, E. (2017). The psychological and academic costs of school-based racial and ethnic microaggressions. *American Educational Research Journal, 54*(6), 1316–1344.

Kena, G., Musu-Gillette, L., Robinson, J., Wang, X., Rathbun, A., Zhang, J., Wilkinson-Flicker, S., Barmer, A., & Dunlop Velez, E. (2015). *The condition of education 2015.* U.S. Department of Education, National Center for Education Statistics. https://nces.ed.gov/pubsearch/pubsinfo.asp?pubid=2015144

Kendi, I. X. (2016). *Stamped from the beginning: The definitive history of racist ideas in America.* Bold Type Books.

Kendi, I. X. (2019). *How to be an anti-racist.* One World.

Kesner, J. E (2000). Teacher characteristics and the quality of child–teacher relationships. *Journal of School Psychology, 38*(2), 133–149.

King, C., Gross, E., Wahi, B., Hogenson, S., & Verbugge, J. (2021). *Data and racial equity in early childhood policy advocacy: Alliance for Early Success webinar series.* Alliance for Early Success. https://earlysuccess.org/data-and-racial-equity-in-early-childhood-policy

King, M. L., Jr. (1967). *Where do we go from here? Chaos or community?* Beacon Press.

Kirmayer, L. J., Gone, J. P., & Moses, J. (2014). Rethinking historical trauma. *Transcultural Psychology, 51*(3), 299–319.

Kirwan Institute for the Study of Race and Ethnicity. (n.d.). *State of the science: Implicit science review.* https://kirwaninstitute.osu.edu/sites/default/files/2019-06//SOTS-Implicit_Bias.pdf

Ko, S. J., Ford, J. D., Kassam-Adams, N., Berkowitz, S. J., Wilson, C., Wong, M., Brymer, M. J., & Layne, C. M. (2008). Creating trauma-informed systems: Child welfare, education, first responders, health care, juvenile justice. *Professional Psychology: Research and Practice, 39*(4), 396–404.

Koch, A., Brierly, C., Maslin, M., & Lewis, S. (2019). *European colonization of the Americas killed 10 percent of world population and caused global cooling.* The World. https://theworld.org/stories/2019-01-31/european-colonization-americas-killed-10-percent-world-population-and-caused

Kubota, R., & Lin, A. (Eds.). (2009). *Race, culture, and identities in second language education: Exploring critically engaged practice.* Routledge.

Kumar, R., Karabenick, S. A., & Burgoon, J. N. (2015). Teachers' implicit attitudes, explicit beliefs, and the mediating role of respect and cultural responsibility on mastery and performance-focused instructional practices. *Journal of Educational Psychology, 107*(2), 533–545.

Ladd, G. W., Birch, S. H., & Buhs, E. S. (1999). Children's social and scholastic lives in kindergarten: Related spheres of influence? *Child Development, 70*(6), 1373–1400.

Ladson-Billings, G. (1995). But that's just good teaching! The case for culturally relevant pedagogy. *Theory Into Practice, 34*(3), 159–165.

Lawrence, K., & Keleher, T. (2004). *Chronic disparity: Strong and pervasive evidence of racial inequalities: Poverty outcomes.* https://www.intergroupresources.com/rc/Definitions%20of%20Racism.pdf

Lebron, D., Morrison, L., Ferris, D., Alcantera, A., Cummings, D., Parker, G., & McKay, M. (2015). *Facts matter! Black lives matter! The trauma of racism*. The McSilver Institute for Poverty Policy and Research.

Lee, R. M., Gamsey, P. G., & Sweeney, B. (2008). Engaging young children in activities and conversations about race and social class. *Young Children, 63*(6), 68–76.

Leonardo, Z. (2004). The color of supremacy: Beyond the discourse of "white privilege." *Educational Philosophy and Theory, 36*(2), 137–152. https://doi.org/10.1111/j.1469-5812 .2004.00057.x

Lesane-Brown, C. L., Scottham, K. M., Nguyên, H. X., & Sellers, R. M. (2006). *The racial socialization questionnaire-teen (RSQ-t): A new measure for use with African American children* [Unpublished manuscript]. Department of Psychology, Rice University.

Li, W. (2019). *The growing racial disparity in prison time*. The Marshall Project. https:// www.themarshallproject.org/2019/12/03/ the-growing-racial-disparity-in-prison-time

Lipset, S. M. (1996). *American exceptionalism: A double-edged sword*. W. W. Norton.

Losen, D. J., & Gillespie, J. (2012). *Opportunities suspended: The disparate impact of disciplinary exclusion from school*. The Center for Civil Rights Remedies, The Civil Rights Project, University of California at Los Angeles. http://civilrightsproject.ucla.edu/resources /projects/center-for-civil-rights-remedies /school-to-prison-folder/federal-reports /upcoming-ccrr-research/losen-gillespie -opportunity-suspended-2012.pdf

Luthar, S. S., & Sexton, C. C. (2004). The high price of affluence. *Advances in Child Development and Behavior, 32*, 125–162.

Magnuson, K. A., & Waldfogel, J. (2005). Early childhood care and education: Effects on ethnic and racial gaps in school readiness. *The Future of Children, 15*(1), 169–196.

Malik, R. (2017). *New data reveal 250 preschoolers are suspended or expelled every day*. Center for American Progress. https:// www.americanprogress.org/article/new -data-reveal-250-preschoolers-suspended -expelled-every-day/

Mandalaywala, T. M., Tai, C., & Rhodes, M. (2020). Children's use of race and gender as cues to social status. *PLoS One, 15*(6), Article e0234398.

Mattheis, A. (2021). Brown v. Board of Education of Topeka, Kansas. In Z. A. Casey (Ed.), *Encyclopedia of critical whiteness studies in education* (pp. 81–88). Koninklijke Brill NV.

Maxwell, K. L., & Clifford, R. M. (2006). Professional development issues in universal prekindergarten. In E. Ziegler, W. Gilliam, & S. M. Jones (Eds.), *A vision of universal preschool*

education (pp. 169–193). Cambridge University Press.

McCarthy, C. (2020). *How racism harms children*. Harvard Health.

McDonald, R. I., & Crandall, C. S. (2015). Social norms and social influence. *Current Opinion in Behavioral Sciences, 3*, 147–151.

McGhee, H. C. (2021). Bacon's rebellion. In I. X. Kendi & K. N. Blain (Eds.), *Four hundred souls: A community history of African America, 1619–2019* (pp. 51–54). Penguin Random House.

McIntosh, K., Girvan, E. J., Fairbanks Falcon, S., McDaniel, S. C., Smolkowski, K., Bastable, E., Santiago-Rosario, M. R., Izzard, S., Austin, S. C., Nese, R. N. T., & Baldy, T. S. (2021). Equity-focused PBIS approach reduces racial inequities in school discipline: A randomized controlled trial. *School Psychology, 36*(6), 433–444.

McIntosh, P. (1988). *White privilege: Unpacking the invisible knapsack* [Essay]. https:// psychology.umbc.edu/wp-content/uploads /sites/57/2016/10/White-Privilege _McIntosh-1989.pdf

McNamee, S. J., & Miller, R. K., Jr. (2014). *The meritocracy myth* (3rd ed). Rowman & Littlefield.

McWayne, C. M., Cheung, K., Wright, L. E. G., & Hahs-Vaughn, D. L. (2012). Patterns of school readiness among head start children: Meaningful within-group variability during the transition to kindergarten. *Journal of Educational Psychology, 104*(3), 862–878. https://doi.org/10.1037/a0028884

Meece, D., & Wingate, K. O. (2009/2010, Winter). Providing early childhood teachers with opportunities to understand diversity and the achievement gap. *SRATE Journal, 19*(1), 36–43.

Meek, S. E., & Gilliam, W. S. (2016). *Expulsion and suspension as matters of social justice and health equity* [Discussion paper]. National Academy of Medicine, Washington, DC. https://nam.edu/expulsion-and-suspension -in-early-education-as-matters-of-social -justice-and-health-equity/

Melzi, G., McWayne, C., & Ochoa, W. (2020). Family engagement and Latine children's early narrative skills. *Early Childhood Education Journal, 5*, 83–95. https://doi.org /10.1007/s10643-020-01132-7

Menakem, R. (2017). *My grandmother's hands: Racialized trauma and the pathway to mending our hearts and bodies*. Central Recovery Press.

Mendez, J. L., & LaForett, D. R. (2020). Understanding the impact of poverty and implications for assessment with young children from low-resource backgrounds. In V. C.

Alfonso, B. A. Bracken, & R. J. Nagle (Eds.), *Psychoeducational assessment of preschool children* (5th ed., pp. 399–420). Routledge.

Mersky, J. P., Choi, C., Plummer Lee, C., & Janczewski, C. E. (2021). Disparities in adverse childhood experiences by race/ethnicity, gender, and economic status: Intersectional analysis of a nationally representative sample. *Child Abuse & Neglect, 117,* 105066. https://doi.org/https://doi.org/10.1016/j .chiabu.2021.105066

Michie, G. (2012). *We don't need another hero: Struggle, hope, and possibility in the age of high-stakes schooling.* Teachers College Press.

Miller, A. (2021). *Math is racial oppression and white babies are racist: $6 million federal grant a deliberate attempt to program wokeism into children.* https://idahofreedom .org/math-is-racial-oppression-and-white -babies-are-racist-6-million-federal-grant -a-deliberate-attempt-to-program -wokeism-into-children/

Miller, E. (2021). Early childhood education and whiteness. In Z. A. Casey (Ed.), *Encyclopedia of critical whiteness studies in education* (pp. 152–158). Koninklijke Brill NV.

Modica, S., Ajmera, M., & Dunning, V. (2010). Culturally adapted models of early childhood education. *Young Children, 65*(6), 20–26.

Moore, M. (2008). Appreciative inquiry: The why? The what? The how? *Practice Development in Health Care, 7*(4), 214–220.

Morris, M. W. (2016). *Pushout: The criminalization of Black girls in schools.* The New Press.

Morrison, S. G. (2008). *Fundamentals of early childhood education* (5th ed.). Pearson Education.

Murray, C., & Murray, K. (2004). Child level correlates of teacher–student relationships: An examination of demographic characteristics, academic orientations, and behavioral orientations. *Psychology in the Schools, 41*(7), 751–762.

National Association for the Education of Young Children. (2011). *2010 standards for initial early childhood preparation.* https:// www.naeyc.org/sites/default/files/globally -shared/downloads/PDFs/our-work /higher-ed/NAEYC-Initial-Professional -Preparation-Standards-Summary.pdf

National Association for the Education of Young Children. (2019). *Advancing equity in early childhood education: A position statement of the National Association for the Education of Young Children.* https://www .naeyc.org/resources/position-statements /equity

National Association for the Education of Young Children (2020). *Position statement: Developmentally appropriate practice.* https:// www.naeyc.org/sites/default/files/globally -shared/downloads/PDFs/resources /position-statements/dap-statement_0.pdf

National Association of Child Care Resource and Referral Agencies (NACCRRA). (2008). *Parents' perceptions of child care in the United States.* https://www.childcareaware .org/wp-content/uploads/2015/10/2009 _parents_perception_report-r3.pdf

National Black Child Development Institute, Inc. (2013). *Being black is not a risk factor: A strengths-based look at the state of the black child.* https://www.nbcdi.org/sites/default /files/import_files/being-black-not-risk -factor.pdf

National Center for Education Statistics. (2018). *Fast facts: Race and ethnicity of college faculty.* https://nces.ed.gov/fastfacts /display.asp?id=61

National Center on Early Childhood Quality Assurance. (2017). *Quality Compendium 2017.* QRIS fact sheet. https://childcareta .acf.hhs.gov/sites/default/files/public/qris _datasystems_2017.pdf

National Center on Early Childhood Quality Assurance. (n.d.). *QRIS resource guide: About QRIS.* https://ecquality.acf.hhs.gov/about-qris

National Center on Program Management and Fiscal Operations. (n.d.). *Community assessment matrix.* https://eclkc.ohs.acf.hhs.gov /sites/default/files/pdf/no-search/ca -appendix-a-1.pdf

National Survey of Children's Health (NSCH). (2016). *About the National Survey of Children's Health.* https://www.childhealthdata .org/learn-about-the-nsch/NSCH

Neblett, E. W., Jr., Rivas-Drake, D., & Umana-Taylor, A. J. (2012). The promise of racial and ethnic protective factors in promoting ethnic minority youth development. *Child Development Perspectives, 6*(3), 295–303.

Neblett, E. W., Jr., White, R. L., Ford, K. R., Philip, C. L., Ngyugên, H. X., & Sellers, R. M. (2008). Patterns of racial socialization and psychological adjustment: Can parental communications about race reduce the impact of racial discrimination? *Journal of Research on Adolescence, 18*(3), 477–515.

Neito, S., & Bode, P. (2012). *Affirming diversity: The sociopolitical context of multicultural education* (6th ed.). Pearson Education.

Neitzel, J. (2020). *Achieving equity and justice in education through the work of systems change.* Lexington Books.

Neville, H. A., Gallardo, M. E., & Wing Sue, D. (2016). *The myth of racial colorblindness: Manifestations, dynamics, and impact.* American Psychological Association.

No Child Left Behind Act of 2001, Pub. L. 107-110, 20 U.S.C. § 6319 (2002).

Norris, A. (2021). *Hair discrimination and global politics of anti-blackness, Part 1.* https://www.aaihs.org/hair-discrimination-and-global-politics-of-anti-blackness-part-1/

North Carolina Department of Health and Human Services. (2018). *State agency collaboration on early childhood education/ transition from preschool to kindergarten session law 2017-57, Section 11B.2.(d). Report to the Joint Legislative Oversight Committee on Health and Human Services and Legislative Education Oversight Committee.* https://www.ncleg.gov/documentsites/committees/JLOCHHS/Handouts%20and%20Minutes%20by%20Interim/2017-18%20Interim%20JLOC-HHS%20Handouts/Reports%20to%20JLOC-HHS/January%202018/SL%202017-57,%20Section%2011B.2.(d)%20PreK%20to%20K%20Transition%20Jan%202018.pdf

Ocen, P. A. (2015). (E)racing childhood: Examining the racialized construction of childhood and innocence in the treatment of sexually exploited minors. *UCLA Law Review, 62*(6), 1580.

Okonofua, J. A., & Eberhardt, L. J. (2015). Two strikes: Race and the disciplining of young students. *Psychological Sciences, 26*(5), 617–624.

Okun, T. (1999). *White supremacy culture.* https://www.dismantlingracism.org/

Okun, T. (2021). *White supremacy culture.* https://www.dismantlingracism.org

Onyeka-Crawford, A., Patrick, K., & Chaudhry, N. (2017). *Stopping school pushout for girls for color.* National Women's Law Center. https://nwlc.org/wp-content/uploads/2017/04/final_nwlc_Gates_GirlsofColor.pdf

Oxford Dictionary. (2021). *Resilience.*

Pacini-Ketchabaw, V., & Bernhard, J. K. (2012). Revisioning multiculturalism in early childhood education. In N. Howe & L. Prochner (Eds.), *Recent perspectives on early childhood education and care in Canada* (pp. 159–180). University of Toronto Press.

Patterson, K. B., & Runge, T. (2002). Smallpox and the Native American. *American Journal of Medical Science, 323*(4), 216–222.

Peck, M. S. (2010). *The different drum: Community making and peace.* Simon & Schuster.

Peisner-Feinberg, E., LaForett, D., Schaaf, J., & Hildebrandt, L. (2013). *Local variations in enrollment processes in Georgia's pre-K program: Findings from the 2012–2013 evaluation study.* The University of North Carolina, Frank Porter Graham Child Development Institute.

Peisner-Feinberg, E. S., Van Manen, K. W., & Mokrova, I. L. (2018). *Variations in enrollment practices in the NC pre-K program: 2016–2017 statewide evaluation.* The University of North Carolina, Frank Porter Graham Child Development Institute.

Penn, H. (2002). The World Bank's view of early childhood. *Childhood: A Global Journal of Child Research, 9*(1), 118–132.

Perkins, L. M. (1983). The impact of the "cult of true womanhood" on the education of black women. *Journal of Social Issues, 39*(3), 17–28.

Perry, B. D. (2006). The neurosequential model of therapeutics: Applying principles of neurodevelopment. In N. B. Webb (Ed.), *Working with traumatized youth in child welfare* (pp. 27–52). Guilford.

Petras, H., Masyn, K. E., Buckley, J. A., Ialongo, N. S., & Kellam, S. (2011). Who is most at risk for school removal? A multilevel discrete-time survival analysis of individual- and context-level influences. *Journal of Educational Psychology, 103*(1), 223–237. https://doi.org/10.1037/a0021545

Pew Research Center. (2021). *Majority of Latinos say skin color impacts opportunity in America and shapes daily life.* https://www.pewresearch.org/hispanic/wp-content/uploads/sites/5/2021/11/RE_2021.11.04_Latinos-Race-Identity_FINAL.pdf

Pierson, E., Simoiu, C., Overgoor, J., Corbett-Davies, S., Jenson, D., Shoemaker, A., Ramachandran, V., Barghouty, P., Phillips, C., Shroff, R., & Goel, S. (2020). A large-scale analysis of racial disparities in police stops across the United States. *Nature Human Behavior, 4*(7), 736–745.

Pine, G. J., & Hilliard, A. G. III. (1990). Rx for racism: Imperatives for America's schools. *Phi Delta Kappan, 71*(8), 593–600.

Quesenberry, A. C., Hemmeter, M. L., Ostrosky, M. M., & Hamann, K. (2014). Child care teachers' perspectives on including children with challenging behavior in child care settings. *Infants & Young Children, 27*(3), 241–258.

Quiros, L., & Dawson, B. A. (2013). The color paradigm: The impact of colorism on racial identity and identification of Latinas. *Journal of Human Behavior in the Social Environment, 23*(3), 287–297.

Ray, A., Bowman, B., & Robbins, J. (2006). *Preparing early childhood teachers to success-

fully educate all children: The contribution of four-year undergraduate teacher preparation programs (Report to the Foundation for Child Development). Erikson Institute.

Reardon, S. F., Grewal, E. T., Kalogrides, D., & Greenberg, E. (2012). Brown fades: The end of court-ordered school desegregation and the resegregation of American public schools. *Journal of Policy Analysis and Management, 31*(4), 876–904.

Reyes, C. R., & Gilliam, W. S. (2021). Addressing challenging behaviors in challenging environments: Findings from Ohio's early childhood mental health consultation system. *Development and Psychopathology, 33*(2), 634–646. https://doi.org/10.1017/S0954579420001790

Rhode, D. L. (2016). *Appearance as a feminist issue* (SMU Law Review 69, Rev 697). https://scholar.smu.edu/smulr/vol69/iss4/2

Roediger, D. R. (1991). *The wages of whiteness.* Verso.

Rohr, R. (2018). *All things new.* https://cac.org/all-things-new-2018-11-18/

Romero, A. J., Cuéllar, E., & Roberts, R. E. (2000). Ethnocultural variables and attitudes toward cultural socialization of children. *Journal of Community Psychology, 28*(1), 79–89.

Rosenbaum, A. (2018). Personal space and American individualism. *Brown Political Review.* https://brownpoliticalreview.org/2018/10/personal-space-american-individualism/

Rudman, L. A. (2004). Sources of implicit attitudes. *Current Directions in Psychological Science, 13*(2), 79–82.

Ryan, S. (2021). American Indian boarding schools. In Z. A. Casey (Ed.). *Encyclopedia of critical whiteness studies in education* (pp. 23–32). Koninklijke Brill NV.

Sacks, V., & Murphey, D. (2018). *The prevalence of adverse childhood experiences, nationally, by state, and by race or ethnicity.* Child Trends. https://www.childtrends.org/publications/prevalence-adverse-childhood-experiences-nationally-state-race-ethnicity

Saloviita, T. (2020). Teacher attitudes towards the inclusion of students with support needs. *Journal of Research in Special Educational Needs, 20*(1), 64–73.

Saluja, G., Early, D. M., & Clifford, R. M. (2002). Demographic characteristics of early childhood teachers and structural elements of early care and education in the United States. *Early Childhood Research and Practice, 4*(1). https://www.researchgate.net/publication/26390917_Demographic_Characteristics_of_Early_Childhood_Teachers_and_Structural_Elements_of_Early _Care_and_Education_in_the_United _States

Sanders, K., & Downer, J. (2012). Predicting acceptance of diversity in pre-kindergarten classrooms. *Early Childhood Research Quarterly, 27*(3), 503–511.

Saracho, N. O. (2012). Early childhood teacher preparation programmes in the USA. *Early Child Development and Care, 183*(5), 571–588.

Schmit, S., & Walker, C. (2016). *Disparate access: Head Start and CCDBG data by race and ethnicity.* CLASP. https://www.ccf.ny.gov/files/1914/5625/2696/Disparate-Access.pd.pdf

Schofield, J. W. (2007). The colorblind perspective in school: Causes and consequences. In J. A. Banks & C. A. McGee Banks (Eds.), *Multicultural education: Issues and perspectives* (pp. 259–277). Wiley.

Schwarz, E. D., & Perry, B. D. (1994). The posttraumatic response in children and adolescents. *Psychiatric Clinics of North America, 17*(2), 311–326.

Scottham, K. M., & Smalls, C. P. (2009). Unpacking racial socialization: Considering female African American primary caregivers' racial identity. *Journal of Marriage and Family, 71*(4), 807–818.

Sellers, R. M., Smith, M. A., Shelton, J. N., Rowley, S. A. J., & Chavous, T. M. (1998). Multidimensional model of racial identity: A reconceptualization of African American racial identity. *Personality and Social Psychology Review, 2*(1), 18–39.

Sensoy, Ö., & DiAngelo, R. (2017). *Is everyone really equal? Introduction to key concepts in social justice education* (2nd ed.). New York: Teachers College Press.

Shapiro, A., Martin, E., Weiland, C., & Unterman, R. (2019). If you offer it, will they come? Patterns of application and enrollment behavior in a universal prekindergarten context. *AERA Open, 5*(2), 1–22. https://doi.org/10.1177/2332858419848422

Shockley, K. G., & Banks, J. (2011). Perceptions of teacher transformation on issues of racial and cultural bias. *Journal of Transformative Education, 9*(4), 222–241.

Skiba, R., Arrenondo, M. I., & Williams, N. T. (2014). More than a metaphor: The contribution of exclusionary discipline to the school-to-prison pipeline. *Equity and Excellence in Education, 47*(4), 546–564.

Skiba, R. J., Horner, R. H., Chung, C.-G., Karega Rausch, M., May, S. L., & Tobin, T. (2011). Race is not neutral: A national investigation of African American and Latino disproportionality in school discipline. *School Psychology Review, 40*(1), 85–107.

Skiba, R. J., Michael, R. S., Nardo, A. C., & Peterson, R. L. (2002). The color of discipline: Sources of racial and gender disproportionality in school punishment. *The Urban Review, 34*(4), 317–342.

Skiba, R., Simmons, A., Ritter, S., Gibbs, A., Rausch, M. K., Cuadrado, J., & Chung, C.-G. (2008). Achieving equity in special education: History, status, and current challenges. *Exceptional Children, 74*(3), 264–288.

Sleeter, E. C. (2017). Critical race theory and the whiteness of teacher education. *Urban Education, 52*(2), 155–169.

Slopen, N., Shonkoff, J. P., Albert, M. A., Yoshikawa, H., Jacobs, A., Stoltz, R., & Williams, D. R. (2016). Racial disparities in child adversity in the U.S.: Interactions with family immigration history and income. *American Journal of Preventive Medicine, 50*(1), 47–56.

Smith, D. G., & Schonfeld, N. B. (2000). The benefits of diversity: What the research tells us. *About Campus, 5*(5), 16–23.

Smolkowski, K., Girvan, E. J., McIntosh, K., Nese, R. N. T., & Horner, R. H. (2016). Vulnerable decision points for disproportionate office discipline referrals: Comparisons of discipline for African American and White elementary school students. *Behavioral Disorders, 41*(4), 178–195.

Soler Castillo, S., & Pardo Abril, N, G. (2009). Discourse and racism in Columbia. In T. A. Van Dijk (Ed.), *Racism and discourse in Latin America* (pp. 131–170). Lexington Books.

Spencer, M. B., & Horowitz, F. D. (1973). Effects of systematic social and token reinforcement on the modification of racial and color concept attitudes in black and in white preschool children. *Developmental Psychology, 9*(2), 246–254. https://doi.org/10.1037/h0035088

Staats, C., Capatosto, K., Wright, R., & Contractor, D. (2015). *State of the science: Implicit bias review 2015.* Kirwan Institute for the Study of Race and Ethnicity.

Statman-Weil, K. (2020). *Trauma-responsive strategies for early childhood.* Redleaf Press.

Stevenson, H. D. (1994). Racial socialization in African American families: The art of balancing intolerance and survival. *The Family Journal 2*(3), 190–198

Stone, M. H., & Noblit, G. W. (2009). *Cultural responsiveness, racial identity and academic success: A review of literature.* The Heinz Endowments. https://www.heinz.org/userfiles/library/crea_executive%20summary.pdf

Strain, P., McGee, G., & Kohler, F. (2001). Inclusion of children with autism in early intervention environments: An examination of rationale, myths, and procedures. In M. J. Guralnick (Ed.), *Early childhood inclusion: Focus on change* (pp. 337–363). Paul H. Brookes Publishing Co.

Substance Abuse and Mental Health Services Administration. (2014). *SAMHSA's concept of trauma and guidance for a trauma-informed approach* (HHS Publication No. [SMA] 14-884).

Sugai, G., O'Keefe, B. V., & Fallon, L. M. (2012). A contextual consideration of culture and school-wide positive behavior support. *Journal of Positive Behavior Interventions, 14*(4), 197–208.

Syed, S. (2019). *Request for applications. Universal pre-K application and enrollment project: Technical assistance and coaching.* North Carolina Early Childhood Foundation. https://buildthefoundation.org/2019/08/request-for-applications-universal-pre-k-application-and-enrollment-project-technical-assistance-and-coaching/

TED. (2014, May). Color blind or color brave?/*Mellody Hobson* [Video]. https://www.ted.com/talks/mellody_hobson_color_blind_or_color_brave?language=en

Terrell, F., Terrell, S. L., & Miller, F. (1993). Level of cultural mistrust as a function of educational and occupational expectations among black students. *Adolescence, 28*(111), 573–578.

Terrill, M., & Mark, D. L. H. (2000). Preservice teachers' expectations for schools with children of color and second-language learners. *Journal of Teacher Education, 51*(2), 149–155.

Thandeka. (2006). *Learning to be white: Money, race, and God in America.* Continuum International Group.

Thomas, A. J., & Speight, S. L. (1999). Racial identity and racial socialization attitudes of African American Parents. *Journal of Black Psychology, 25*(2), 152–170.

Tierney, A. L., & Nelson, C. A. III. (2009). Brain development and the role of experience in the early years. *Zero to Three, 30*(2), 9–13.

Tileston, W. D. (2010). *What every teacher should know about diverse learners* (2nd ed.). Corwin Press.

Tobin, T. J., & Vincent, C. G. (2011). Strategies for preventing disproportionate exclusions of African American students. *Preventing School Failure, 55*(4), 192–201.

Todd, A. R., Thiem, K. C., & Neel, R. (2016). Does seeing faces of young black boys facilitate the identification of threatening stimuli? *Psychological Science, 27*(3), 384–393.

Unger, R. K. (1979). Toward a redefinition of sex and gender. *American Psychologist, 34*(11), 1085–1094.

University of California, San Francisco. (2021). *Racial equity & anti-black racism.* https://mrc.ucsf.edu/racial-equity-anti-black-racism

University of California San Francisco Multicultural Resource Center. (2022). *UCSF definition of racism.* https://mrc.ucsf.edu/racial-equity-anti-black-racism

University of Pittsburgh School of Education Race and Early Childhood Collaborative. (2016). *Positive racial identity development in early education: Understanding PRIDE in Pittsburgh.* University of Pittsburgh. https://www.racepride.pitt.edu/

University of Southern California. (2017). *SMART goals: A how to guide.* https://www.ucop.edu/local-human-resources/_files/performance-appraisal/How%20to%20write%20SMART%20Goals%20v2.pdf

U.S. Department of Education Office for Civil Rights. (2014a). *Civil rights data collection. Data snapshot: Early childhood education* (Issue Brief No. 2). http://www2.ed.gov/about/offices/list/ocr/docs/crdc-early-learning-snapshot.pdf

U.S. Department of Education Office for Civil Rights. (2014b). *Civil right data collection. Data snapshot: School discipline* (Issue Brief No. 1). https://ocrdata.ed.gov/assets/downloads/CRDC-School-Discipline-Snapshot.pdf

U.S. Department of Education Office for Civil Rights. (2016a). *2013–2014 civil rights data collection: Key data highlights on equity and opportunity gaps in our nation's public schools.* https://ocrdata.ed.gov/assets/downloads/2013-14-first-look.pdf

U.S. Department of Education Office for Civil Rights. (2016b). *Data snapshot: School discipline.*

U.S. Department of Education Office for Civil Rights. (2021). *Discipline practices in preschool: 2017–18 civil rights data collection.* https://www2.ed.gov/about/offices/list/ocr/docs/crdc-DOE-Discipline-Practices-in-Preschool-part1.pdf

van Ryn, M., Hardeman, R., Phelan, S. M., Burgess, D. J., Dovidio, J. F., Herrin, J., Burke, S. E., Nelson, D. B., Perry, S., Yeazel, M., & Przedworski, J. M. (2015). Medical school experiences associated with change in implicit racial bias among 3547 students: A medical student CHANGES study report. *Journal of General Internal Medicine, 30*(12), 1748–1756.

Vittrup, B. (2016). Early childhood teachers' approaches to multicultural education & perceived barriers to disseminating anti-bias messages. *Multicultural Education, 23*(3–4), 37–41.

Wadsworth, M. E., & Santiago, C. D. (2008). Risk and resiliency processes in ethnically diverse families in poverty. *Journal of Family Psychology, 22*(3), 399–410.

Wakefield, W. D., & Hudley, C. (2009). Ethnic and racial identity and adolescent well-being. *Adolescent Mental Health, 46*(2), 147–154.

Wallerstein, N., Duran, B., Oetzel, J. G., & Minkler, M. (Eds.). (2017). *Community-based participatory research for health: Advancing social and health equity* (3rd ed.). Jossey-Bass.

Weber, P. J. (2015, October 5). Publisher apologizes for textbook calling slaves "workers." *Associated Press.* https://apnews.com/article/ce1eaa40c7504c9d8e772241f07d6965

Weinberg, M. (1977). *A chance to learn: A history of race and education in the United States.* Cambridge University Press.

Welter, B. (1966). The cult of true womanhood: 1820–1860. *American Quarterly, 18*(2), 151–174.

White, A., & Wanless, S. B. (2019). "P.R.I.D.E.: Positive Racial Identity Development in Early Education." *Journal of Curriculum, Teaching, Learning and Leadership in Education, 4*(2). https://digitalcommons.unomaha.edu/ctlle/vol4/iss2/9

White House. (2014). *2014 native youth report.* Office of the President. https://obamawhitehouse.archives.gov/sites/default/files/docs/20141129nativeyouthreport_final.pdf

White-Johnson, R. L., Ford, K. R., & Sellers, R. M. (2010). Parental racial socialization profiles: Association with demographic factors, racial discrimination, childhood socialization, and racial identity. *Cultural Diversity and Ethnic Minority Psychology, 16*(2), 237–247.

Wildenger, K. L., & McIntyre, L. L. (2011). Family concerns and involvement during Kindergarten transition. *Journal of Child and Family Studies, 20,* 387–396.

Wildman, S., & Davis, A. (1995). Language and silence: Making systems of privilege visible. *Santa Clara Law Review, 35*(3), 881–906.

Williams Shanks, T. R., & Robinson, C. (2013). Assets, economic opportunity, and toxic stress: A framework for understanding child and educational outcomes. *Economics of Education Review, 33,* 154–170.

Winkler, E. N. (2009). Children are not color-blind. *PACE, 3*(3), 1–7.

Wright, K. (2021). The Virginia slave codes. In I. X. Kendi & K. N. Blain (Eds.), *Four hundred souls: A community history of African America, 1619–2019* (pp. 77–81). Penguin Random House.

Wu, S.-C., Pink, W., Crain, R., & Moles, O. (1982). Student suspension: A critical reappraisal." *The Urban Review, 14,* 245–303.

York, S. (2016). *Roots and wings: Affirming culture and preventing bias in early childhood programs.* Redleaf Press.

Yosso, T. J. (2005). Whose culture has capital? A critical race theory discussion of community cultural wealth. *Race Ethnicity and Education, 8*(1), 69–91. https://doi.org/10.1080/1361332052000341006

Zeng, S., Corr, C. P., O'Grady, C., & Guan, Y. (2019). Adverse childhood experiences and preschool suspension expulsion: A population study. *Child Abuse & Neglect, 97,* 104149. https://doi.org/10.1016/j.chiabu.2019.104149

Zeng, Z., & Minton, T. D. (2021). *Jail inmates in 2019* (Report NCJ 255608). U.S. Department of Justice, Bureau of Justice Statistics.

Zero to Three. (2017). *Early childhood mental health consultation: Policies and practices to foster the social-emotional development of young children.* https://www.zerotothree.org/resources/1694-early-childhood-mental-health-consultation-policies-and-practices-to-foster-the-social-emotional-development-of-young-children#downloads

Index

Page numbers followed by *f* indicate figures.

AAVE, *see* African American Vernacular
    English
Abecedarian Study, 64
ACEs, *see* Adverse childhood experiences
Academic achievement, Whiteness and, 122,
    124
Academic skills, for school readiness, 83, 85
Acknowledgment, and racial healing, 25
Additive level, for multicultural content, 76–77
Adultification, 3, 58, 67–68, 91
Adverse childhood experiences (ACEs), 53, 101
Affirmation, daily, 83, 84–85
African American Vernacular English
    (AAVE), 147–148
Afrocentric lens, 81
all about love (hooks), 22, 133
Allyship, co-conspirator *versus*, 49
American Genocide, 14, 15, 20, 52, 54–55, 131
Anti-bias curriculum, 78–79
*Anti-Bias Curriculum: Tools for Empowering
    Young Children* (NAEYC), 78
Anti-bias education
    criticism of, 79
    developmentally and culturally responsive,
        77–78
    early, 78–79
    see also Culturally responsive anti-bias
        education
Anti-Blackness, 18–19
    acknowledging and interrupting biases of,
        93
    colorism and, 16–18
    confronting and addressing, 14–15, 24
    definition of, 18, 106
    and family engagement, 91, 93
    and Latine people, 19–20
    manifestations of, 106
    and suspensions/expulsions, 3, 66–68
Anti-racism
    commitment to, 11–12, 36, 37, 141
    defining and describing, 36–37
    work required for, 49–50 (*see also* Equity
        work)
Anti-racist education, 79
Anti-racist resources, 155–158
Application processes, 98–99
Appreciative inquiry approach, 137–140

Art
    diverse representation in, 80, 92
    educator uses of, 116–118
    empowerment through, 116–117
    positive racial identity and, 115–118
*Art From Her Heart, Folk Artist Clementine
    Hunter* (Whitehead), 117
Aspirational capital, 102
Assessment methods, 100
Assets, cultural, 102
Atonement, 25
Audit, cultural, 92
Authentic self, developing, 125

Bacon's Rebellion, 42–43
Bearden, Romare, 117
Behavior characterization, 109
Behavioral expectations
    implicit bias and, 67
    Whiteness bias in, 48
"Beloved community," 12, 24, 128, 137, 141
Bias
    implicit (*see* Implicit bias)
    preparation for, 110
Biden, Joseph R., 46
BIPOC (Black, Indigenous, and People of
    Color)
    definition and use of term, 37–38
    self-worth and identity of, 35–36
Black bodies, 60
Black boys
    expectations of/attitudes toward, 18–19,
        67–68, 91, 106
    implicit bias and, 67
    suspension and expulsion of, 2, 65, 67–68,
        69, 91, 100
    see also Black children
Black children
    access to high-quality care/programs, 5–6,
        30, 64, 123
    adultification of, 3, 58, 67–68, 91
    adverse childhood experiences of, 53
    anti-Blackness and, 18–19
    conceptualization of race by, 76
    culturally consonant character education
        for, 83, 86